TWAYNE'S WORLD AUTHORS SERIES
A Survey of the World's Literature

Sylvia E. Bowman, Indiana University
GENERAL EDITOR

NEW ZEALAND

Joseph Jones, University of Texas, Austin
EDITOR

Janet Frame

TWAS 415

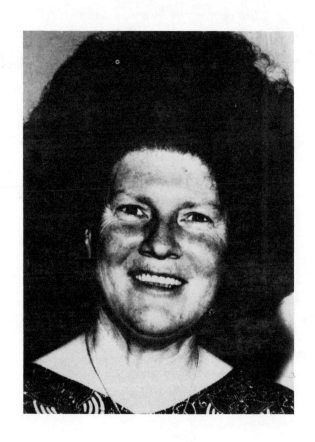

Janet Frame

JANET FRAME

By PATRICK David EVANS

University of Canterbury
Christchurch, New Zealand

TWAYNE PUBLISHERS
A DIVISION OF G. K. HALL & CO., BOSTON

Library of Congress Cataloging in Publication Data

Evans, Patrick David, 1944–
    Janet Frame.

    (Twayne's world authors series ; TWAS 415 : New
Zealand)
    Bibliography: p. 221–25.
    Includes index.
    1. Frame, Janet—Criticism and interpretation.
I. Title.
PR9639.3.F7Z645   823   77-4752
ISBN 0-8057-6254-X

PR
96 39.3
F7
Z645

Contents

About the Author

Patrick Evans was born in India in 1944. His father had been in the Indian Army, but, after the partition of the subcontinent in 1947, emigrated with his wife and twin sons to New Zealand. After living briefly in many New Zealand towns, the family settled permanently in Christchurch. Educated in state schools, Patrick Evans took an M.A. (Hons) in English literature at the University of Canterbury in 1968, and in 1974 gained a Ph.D. in American literature from the same university. After passing through Christchurch Teachers' College, he taught in a secondary school for a year before taking a position as a lecturer in the English Department at the University of Canterbury in 1970. His teaching interests are in New Zealand and American literature, Romantic poetry, Victorian fiction, and the contemporary novel. Publications include *An Inward Sun* (1971), a study of some of Janet Frame's novels, and several articles on New Zealand and Australian literature which have been published in Australasian journals.

Preface

I was first drawn to the writing of Janet Frame about ten years ago, when I was an undergraduate. Raised on a diet of Great English Writers who really *were* English, I had, I suppose, lapsed into the colonial's characteristic modesty concerning his country's writers, and was doubtful that any New Zealand author of worth could ever exist. *Owls Do Cry* (the novel nearly everybody reads first when coming to Janet Frame) broke my despondent mood, for in it I found an author who articulated recognizable local experiences in a manner which immediately carried them beyond the provincial pale and onto a plane of universality. As I explored her writing further, I began to see that her vision unfolded slowly from story to story and from novel to novel, gaining definition in an evolutionary way as new material appeared. I found that her art had coherence and weight. This, I imagined, would be matched by an attendant volume of criticism that had accumulated over the years. It was therefore with considerable surprise that I discovered that almost no such criticism existed at all.

Janet Frame published her first short story in 1946; the first substantial critical approaches to her fiction appeared only in 1970. It is a slight exaggeration, admittedly, to place a quarter of a century between stimulus and response: she was not widely known as a writer until the publication of her first novel in 1957, and since then each of her publications has been warmly and sometimes intelligently reviewed in literary magazines and newspapers both within New Zealand and overseas. Nevertheless, it may fairly be said that while Janet Frame has published thirteen volumes of poetry and prose—some of which have been translated into French, Spanish, and German—that while she has written numerous uncollected poems, stories, and nonfiction articles, has won more awards and scholarships than most writers dream of, and has been widely acclaimed overseas, she has nevertheless been neglected by the very critics who should be best placed to understand her—in short, by those who have experienced a similar upbringing and who know what it is to grow up as a New Zealander. Recognition and acceptance have tended to come first from overseas: from Stanley Edgar

Hyman in America, from Robert T. Robertson in Canada, from V. Dupont in France, and from Anna Rutherford in Denmark.

Why has this been so? In part, it is the result of that very universality which has made her writing so readily understandable to the overseas critic with no knowledge whatsoever of the New Zealand experience. This universality is, in a sense, a rather unfashionable quality for a New Zealand writer to have, for we tend still to demand a reflection of ourselves in the fiction our writers produce; we have a narcissistic thirst for identity which has sociological rather than purely artistic implications. Janet Frame has without doubt numerous judgments of this sort to make—they are the very basis of her vision—but she does not make them in a sociological manner, thus deceiving the summer soldiers of the reading public. Further, she has carefully concealed many of the details of her early years, and so we have almost no sense of the formative influences upon her mind as we do, say, with Frank Sargeson or J. K. Baxter, to give only two examples.

New Zealand's size and accessibility are such that the artist, if he so wishes, can slip out of his vocation and become a public figure and general commentator upon life. One can think of no one less likely to degenerate into this role of public sage than Janet Frame. A reluctant correspondent (especially with academics seeking information about the writer's art) and one who does not readily grant interviews, she has never spoken of many parts of her life and refuses to discuss the genesis and meaning of her novels in the way in which some artists are all too ready to do. While one can only admire the single-mindedness of her integrity and her refusal to meddle with the process of creation after it has occurred, it does make for major problems when the critic seeks to construct a biographical base for a discussion of her art. The extreme difficulty of doing this has obviously deterred many critics, at the same time propelling others into stratospheres of hypothesis and conjecture. The full story of her life and its relationship to her art will undoubtedly be told one day; almost certainly, this will be by way of an autobiography rather than an authorized biography. But this event lies well in the future, it seems, and until its occurrence a gap will remain in New Zealand literary criticism.

This book is a modest attempt to cover that gap with a rope bridge, as it were, until a more permanent structure can be formed. This metaphor is not inspired by false modesty but rather by its aptness: rope bridges are flimsy and no fun to cross; their users are all too aware that important details are missing from them; but, as a rule, they get the traveller across the chasm. The traveller across this critical rope bridge will often sense my limitations and restrictions in the biographical remarks I make, and from time to time may sense a certain momentary fading of subject from writer. But he may be assured that there are no missing sections and no parts sustained by sleight of hand, for what is presented here is a coherent narrative of the life of Janet Frame in which no period is unaccounted for and for which each date or fact put forward has been carefully verified. It is obvious that certain areas of her life are more significant to the development of her art than others, and I have attempted in particular to give as clear details as possible of her childhood years in Oamaru, since so much of her fiction stems from recollections of these years. Thus, the reader familiar with this fiction will be able to "place" many of its childhood sequences in a chronological and factual context for the first time.

The outline of her more recent years as a recognized writer will be useful, I hope, in providing a context for the later work, which until now might well have been considered to have been written in a vacuum. It is not insignificant, I think, to be told that *The Rainbirds* was written in a city in which, as a young woman recently away from her home, she had once experienced prolonged periods of loneliness and unhappiness as well as a sense of social exclusion. Similarly, *Intensive Care* becomes a more easily understood and moving novel if we understand that at its conception its author had been travelling in America during the widely publicized war in Vietnam, and had there witnessed both the social protest against the war and the televised horror of the war itself. I hope that the reader of this book will leave its last pages to turn back to all of Janet Frame's works with a sense of the individuality of each and with a stronger awareness of the character of their creator and the conditions behind their composition.

The nature of Janet Frame's art caused me certain difficulties in devising a critical framework in which it might be fairly contained. Since my main concern was to record how her art grew out of her life, I considered the possibility of dealing with both aspects together, chapter by chapter. But I feared that the narrative of Janet Frame's life, important in itself because not widely known before, might fade if it were presented simply as a series of adjuncts to the important business of literary analysis and comment; consequently, I have placed it separately, after all, in a couple of initial chapters. My emphasis in these, it will be seen, is upon the question of how a New Zealander brought up in a small town develops into an artist when all the pressures are towards a "normal" career as schoolteacher, librarian, or housewife. Thus, the referent of these early chapters is always literary, not simply a journalistic interest in personal details. As a watershed between these two chapters, I have selected Janet Frame's long spell in hospital which began in 1947 and which she herself recognized as an important period of development in which she moved from what she has called "this" world (the everyday world of society with its common values and mass culture) to "that" world (the private and possibly idiosyncratic world of the gifted, imaginative individual).

I was also tempted to discuss her work thematically, but since I did not wish to portray any part of it as less than a coherent entity, I have tried to follow the rhythms by which her writing seems to have evolved, treating each work individually yet trying to demonstrate that the works interrelate within different periods of development. I have made references to her juvenilia, since this has not been discussed before, and have related minor fiction of Janet Frame's "English" period (1958–1963) to the major, since both are a part of a single creative outburst. The more recent fiction, it will be seen, subdivides itself into similar groupings, while the poetry is treated separately, partly because of the difficulty of dating individual poems. But always, the desire to show the wholeness of her achievement, its overall shape and worth, is predominant.

PATRICK EVANS

Christchurch, New Zealand

Acknowledgments

One of the most remarkable aspects of the compilation of this study has been the almost universal cordiality and kind willingness to help which have been shown by people I have approached for their recollections of Janet Frame and her family. Certainly, this has become to a large extent "their" book, since without their recollections, work, and goodwill it would have been very sketchy indeed. Their response suggests, perhaps, a feeling that a book of this sort is overdue.

I am particularly grateful to two people whose constant interest has helped me over many hurdles in my research. I thank Janet Gibson of Oamaru, formerly a teacher of Janet Frame, for her invaluable help in providing information which I could have obtained from no other source, and for indicating to me many important avenues of research which I would not otherwise have seen. I have been exceptionally fortunate in having been attended by her unflagging interest in this project. I also thank Frank Sargeson for his cheerful and witty salvoes of information, in which many of my hunches and half-formed ideas have been returned to me as verified facts. The checking of dates relating to Miss Frame's recent years has been greatly aided by his help.

I also thank Miss J. J. Jarrold, Principal of the Waitaki Girls' High School in Oamaru, and her clerical staff, for their trouble in unearthing for me records of Janet Frame's years at that school. I am grateful for similar research into records and documents undertaken for me by the University of Otago and Dunedin Teachers' College, as well as by the Oamaru and Dunedin staff of the New Zealand Department of Justice. For particular items of information I thank Mrs. P. Hill of Christchurch, Dr. L. O. Jones of the University of Otago, Mr. Bill Meehan and Mrs. Judith Powell of Dunedin, Mrs. A. J. Hubbard of Timaru, and Miss D. Logie, Mr. K. Small, and Mrs. J. Banks-Kirkness, all of Oamaru.

I am very grateful to Barbara Lyon, of the Reference section of the University of Canterbury Library, for compiling the bibliography of Janet Frame's works which appears in this volume. This is the first bibliography of the writer's publications to have been yet compiled, and I am glad that such a thorough piece of research, which will provide a basis for future bibliographies, has been allowed to become incorporated into this study. I also thank the Interloan section of the Library for their help and advice over a long period.

I thank and acknowledge Mr. Ian Cross, editor of the *New Zealand Listener*, for permission to quote from material published in that magazine, and am similarly grateful to the Caxton Press of Christchurch, for permission to quote from various volumes of *Landfall* and *The Lagoon*, and to the Pegasus Press of Christchurch, who have the distinction of publishing Janet Frame's first novel, in 1957. Particular thanks and acknowledgements go to George Braziller Inc., of New York, for permission to quote from the works of Janet Frame.

I especially thank my friend and colleague, K. K. Ruthven, who, when problems arose and highly professional advice was needed, never failed to be there.

Chronology

Church Memorial Award.

1961 *Faces in the Water* published, and wins the Hubert Church Memorial Award.

1962 *The Edge of the Alphabet* published.

1963 *Scented Gardens for the Blind* published, as well as two volumes of short stories, *The Reservoir* and *Snowman, Snowman*. August, death of Janet Frame's father in Oamaru, followed by her return to New Zealand in November.

1964 April–August. Broadcasts a series of radio talks and completes *The Adaptable Man*, begun in England. Travels briefly overseas again.

1965 *The Adaptable Man* published. Lives in Opoho, Dunedin, and holds the Robert Burns Fellowship at the University of Otago, where she writes *The Rainbirds*.

1966 *A State of Siege* published.

1967 Lives and works at the Yaddo Foundation, a writers' colony in Saratoga Springs, New York. Visits England briefly and travels further in the United States. Publishes a volume of poetry, *The Pocket Mirror*, and a selection of stories, *The Reservoir and Other Stories*.

1968 Returns to Dunedin.

1969 Works again at the Yaddo Foundation. A brief trip to England is followed by three months at the McDowell Colony, Peterborough, New Hampshire. *The Rainbirds* published (under the American title of *Yellow Flowers in the Antipodean Room*). Publishes a book for children, *Mona Minim and the Smell of the Sun*. Works on *Intensive Care*.

1970 Returns to Dunedin. *Intensive Care* published.

1971 Travels in the United States and works on *Daughter Buffalo* at the Yaddo Foundation.

1972 Returns to Dunedin, where she completes *Daughter Buffalo*. Shifts in July to the Whangaparoa Peninsula, north of Auckland. *Daughter Buffalo* published.

1973 Changes surname to Clutha. Awarded Winn-Menton Scholarship for 1974. November, travels to France. *Daughter Buffalo* wins the Hubert Church Memorial Award.

1974 Works at Menton, returning to New Zealand later in the year via the United States.

1975 Shifts to Glenfield in Auckland.

CHAPTER 1

Life in "This" World

I *Early Days in Oamaru*

NEW Zealand sprang to life in the middle decades of the nineteenth century, when its great natural harbors and rolling, barren tussock land—until then the home of the Maori, the whaler, the gentleman sheep farmer, and the adventurer—became imprinted with the formal grid pattern of streets planned by Englishmen living twelve thousand miles away. For New Zealand was in a sense the "invention" of civilized, melioristic minds in Britain, and for years it was destined to bear the mark and manner of the towns and counties of the United Kingdom. These characteristics augmented the existing variations of the new Britain of the South Pacific and helped the quicker establishment of distinctive regions; of these, none became more distinctive, perhaps, than Otago province, in the south of the South Island. Otago's capital, Dunedin, had been established as a Presbyterian community and soon acquired an unmistakably Scottish flavor brought by thousands of immigrants from north of the Cheviots, who soon far outnumbered settlers from any other part of the world. Hamlets, farms and rivers in the province were given Scottish names—Cromwell, Naseby, Roxburgh, Outram, Wyndham—to commemorate the far-distant birthplaces of young men and women who would live and die in the new land. To help absorb the flow of migrants in the 1860's and 1870's, a new town called Invercargill was built in the south of the province, and young Scots stepping from the decks of their ships in Dunedin were likely to be sent there or, purely by chance, northwards eighty miles from Dunedin to a remarkable new town which had sprung up on the eastern coast under the name of Oamaru. As arbitrarily as this, in the early 1870's, a young blacksmith from the Clyde valley found himself beginning a new life amongst thousands of other such immigrants in Oamaru. Generations back, his family had been known as Fraëm; generations hence, his form of the name would be indelibly a part of the town which had become his chance home. He was Alexander Frame.[1]

Oamaru had plenty of opportunities for a blacksmith, or for anyone who had a trade, for it was bursting with growth in every direction during the 1870's. And yet its very existence was improbable: without a natural port, it had a roadstead better known for wrecking ships than for allowing them to unload; its central river was too tiny to allow river traffic but sufficiently wide to make it difficult for the town to expand onto its far bank for some time; and the town constantly stood second to Dunedin in the queue for government development revenue. Its very existence was an expression of the wealth and influence of its hinterland, upon whose rolling, bare hills large runholders reared sheep and grew wheat. Oamaru was "their" port and "their" town, and from its first years (it was established in the late 1850's) began to symbolize their prosperity and power in its very buildings: for the region was soon found to possess vast quantities of a pale, easily worked limestone that was more durable than wood or brick and more easily worked than stone.

Just as the wealth of the town came, in a sense, from the ground, so too did the material which showed that wealth; barely a decade after the first dwellings had been constructed there, its main street boasted an edifice that was quite unparalleled in the colonial towns of the times. This was the Bank of Otago building, finished in Oamaru stone and resembling—as it still does today—a strayed Greek temple, complete with Corinthian columns. Few things as impressive could have been found in the much larger settlements of the country farther to the north, particularly if the observer ignored the fact that its depth was only half its frontal width. Opposite the bank a tiny stone Post Office was built, which for all its diminutive size was equipped with a two-storey tower, Georgian in style if not in scale. The nearby jail, also built in the early 1870's, utilized the stoutness of the local stone and a rather ambitious Y-shaped design, all executed in a vaguely Queen Anne style. Soon the main street became crowded with similarly impressive buildings; hotels multiplied and independent businesses and industries were established by the end of the decade. Thus, before many larger cities had managed to build anything intended to endure, Oamaru had the appearance and atmosphere of a much larger and more substantial community than it actually was. At no stage did it quite resemble a frontier town; it still looks today like a part of a much larger city, and has never lost its initial solid confidence and the conservatism which comes from owning property.[2]

In 1877, Alexander Frame made one of the family's rare sorties into one of these stone institutions: on the eleventh of May that year he married Mary Paterson, a young girl from Paisley in Scotland, the groom managing to sign his name but the bride marking hers with a cross.[3] Literacy was perhaps the last of her needs: during the next two decades she busily bore and helped raise eleven children, amongst the last of whom, born in February 1894, was a son christened George Samuel.[4] The town, growing steadily in size and now the home of numerous industries, offered the children of Alexander and Mary Frame many kinds of employment as they grew out of childhood; but the very nature of its progress made it unlikely that any of them should be able to follow their father's trade.

As Oamaru had become a link in a railway system that covered both parts of the country, almost inevitably George Frame became a locomotive engineman before he was twenty, at the beginning of the Great War. It was a job which condemned him to years of wandering from one railway settlement to another as he was moved amongst different runs. But eventually his job took him to Wellington, the country's capital, and gave him the advantage of meeting the woman he was to marry in 1916.

This was Lottie Clarice Godfrey, two years his senior, who had been born in Picton, a tiny seaside township at the north of the South Island. A woman of remarkable intelligence and character, she showed literary interests from the first. Her mother's maiden name of Joyce suggests exciting possibilities, which investigation, alas, does not bear out. But after leaving school at an early age, she brushed against another literary figure when she went into service as a maid at the Picton home of the family of Katherine Mansfield, for many years acknowledged as New Zealand's finest writer. This early, though distant, contact seems to have been an inspiration: for the rest of her life Mrs. Frame was putting pen constantly to paper in a relentless pursuit of poetry and prose.[5]

The years immediately following the Great War involved the Frames in the more mundane and day-to-day business of making a living. They moved south again, but to Dunedin, not Oamaru; there Mr. Frame continued his job on the railways and, on December 15,

1920, his wife bore their first child, a daughter whom they named
Myrtle Jean. Two more children were born during their years in
Dunedin: their only son, named after the father, on April 22, 1922;
and on August 28, 1924, Janet Paterson Frame, their second daughter and the subject of this study.[6]

II   *Childhood*

Not long after the birth of Janet Frame, her parents took the three
children to Outram, the first of a series of small, rather lonely towns
in South Otago and Southland which were to be their homes for the
next five years. There, on May 10, 1926, the third daughter of the
family, Isabel May, was born. After Outram came Glenham, farther
south, and later Wyndham, where a fifth child, Phyllis Mary Evelyn
June, was born on June 30, 1928. Mrs. Frame, obviously determined that this should be her last child, used up all her favorite
names on her; she was always to be known as June, while Janet
Frame was known in her early years as Jean, the second name of her
older sister.[7]

Janet Frame claims to have written her first story during these
years, "on the banks of the Mataura river, after a meal of trout and
billy tea."[8] It is a few sentences long:

Once upon a time there was a bird. One day a hawk came out of the sky and
ate up the bird. The next day a big bogie came out from behind the hill and
ate up the hawk for eating up the bird.[9]

Although this is probably insufficiently telegrammatic for a child of
three, it nevertheless articulates perfectly the sense of loneliness
and threat that was obviously the product of bleak early years spent
moving about "the wilds of Southland," as she later described
them.[10] Each of their homes was a flimsy railway cottage, pene-
trated by the freezing Antarctic winds of winter and surrounded at
that time by drifts of snow. Many years later, she described Wyndham in a poem about her childhood there:

I see the weathered grey sheep pens, their gates askew,
still standing not used now, scattered with old sheep dirt
like shrivelled berries of deadly nightshade
that lead me to suppose a spreading sheep tree grew here.
I cannot remember. The wildest tree was the sky. Also,
deadly nightshade is poisonous, and sheep are not, are they?

The trains used to pass here. Wyndham station is closed now
and the railway lines like iron thorns are lifted
from their sleeper beds. The stranded station hangs
a sheltering verandah over no human traveller
for the track is overgrown with grass and it is grass, rooted on the platform,
stay-at-home, that meets only the wind passing through
with hospitality of plaintive moan and sigh. . . .[11]

Such images as these obviously impressed themselves on the mind
of the young girl, and remained indelibly to dominate her later
fiction. Thus, Janet Frame's artistic vision came early to her, fos-
tered by the insularity of a family which turned inward from the
barrenness without.

The year 1930 marked a sudden and substantial change in the
lives of the Frame family, for in that year their father was transferred to the Oamaru run. There they were able to resume links with
the town which was to be a permanent home for all but Janet and
June and which provided the children with a background for their
childhood years and early adolescence. Oamaru had by this stage
fulfilled all of its early promise, and had developed into a thriving,
bustling town whose sturdy buildings had increased in number
along its broad main street and were now appearing in the smaller
roads which led from either side of it. In the 1920's, the New Zealand farmer was particularly prosperous, and, as the chief town of a
wealthy farming area, Oamaru enjoyed much of that prosperity.
Increasingly it had become institutionalized, in the sense that it
gave prominence to buildings like the early Bank of Otago or the
Post Office, which had long since been joined by similar edifices—
County and Borough Council offices, law courts, a police station, a
library, more banks, substantial office buildings—which, standing
side by side, disguised their relative shallowness and augmented the
town's considerable appearance. For every agency which helped the
town to function, there seemed to be an impressive stone building.[12]

The Frames rented a small wooden weatherboard bungalow at 56
Eden Street, a few blocks along one of the side roads which ran
inland from the main street of the town and uphill. The house was
about a mile from the railway yards, to and from which Mr. Frame
cycled daily. The three oldest children, who had begun school at
Wyndham, transferred to Oamaru North School, which involved a
walk of a little over half a mile. The house which was to be their

childhood home was distinctive, but rather more in detail than in kind. Literally thousands of such dwellings were built throughout New Zealand in the 1880's and 1890's: quite square, with a central corridor running from front to back and a verandah at the front encasing paired sash windows which were separated by a central front door—the whole dwelling a box containing four rooms and less formal additions at the rear. But the house was in poor condition, in need of paint and many repairs and, like many rented homes, difficult to improve. In a later story, Janet Frame called it "the funny little house with the rusty roof and the cracked front window,"[13] giving an adequate image of its generally run-down appearance. The land behind the house rose immediately upward, towards the hillside behind, which in winter months robbed the houses on the north side of Eden Street of the late sun. Most of these houses resembled the one the Frames lived in, although they were in better condition. The early settlement of the area was evident in the house next door to them, a two-roomed dwelling belonging to the 1860's. The Oamaru Reserve lay over the hill, and for years it was to be Janet's task morning and night to find and milk their two cows there. The Frame children came to know the neighboring hills intimately.[14]

But the arrival of the Frame family in the proud, propertied town coincided with the arrival of the world Depression in New Zealand. Almost overnight thousands of families were forced into poverty and unemployment, which lasted for five years. Oamaru was particularly badly hit: when the farmers prospered, the town prospered, and when the bottom fell out of the farmers' overseas markets, the town nearly collapsed too. Businesses which for years had supplied the farmer or helped export his products found themselves empty; futile and poorly paid jobs were devised, upon which men worked for alternate weeks; children ready to leave school were forced to remain there until the very schools themselves were threatened with closure as an economy measure. Poverty of this sort was not a fresh experience for the Frames; they managed to survive by various means, and must have been the only family in New Zealand whose mother sold her poetry from door to door in order to supplement their income. Gradually, the community recovered, and by the late 1930's all of its old pride and materialism had returned. But for the Frames, the Depression never ended.[15]

They formed a remarkably self-sufficient family, and their simple pleasures in each other compensated for their lack of material goods. Although the early stories Janet was to write reflect a typically New Zealand childhood, with friendly warfare between rival gangs, children's games, and expeditions into the local countryside, the five children were usually sufficient to provide company for one another without the inclusion of neighboring children. Janet and her immediately younger sister, Isabel, became particularly close to each other, often spending long hours walking together on the treeless hills beyond their home; it was here that Janet Frame's love and knowledge of nature were bred.[16] When not there, the children's focus was their home, something of whose untidy warmth comes through in this description of her childhood reading matter:

On the shelves in the kitchen at home there were none of the books which my mother was able to remember and recite from: Hawthorne, Mark Twain, Dickens, and the American poets. My mother had come from a home where there were many books to one where there were few; in a way, her marriage was a migration; she retained passages of prose and poetry and recited them as if they were vivid memories of a homeland she would never see again. Our bookshelf had Grimm's *Fairy Tales* with its dark small print enhancing the terror of many of the tales, and with occasional pages stiffened and curled as if they had been exposed to the weather, as they had been, for Grimm's *Fairy Tales* and Ernest Dowson's *Poems,* and George Macdonald's *At The Back of the North Wind* had been found in the town rubbish dump. The other family books were twelve volumes of Oscar Wilde (which my father had bought in an auction in Wyndham, in a "lot" which included Oscar Wilde, a yellow and black chiming clock, a pair of hedge shears, and a bagpipe record, The Wee Macgregor), *Christendom Astray,* my mother's Christadelphian manual, the Bible, God's Book (a luridly illustrated account of the creation and the prophets and the Latter Days), the doctor's Book, an equally luridly illustrated account of the human body in sickness; a collection of school books and prizes, and one "foreigner" which I never read: it was pale blue with white stripes down the cover and the spine, and its title was *To Pay the Price.*[17]

The children's father was pleasantly idiosyncratic in his manner of relaxation at home. At various times he played bagpipes, danced, painted amateurishly in oils, and embroidered on velvet; he was also an ardent member of the railwaymen's union and the Labor Party. Mrs. Frame, a large and kindly woman, relaxed by writing her stories and poems, many of which were sold to Australian magazines during the 1930's and the war years.[18] Rather than emulating their father's doubtful musical achievements, the children became readers and writers like their mother. When Janet came first in her class during her final year at primary school, her prize of a year's membership in the local library enabled her to flood house and family with books.

My mother (excited at the thought of communicating with the characters and poems of her past begged, "Bring home Charles Dickens, bring home Nathaniel Hawthorne, Henry Wadsworth Longfellow, John Greenleaf Whittier, Mark Twain (that is, kiddies, Samuel Clemens)." My mother would never dream of giving a writer anything but his or her full Christian name and surname. I dutifully "brought home" the favourites including 'a William book' for my brother who was ill, and "something about the sea" for my father. The library tradition was begun.[19]

This was an important occasion in another way: hitherto the family had not been able to afford membership in the large, stone library on the main street; now they had access to at least one of the town's institutions from which their poverty had previously excluded them. When Janet's subscription expired, its annual renewal became the only luxury the family allowed itself.

This was the period of life which she constantly recalled in her later fiction. Nearly always, a feeling of being different and shame at a sensed inferiority dominate these stories. In one of the earliest, called "Child," the narrator befriends another girl at school who seems to have a better and more privileged life than her own; the narrator feels ashamed of her "big mother with a blue pinny to shake at you as if it were wheat for a little fowl."[20] Another early story recalls a father's careful preservation of his only suit, and explains:

Of course it was in the days of the depression, and that's why my father cared so much. That's why we had footnotes on our bill, too, from the draper's shop at the corner, and that's why we had mince for dinner nearly every day, and specked fruit from the Chinaman's and stale cake from Dent's whenever visitors came, and I suppose that's why we wore our aunt's old clothes, dark reds and browns and purples, morocain and voile mostly.[21]

"Miss Gibson and the lumber room" refers to a broken rag doll which belongs to the narrator, her desire for a wristwatch, the modesty of her reading matter, and a pair of dull parents who live in a cluttered home. "Royal Icing" describes a mother who "had no money and no clothes except for an old sack tied around her waist, and a costume, with moth balls in the pockets, hanging in the front wardrobe. Her titties were flat and heavy against her tummy. Her legs had varicose veins."[22] The icing set her husband brings her after years of modest living remains on the sideboard, a sacrosanct emblem of luxuries never experienced. And there are references throughout the childhood stories to beds shared with sisters and to the drudgery of milking the cows twice a day so that the butter could be made. Olive, the central figure of "The Bull Calf," envies her classmates for their freedom from such chores and for their new clothes: "her stockings never lasted, all the other girls bought their stockings at Morton's, and theirs were cashmere, with a purple rim around the top, a sign of quality, while Olive's were made of coarse rayon. She was ashamed of them, she was ashamed of everything and everyone."[23] And in the first novel, *Owls Do Cry,* the children of the family are outsiders: "Francie Withers is dirty. Francie Withers is poor. The Withers haven't a week-end bach nor do they live on the South Hill nor have they got a vacuum cleaner nor do they learn dancing or the piano or have birthday parties nor their photos taken at the Dainty Studios to be put in the window on a Friday."[24]

III *Waitaki Girls' High School*

Early in 1935, at ten and a half years of age, Janet Frame entered the Waitaki Girls' Junior School, which was attached to the High School and lay at a distance of about a mile from her home. A couple of years later, after passing the proficiency examination, she entered the High School, announcing in careful handwriting upon her admission form her intention of becoming a schoolteacher. She was the first of the Frame children to reach High School: her older sister had long since left school and was working for a well-to-do family near home as a housemaid, and her brother had also entered the adult world and was finding it difficult to get a job in the last years of the Depression.[25] The change in Janet Frame's life, caught up in a large and systematically run institution for the first time, was underlined barely a month after her arrival there when Myrtle, her older sister, was drowned in the Oamaru Public Baths on the afternoon of March 5. It was late summer and the baths were crowded: Myrtle was a strong swimmer and may have suffered some kind of seizure while in the water.[26] She was not noticed for some time, and attempts at resuscitation were unsuccessful.

The effects of this tragedy upon a closely knit family were obviously marked and lifelong; their influence upon the mind of a child just entering adolescence is beyond conjecture. Even more than before she and her younger sisters were now thrown together, and the incentive to escape the outside world altogether was increased. Schoolwork was one means of escape, and at the conclusion of her first year at a school noted widely for its scholastic excellence she was placed either first or second in nearly all her subjects. A lowly thirteenth place in Home Science (a course common in New Zealand schools, offering training in cooking and sewing) seems appropriate to one of such an obviously scholarly mind. Similarly high marks, particularly in literature, language, and mathematics, were to distinguish most of the six years she spent at Waitaki Girls' High School.[27] Her favorite teacher there was Janet Gibson, who taught her English and French (and who was later portrayed, rather inaccurately, in "Miss Gibson and the lumber room"). She recalls Janet as a typical member of an alert and intelligent class, remarkable only for her constant smile, the "bright red fuzzy hair"[28] which Janet herself comments on, and of course for her ability in literature and languages. Within school, she and her younger sisters, who came to the High School in subsequent years, were model pupils.

But outside the classroom their attitude became more remote. "I remember at school the teacher used to say, 'You Frame girls, you think you're so different,' " she later recalled. "I suppose we felt different, we were an isolated kind of family. Our hair was different, we always had a lot of hair and that was resented."[29] The solitariness of the children was no affectation, but an expression of an awareness of how different they really were from other children in their classes who came from homes that were tidy and wealthy and who had clothes and possessions that were new. Very few of these children indeed were invited back to the untidy, rusty-roofed house on Eden Street, while invitations from other girls to their homes were as a rule flatly refused, since hospitality would have been not difficult but painful to return. The three girls, and particularly Janet and Isabel, spent much time together; Isabel once told a teacher that, above all else, she liked most to wander for hours over the hills behind their home in the company of Janet.[30] The kind of communion the two girls enjoyed during those years of early teenage is suggested by a pleasant anecdote recalled by one of their teachers: in a fifth-form English class, Isabel submitted an essay of such mystical profundity that no staff member could understand it, and when asked for an interpretation replied, "I knew you wouldn't understand it; Jean would!"[31]

At home, the three girls shared a personal, imaginary world created out of their reading of literature. Its strength and allure is evident:

> In our later years at High School my sisters and I, becoming more ambitious, set to work on our novels, with the titles carefully chosen: *There is Sweet Music, Go Shepherd,* and *The Vision of the Dust,* because I was currently anti-shepherd, anti-sweet music, seeking the poetry in "the heart of the unobvious" by writing about such topics as cellophane paper, factories, ditches, slums, ugliness. There were tragic happenings in our family. Sometimes when it seemed to us that our family was doomed, we would console ourselves by remembering the Brontes and drawing between them and us a grandiose parallel which could not harm, though it might have amused, them, but which may have harmed us into believing that we three girls held, by right, "silk purses" of words. With a background of poverty, drunkenness, attempted murder and near-madness, it was inevitable that we should feel close to the Brontes, once we had read their books and knew the story of their lives. My younger sister . . . was assigned the role of Emily; I, more practical and less outwardly 'passionate' became Charlotte, while my youngest sister, shy, overshadowed in many ways by our "glory," became Anne.[32]

Later, she recalls, she began to retreat increasingly into "my land of Ardenue," an imaginary world hidden even from her sisters and peopled by characters "drawn from objects and people I met in my daily life, with occasional intrusion of characters from fiction."[33] None of the girls made a secret of their desire to be poets (an ambition which provoked occasional suspicion from their more prosaic classmates), and some of their juvenilia remains in the pages of the local newspaper, which encouraged schoolchildren's verse. From about 1940 onward, Janet Frame contributed poems under the pseudonym, "Amera"; most of these suffer from rather precious subject matter and overlush imagery, but are remarkable for their metrical control and general confidence. One in particular is worth seeing in full for its anticipation of the tone and themes of much later writing; it is called "Anzac Evening":

The sunset burns tonight within the sky
As if a thousand poppies had been pressed
In flashing velvet flame above the hills,
And soft the showers of leaves are sweeping by
In murmurs to the distant golden west
Where crimson sunsets die.

And silver ashes, wafted on the breeze,
As slowly creep the shadows o'er each cloud,
Will flutter to the earth and tint the grass
Beneath the groves of silent swaying trees,
Beneath the twilight's dreamy, misted shroud,
When soon the daylight flees.

The perfume of the poppies will drift down,
And linger by the shadows long and deep
That gloom the lonely streets at dead of night,
And houses, dewy cool and neatly brown,
Will wink their eyes and softly fall asleep
In the quiet little town.

I think the poppy embers fall to glow
Upon the graves of soldiers far away.
To gleam and gleam. I think such embers flow
From hearts where sorrow weeps her idle tears
To where the toll of war is marked in grey
That once was white as snow.[34]

In all, Janet Frame enjoyed this pleasant existence for eight years, regularly attending a school whose ways had become very familiar to her and whose academic demands were all too easy to satisfy, living in the same home with the same protecting family. There was some pressure from her parents to leave school and to earn money to help support the family, but the school, recognizing both her special abilities and her special difficulties, provided financial support for her later years there.[35] They were rewarded by good results until the final months of her last school year, when, inexplicably, she sank to the bottom of the class in nearly all her subjects.[36] The years of safe, familiar routine were drawing to an end, and the unnerving, changeful presence of society loomed ahead of her.

IV "This" World

The following year, 1943, was one of change for the entire Frame family. The lease on their Eden Street home expired and their landlord offered to sell it to them, but they preferred to move farther out of town, buying instead an even older house which stood in a valley to the south of Eden Street.[37] The railway line leading from Oamaru to Dunedin passes along a cutting in this valley; Mr. Frame would long have been familiar with the old dwelling which stood fewer than a hundred feet below the railway track. This was "Willow Glen," as it had been known for years, an unpainted cottage beyond the town boundary, far from other buildings and accessible only by means of a long, pine-shrouded drive which was nearly overgrown with grass. Although much smaller than the Frames' former home, it enjoyed a setting that was remarkably similar: hills rose behind and around it, and the familiarity suggested by the adjacent railway cutting and the scattered houses which stood above it was countered by the somber pines and the willows to the south which locked the house and the family into the hillside. It still stands, as a tangible and visible metaphor for the house which had been the Frames' home for their first thirteen years in Oamaru, its every aspect symbolizing the insularity and austerity of the family. It must have seemed like this to many observers: when Janet Frame wrote her first novel, local residents began to call the old house "Where Owls Still Cry."[38]

Janet Frame was not destined to spend much time at "Willow Glen," for her schooldays had ended and what she was later to call "this" world, with its confusions and demands, lay in undisguised enmity before her. Although there was still some family pressure upon her to earn money immediately, she enrolled at Dunedin Teachers' College early in 1943 for a two-year course designed to prepare her to teach children between the ages of five and twelve. This was a choice of career forced upon her, as upon many young New Zealanders of a similar age, by the hard economic facts of university study, which was in these years largely a privilege reserved for those whose parents were wealthy enough to maintain them there. Academic brilliance amongst the less wealthy was catered for by the University Scholarship system, in which Janet Frame had competed late in 1942, together with thousands of other gifted New Zealand schoolchildren. Although she performed extremely well,[39] especially in English and French, she failed to win a scholarship, for the good reason that only five were awarded each year throughout the entire country. A two-year course at a teachers' college offered the only other means of approaching university study, for only in such an institution could a salary—although a small one—be earned while at the same time one could be left a few hours daily for attending lectures. Successful study at university was also a means of promotion in teaching. Thus, for Janet Frame, the imaginative pleasures of literature, and access to the university library with all its resources, became the property of another institution, to be parcelled out, divided, and turned into a yardstick by which a successful career could be measured. The prolonged tug-of-war between inner and outer worlds had begun.

These were not happy years for her. Used to the security of a family now eighty miles away, deprived in particular of the companionship of Isabel (both younger sisters were still at the High School in Oamaru), and lacking sufficient money to make frequent trips north, she found it difficult or unnecessary to make friends, least of all at the Dunedin Teachers' College, which she soon began to dislike strongly.[40] In her spare time, she did alone what she had often done as a child in Oamaru: she wandered about the hills near the outskirts of the town. Here, in the suburb of Opoho in the northern part of Dunedin (where, twenty years later, she was to make a more permanent home), she found a place to suit her mood. "I looked for the poets," she later recalled. "Where were the poets? I spent my free time in the North Dunedin Cemetery, sitting on the tombstones, dreaming, or walking along St. Clair beach, by the lupins and the sandhills."[41] Later, in her second novel, she was to give the fictional Istina Mavet similar experiences:

I liked to eat Carmello chocolate because I was lonely. I bought twelve cushions for sixpence. I sat in the cemetery among the chrysanthemums, bunched in their brownish water inside the slime-coated jam-jars. I walked up and down in the dark city, following the gleaming tram-lines that held and arrowed the street lights and the trams flashed sudden sparks above my head and made it seem, with rainbow splashes of light, that I looked through tears. But the shopwindows were speaking to me, and the rain too, running down inside the window of the fish shop, and the clean moss and fern inside the florists, and the dowdy droopy two-piece sets and old-fashioned coats hung on the aged plaster models in the cheaper shops that could not afford to light their windows, and crowded their goods together, displayed with large warning tickets painted in red.[42]

The alternative to her lonely walks was provided by the writing of poetry and fiction. Something of her ability, as well as her disdain for the institution which governed so much of her life, is seen in an anecdote recalled by an acquaintance who edited the Dunedin Teachers' College literary magazine, *Te Rama,* during Janet Frame's years there. Having made the customary annual call for contributions, the editor was abruptly visited by Janet Frame, who briskly deposited a couple of poems (called "Cat" and "Tunnel Beach") before her and silently left. The editor called upon Joan Stevens, a lecturer at the college (and later Professor of English at Victoria University of Wellington) for advice in evaluating the poems, and both soon agreed on their subtlety and worth. Other staff members were less sure, and many nervously sensed veiled satire in them. Debate raged for a week, until word spread of Miss Stevens's approval, whereupon the doubters began to realize that they had valued the poems all along. The same editor recalls rejecting a short story from the young writer—a rare editorial distinction—on the grounds not of inferiority (on the contrary, it was all too vividly written) but of its unsuitability as the children's story it was intended to be. It described the unexpected arrival of a sea serpent in a child's bath, slithering through the plughole before the child could scramble out. This was adjudged too gruesome even for the young, and unfortunately the manuscript was destroyed at the author's request. As the editor later observed, one destroys an original Janet Frame manuscript just once in a lifetime. [43]

Despite these diversions, her first year of study was highly successful: she passed the first-year English course with an A grade and also scored very well in her French examinations. In 1944, she passed the second-year course in English, but in the absence of an accompanying subject this would not have been accredited to her for the purpose of her teaching career. [44] This shortcoming, together with misgivings apparently felt by those who had trained her, meant that she had little choice of the school in which she was to teach. Instead of being able to return to Oamaru as a schoolteacher, she found herself early in 1945 in a classroom at the Arthur Street school in Dunedin, her only contact with university life being through the course in psychology for which she had enrolled as a part-time student under Dr. John Money, a lecturer who had established the subject at the University of Otago. Neither her teaching nor her university work survived the year: the confusing, contrary demands of classroom and staffroom alike epitomized "this" world, and long before the year ended she had walked away from classroom and school, "from 'this' world to 'that' world where I have stayed, and where I live now,"[45] she later stated. Appropriately, it was an agent of the system who precipitated her departure: her classroom had two doors, and as an Inspector entered through one she vanished through the other, never to return.

"That" world, the world of the imagination, involved an almost complete commitment to literature. Taking a job as a sort of all-purpose maid to four elderly people in a Dunedin boardinghouse,[46] she wrote incessantly in her spare time. Her bedroom was a tiny linen cupboard under the stairs; there, "beneath the shelves piled with linen, I sat on my bed with my newly acquired secondhand typewriter, an aged Barlock whose keys performed a roundabout dance before they reached the paper, and typed slowly, with one finger, for I had never used a typewriter before, most of my *Lagoon* stories."[47] Early in 1946, *The New Zealand Listener* published one of these, the first of her work that could be considered the writing of a mature artist. This was called "University Entrance," a story barely distinguishable in its tone and subject matter from the stories soon to be published in her first collection. Perhaps the most unusual aspect of this story is its curious narrative method, which uses the third person in a manner suggestive of a narrator addressing herself in another form. But the story is not otherwise experimental: set in 1940, it contains characters who are thinly disguised members of the Frame family, down to the gruff and impoverished father and an older sister, "Joan," said to have drowned three years before. The story concerns Doreen, one of the daughters, and her awareness of her family's poverty when her teacher asks her for the two-guinea fee required for her to sit the university entrance examination. Doreen brightly promises to bring the money on the following day, but later plods home knowing that her father cannot afford it. But after summoning up her courage to ask her father for the money she is surprised by his ready agreement, and goes to bed that night feeling more secure than before and able to face the world.

Such successes as these were the high points of her early twenties; the low points can be discerned behind an attempted suicide, which was followed by a period of six weeks spent in hospital.[48] Some comfort had been gained from her sister Isabel, who had followed Janet to Dunedin Teachers' College and to the University of Otago in these years. In the late summer of 1947, the two girls made a holiday trip together to the seaside resort of Picton, their mother's home town and the scene of numerous former holidays. There, on the afternoon of February 17, Isabel, a strong swimmer, left a crowded foreshore and swam a considerable distance into the bay. Then the horrifying events of ten years before began to repeat themselves: the girl was noticed floating in an unusual position, was brought to the shore, and given artificial respiration. But she too had drowned.[49]

It is hardly necessary to comment on the effects of this second tragedy, nor of the cruel way in which its details coincidentally and consistently evoked the death of Myrtle Frame in 1937. To a large extent, these two tragedies were conflated by Janet Frame as she looked back on them in later years, becoming the symbolic death of childhood in her first novel; in *Daughter Buffalo*, by contrast, she confronts them almost directly, but as the loss suffered by a minor character in the novel, and not by herself. The circumstances of the bereavements are not mentioned in this work, and one or two other details are altered slightly; instead, the sense of loss and the nature of the rituals with which humans greet death become the subject of the writing. Her concern with death and its contingency upon life, so dominant in her artistic vision, is born at this point, which becomes a crucial stage in her artistic development.

In the following months, she attempted to come to terms with her loss. She travelled north to Christchurch to work as a maid in a hotel, but her "fear of everyone—the fierce black-clad head waitress, the proprietor, his wife, the guests, a fear intensified in some way by the nightmare of the long Christchurch streets" became more than she could bear alone.[50] She returned home, and in the autumn of 1947 voluntarily entered Seacliff Hospital.[51] She was to remain in hospital for the next eight years. She was then aged twenty-three.

CHAPTER 2

Life in "That" World

I Memory and a Pocketful of Words

ONE of the most striking things about Janet Frame's writing is its
cosmopolitan nature, its confident articulation of experiences
familiar to any reader of English. Although few strong literary
influences stand behind her art, a large body of literature stands at
its side. Few writers have immersed themselves so deeply in the
fiction and poetry of the world, and fewer have turned so sharply
from that fiction to create their own. Recalling this early reading,
she mentions "Beowulf, Marlowe, Shakespeare . . . the metaphysi-
cal and Romantic poets, the novelists—Swift, the Brontës, Hardy;
modern writers—Joyce, Yeats, Eliot, Virginia Woolf, Hopkins,
Dylan Thomas," and, in translation, "Dostoevsky, Tolstoy, Ibsen,
Dante, Kafka and others." These works, and the many others she
read during her twenties,[1] form not simply a world, but *the* world,
embracing all possible acts and emotions and eventualities:

It seems that the whole of humanity and its history of suffering and wonder
are laid out in clearness and understanding. One's sight is made so acute
that one can distinguish the down on the upper lip of Tolstoy's "little
princess"; one can see, with Mitya's agony, the big toe peeping out of his
sock as he stands on trial; there is Marty South at the grave of Giles Winter-
bourne; one can hear her words—"Whenever I get up I'll think of 'ee, and
whenever I lie down I'll think of 'ee again . . . ." There is the interior of
Jude's room; the Ancient Mariner; Lear on the Heath; now it is Midsummer
night, now St. Agnes Eve, now a poet's thirtieth year to heaven, one can
see, side by side, a fairy queen on a bank of wild thyme, a leech-gatherer on
a lonely moor, a saint praying in the sea, his hands warmed by two seals;
here there is a doctor of divinity preaching his sermons at St. Paul's; there, a
poet writing from Northampton County Asylum—"I am yet what I am who
cares or knows?"[2]

32

The world she sketches here, it seems, is for readers, not writers: the writer may visit and revisit, but may not live in the city of words he is helping to build. For Janet Frame, the world of literature is a source of comparisons, generally speaking, but not a source of inspirations.

The years she spent in mental hospitals were, if nothing else, years of literary incarceration. There, she has said, "I was rich beyond calculation . . . for my companions, carried about with me in a little rose-embroidered bag, were Shakespeare and a translation of Rilke's Sonnets to Orpheus." Her interest in Shakespeare was like her interest in most other writers, a reader's interest: "My discoveries about Shakespeare were surprising and personal. I learnt, for instance, that when no one was reading him he invariably read himself—an act consistent with the noise of living made by his unattended works near the gateway of doom."[3] The concept of blindness that occurs in her writing often recalls Gloucester on the cliff, but does not spring from her reading of Shakespeare's plays, which, like many other occupants of the city of literature, simply provide confirmation and illustration of her own ideas.

But the influence of Rilke's "Sonnets to Orpheus" is clearly different, for alone of all works this volume has clearly and substantially affected the style and subject matter of Janet Frame's fiction, particularly the earlier novels, to the extent that Rilke's poetry might be seen as the alembic in which her entire art was formed. The attraction that Rilke's sonnets had for her can be explained by the similarity of her predicament to the poet's, with which she appears to have identified her own. The fifty-five sonnets to Orpheus were written in February 1922, in response to the death of the daughter of one of Rilke's friends. The girl was Wera Ouckama Knoop, whom Rilke had met when she was a child and who died of a glandular disease at the age of nineteen; her death precipitated in Rilke the desire to write a long homage to Orpheus, the mythological figure in whom are united life and death, those two experiences which at first seem so irrevocably opposed. What he saw in the girl's death—the cutting short of a talented, vital, and gifted life—was what confronted Janet Frame herself in the recent loss of a gifted sister of a similar age, a loss made so much less explicable in her case by the earlier and similar death of her older sister. For her, the continued acceptance of life simply had to involve an acceptance of death, which had so forcibly entered her world. Her attraction to the work of Rilke was almost inevitable.

What did the "Sonnets to Orpheus" offer her? Both they and the more substantial "Duino Elegies" which "surround" them set out a vision that seems familiar enough to a contemporary reader. For Rilke sees everyday consciousness in the manner in which a Romantic poet or a later existentialist might envisage it—as a fleeting thing, an unsatisfactory tissue of appearances. In his poetry, everyday experience is portrayed as being merely the lesser part of an ideal existence whose other, ignored part he terms "the invisible." The breathtaking Angel who appears in the Elegies synthesizes the visible and the invisible by his very appearance in human form within the visible world; he terrifies those who deal only in the everyday because he represents a higher degree of reality whose existence has been unsuspected. Death is a part of this higher reality, according to Rilke:

Death is that side of life which is turned away from us, unilluminated by us: we must try to achieve the greatest possible consciousness of our existence, which is at home in both of these unlimited provinces, inexhaustibly nourished out of both . . . . The true form of life extends through both regions . . . there is neither a here nor a beyond, but only the great unity, in which the "Angels," those beings that surpass us, are at home.[4]

Rilke goes on to describe the unification of the two realms of existence as producing "this now first whole, first hale world."[5] The Angel's place in the Elegies is taken by the eponymous god in the Sonnets, for Orpheus's familiarity with the Underworld as well as the everyday symbolizes the union of the visible and the invisible, while his spellbinding gift of song, symbolized by his lyre, stands for the power of art to bring about the desired unification. Looking back at the young girl Wera Knoop through this vision, Rilke idealizes her, too, seizing on her love of dancing and music as evidence of her Orphic ability in the face of oncoming death. Here, for example, he addresses her directly, in the twenty-fifth sonnet of the first part:

Dancer, who all of a sudden, her body rebelling,
stopped, as her youth had been bronzed into art,
mournfully hearkening.—Then, from the Ever-Impelling,
music entered into her altered heart.

> Sickness was near. In the grip of the shadows already,
> darklier thrusted the blood, though defiantly ready
> to surge to its natural spring-tide just as before.

In the twenty-eighth sonnet of Part Two, Rilke tries to suggest some
of the effects of entering upon higher reality through the door of art:
the girl begins

> hearing with all her ears at Orpheus' song.
> And you still moved with motion then imparted,
> And shrank a little when a tree seemed long
>
> In treading with you the remembered pace.
> You knew it still, that passage where the lyre
> Soundingly rose, the unimagined centre . . . .

The theory behind this passage is explained by Rilke himself, who
describes nature as "provisional and perishable" and therefore a fit
companion for man, who is similarly transitory. All everyday things

should be, in the most fervent sense, comprehended by us and transformed. Transformed? Yes, for our task is to stamp this provisional, perish-
ing earth into ourselves so deeply, so painfully and passionately, that its
being may rise again, 'invisibly,' in us. We are the bees of the Invisible.[6]

Where the apparition of the Angel in the Elegies leaves the human
who sees it fainting, Orpheus provides a positive and imitable ideal
in the Sonnets. His song *creates* the world—the "first whole, first
hale" world—and his music entrances nature. A poet does his failing
best to emulate him, so that poetry is a celebration of all nature. The
"Sonnets to Orpheus," accordingly, are amongst the finest poems of
celebration ever written. In the fifteenth sonnet Rilke asks his
reader to

> Dance the orange. Who can forget it,
> The way it would drown in itself,—how, too,
> it would struggle against its sweetness. And yet it
> 's been yours. Been deliciously changed into you.

The thirteenth sonnet is even more explicit about the way in which
poetical exploration of natural objects elevates them:

Banana, rounded apple, russet pear,
gooseberry . . . does not all this convey
Life and death into your mouth? . . . It's there! . . .
Read it on a child's face any day,

when it tastes them. What infinity!
Can't you feel inside your mouth a growing
mysteriousness, and, where words were, a flowing
of suddenly released discovery?

The poet, in Rilke's view, performs a vital function for mankind, showing how to renew and transform everyday life by acknowledging the existence of a higher reality, a fully authentic mode of existence. Implicit in the passages above, too, is a judgment of everyday language, a suggestion that words and things do not truly relate and that the poet's voice alone can make the world whole.

Rilke suggests a modern existentialist philosopher like Heidegger when he stresses the need to embrace death as a concept complementary to life. Any mode of existence that turns from the breathtakingly authentic experience by opting for safe, ritualized, and repetitive behavior is, in a way, dead itself, for "That which would stay what it is renounces existence."[7] In a long passage written to a friend, he laments the tendency of twentieth-century society to move away from the authentic:

Even for our grandparents a "House," a "Well," a familiar tower, their very dress, their cloak, was infinitely more, infinitely more intimate: almost everything a vessel in which they found and stored humanity. Now there come crowding over from America empty, indifferent things, pseudothings, dummy-life . . . . A house, in the American sense, an American apple or vine, has nothing in common with the house, the fruit, the grape into which the hope and pensiveness of our forefathers would enter . . . . The animated, experienced things that share our lives are coming to an end and cannot be replaced. We are perhaps the last to have still known such things.[8]

Rilke was neither the first nor the last to complain of such insidious decadence: the tendency of any industrialized society towards the mass production of commodities, and the consequent effacement of individualism, is a recurring theme amongst social critics.

Rilke's belief that his ancestors were able to enjoy a more intimate relationship with nature than he could reveals a strong generic sense in his thought. In the nineteenth sonnet of the first part of "Sonnets to Orpheus," he indicates that mankind has not even begun to move in the directions he has advocated for it, and in several of the poems there is an urgent sense of the pressing forward of generation upon generation towards a final moment in which the visible world will melt and disperse into the invisible. This is best expressed in the entirety of the seventeenth sonnet of Part One:

> Undermost he, the earth-bound
> root of uprearing
> multitudes, source underground,
> never appearing.
>
> Helmet and hunting-horn,
> words of the aging,
> rage between brothers-born,
> women assuaging.
>
> Branch on branch, time on time,
> vainly they spire . . .
> One free! Oh, climb . . . oh, climb . . .
>
> One, though the others drop,
> curves, as it scales the top,
> into a lyre.

This poem also states that before this long-awaited moment of consummation and fulfillment, the individual poet Rilke himself represents will keep alive the Orphic principle from generation to generation, passing forward to others his superior wisdom, knowledge, and skill.

And Janet Frame is one of those to whom the Orphic principle has been passed. The poetry of Rilke "enters" her artistic world and helps crystallize it as no other writer's has done. This is immediately obvious in the use of names from both the Sonnets and the Elegies in her earlier novels: "laurelled Daphne," mentioned in the twelfth sonnet of Part Two, gives her name to the narrator of the first novel; Toby, her brother, derives from Tobias in the second Elegy; the narrator of *Scented Gardens for the Blind*, Vera Glace, bears the same first name as the young girl whose death provoked Rilke to write the Sonnets. The third novel, *The Edge of the Alphabet*, contains direct quotations from the Sonnets. These echoes are almost obligatory acknowledgments of the wider influence of Rilke's poetry in helping form the fictional world of the novels.[9]

From the outset, Janet Frame's central figures are confident in their possession of superior gifts. They are not outcasts from society but misunderstood prophets who stand apart to assert their superiority and to protect their gifts. New Zealand fiction, like much of twentieth-century literature, has depicted many lonely outcasts; but it is not until the growth of Janet Frame's work that the *worth* of individualism, the rewards that the lone imagination can provide, is demonstrated in the very texture of the fiction. Thus Daphne's voice in the first novel is lyrical, differentiated from the main body of the text by typographical means, for it is the poet's voice which utters imaginative truths. And throughout the subsequent fiction the lyrical voice is repeatedly heard: no other novelist bursts so frequently into song, for no other novelist has such a need to remind the reader of the point upon which her imaginative world balances. It is illuminating that she always thought of herself as a poet, even when writing short fiction, for it is a role which suggests that language has a place as one of the subjects of her fiction.

Rilke's belief in the need to embrace death as a complementary pole to life offered Janet Frame another valuable literary precedent. In her own work, death becomes not simply a pole complementing life but the central part of her vision, a focus for all of life. This increased emphasis upon death stems both from her personal need to confront her own bereavements and from a desire to show how paltry the life is that is led without any acknowledgment of the more majestic and disturbing aspects of existence. Death, like mental breakdown and sickness, becomes a metaphor for the imaginative act which alone will help in the survival of bereavement. Her fiction constantly assaults those ways in which society combats every opportunity it is given to live authentically: schools and scented gardens, mirrors and mindless religion, sports, newspapers, radio and television, and so on. From New Zealand to England to North America, her novels depict a society in a state of atrophy and etiolation, so reluctant to become "whole" or "hale" that it can be truly depicted only as Janet Frame depicts it, through images of freezing snow and the stillness of stone. Much of her fiction, because of the accuracy and sharpness with which she depicts society, is direct social satire, a fact often unacknowledged by her readers.

It is possible that this fiction might have been no more than clever social comment if her knowledge of the "Sonnets to Orpheus" had not encouraged her to explore the causes of the social malaise she perceived. There is a point at which her fiction quite suddenly begins to resonate more clearly, to indicate wider themes and meanings and to transcend the autobiographical. This is in *Scented Gardens for the Blind*, which immediately follows the artistic agony of Zoe Bryce at the end of *The Edge of the Alphabet* as a sort of resolution of all the problems confronted there. In this fourth novel, modern society is seen for the first time as the product of countless years of struggle by individuals to communicate with one another in a way that renders everyday language unnecessary and themselves whole; this struggle has failed so far, and as a result man has worked out his frustrations in organizing mass war and destroying his fellows. As Rilke stated, the struggle has not yet meaningfully begun in which human beings will learn to communicate through a new language, but the conclusion of this novel suggests that the first sounds have been heard.

This weight of concern marks Janet Frame's subsequent work, ensuring its standing as major literature with a statement to make about contemporary man and not simply contemporary man in New Zealand. The feeling that she has particular insights into the mind of the twentieth century, the age of war and organized death, may be owed greatly to the influence on her of Rilke's poetry. Amid the self-doubts which afflict any creative artist, communion with a writer of a similar mind must have been a source of confidence and a reassurance that her own work was developing along significant lines.

II   *Lagoons and Reservoirs*

As well as reading voluminously during her years in hospital, Janet Frame continued to write, encouraged by John Money, her former lecturer in psychology and now a close friend.[10] In 1950 he collected twenty-four of her stories and sketches and persuaded the Caxton Press in Christchurch to publish them under the title of their main story, "The Lagoon." Her first publication in book form received interested attention, and considerable promise for the future was detected in its pages.[11]

The title story is a recollection of childhood visits to a grandmother in Picton. The pleasures of the company of the colorful and straightforward old woman are represented by the tidal lagoon whose delights she points out to the child: crabs, dirty seaweed, and sandcastles. Nevertheless, the child senses that "that wasn't the real story,"[12] that her grandmother withholds a truth about herself that will not be understood until the child is an adult herself. Many years later, grown to adulthood, she travels once again to Picton after the death of the old grandmother to stay with her aunt and uncle, who reveal to her the old woman's secret. "Your grandmother was a murderess," the aunt tells the girl. "She drowned her husband, pushed him in the lagoon."[13] This suggestion of a family taint is concealed as the story ends with a return to the childhood images of sandcastles and fishing.

This pattern, in which images of a happy and secure childhood recede momentarily to admit a terrifying image of the pain of adult life, dominates nearly all the stories in *The Lagoon*. Rather than being seen as an autobiographical record of Janet Frame's grandmother, this story ought to be viewed as a metaphor which makes experience less direct. The beach setting at Picton and the reference to drowning tell us all we need to know about its referents: it is a working-out of the shock of the death of her favorite sister. Picton's beach, with its memories of childhood and summer play, is like the still lagoon which lies within it; but it is a tidal lagoon, linked with the sea which, the writer knows, will later betray the playing child. Thus a taint is sensed even during the remembered idyll of childhood, but is focused upon the grandmother, whose murder of her husband in the lagoon (in itself an unlikely event) is a metaphor for the later tragedy which destroys the innocence of any memories of the place.

The strongly autobiographical interest of this story is typical not only of most of the others in this collection but of much of the longer fiction which follows. Several years after the events, she was still coming to terms with the tragedies of her childhood and youth by means of her fiction. One cannot help but be struck by the imagery of water in the titles of some of her earlier volumes: *The Lagoon*, *Faces in the Water*, *The Reservoir*. A central idea in *The Edge of the Alphabet* is of the "incident in mid-ocean" (to borrow the title of a parallel story), in which a special revelation is made to a traveller upon waters. Some of the implications of this metaphor, particularly in the second novel, will be examined in later chapters. Only an understanding that many references in this earlier fiction are disguised incidents in the writer's own life will enable the reader to understand the work fully.

At times the *Lagoon* stories are quite openly autobiographical, although events in them are very slightly altered. The second story, "The Secret," features the first appearance in her fiction of the figure of an adored sister, here named however after her older sister, Myrtle, and not after Isabel. The pattern of the first story appears here, the playful world of childhood momentarily receding to admit terror. The mother figure in this story solemnly tells its girl-narrator that her sister, Myrtle, has a heart weakness and "may go at any time." "That meant die and death, but Myrtle couldn't die. Gosh we had fun together."[14] But at night, in the bed she shares with her sister, the narrator awakes convinced that her sister's heart has stopped during sleep. "The shadow of the plum-tree outside was waving up and down on the bedroom wall, and the dark mass of coats at the back of the door made fantastic shapes of troll and dwarf," the child observes;[15] but, reaching out, she feels the steady heartbeat of the sleeping girl beside her, and, curling up in the bed's reassuring warmth, no longer sees a threat in the shadow of the plum tree, but thinks once more as a child: "I thought tomorrow there'll be a ripe plum on the plum-tree, Myrtle and I will eat it. And then I fell asleep."[16] Once again, we see a looming adult world of pain and suffering momentarily repelled by the child's return to womblike security.

The third story, "Keel and Kool," presents the death of a sister as an undeniable event which has recently occurred. Winnie, a young girl, has gone with her parents on a picnic near a river; with them is Joan, a girl from a neighboring family. Gradually, behind the trivial business of putting the camera away, shaking the rug, watching the father going off to fish in the river and the mother settle down with a women's magazine, it is revealed that the family is obsessed by the recent death of Eva, their oldest child. The two girls play among the pines, Winnie anxiously aware of Joan's former intimacy with the dead girl and that she herself is an inadequate substitute. She refuses to play with Joan and yearns instead for somewhere to escape, although she knows that "Perhaps she would never find anywhere to go."[17] It is a lonely prediction made by a child who cannot accept the prospect of adult life with her parents dead, like her sister; and in the last paragraphs she climbs a tree—a dark pine—to watch "a

seagull white as chalk, circling and crying Keel Keel Come home
Kool, come home Kool. And Kool would never come home, ever."[18]

Seagulls, naturally, are to be associated with that treacherous
element, the sea; but they are also a part of the vision which she
later expressed aphoristically when trying to explain why she came
to write fiction: "The story of How I Began writing could be condensed into two lines: *A Hawk Came out of the Sky* and *I Knew a
man who knew a man who knew a locksmith.*"[19] In *The Lagoon*,
sudden death or pain intrude often in the form of dark or threatening birds, as in "Swans," in which some children are preparing for a
midweek visit to their favorite beach with their mother, a trip they
usually make on weekends with their mother and father together.
Just before leaving to catch the train, one of the girls finds their cat,
Gypsy, ill in the laundry; they feed and cover it, and then depart.
But on the journey, the girls find themselves disturbed by the
strangeness of travelling without their father and cannot understand
why so few people are at the beach when they arrive there. The
beach they are used to is warm, secure, and predictable, and when
they think of it they know "that never would they grow up and be
people in bulgy dresses, people knitting purl and plain with the ball
of wool hanging safe and clean from the neat brown bag with hollyhocks and poppies on it. Hollyhocks and poppies and a big red
initial, to show that you were you and not the somebody else you
feared you might be."[20] But the deserted beach that awaits them
with its "wrong sea"[21] means change and growth, and this deeply
disturbs the young girls. When they finally leave the beach at the
end of their long stay they wade through a lagoon, and suddenly
confront a forbidding image of their own experience. They have just
been taking comfort from the presence of their mother ("Everything
was warm and secure and near, and the darker the world outside got
the safer you felt for there were mother and father always, for
ever"[22]), when they see a flock of swans upon the darkening water:

It was dark black water, secret, and the air was filled with murmurings and
rustlings, it was as if they were walking into another world that had been
kept secret from everyone and now they had found it. The darkness lay
massed across the water and over to the east, thick as if you could touch it,
and soon it would swell and fill the earth . . . .
   They looked across the lagoon then and saw the swans, black and shining,
as if the visiting dark tiring of its form, had changed to birds, hundreds of

them resting and moving softly about on the water. Why the lagoon was filled with swans, like secret sad ships, secret and quiet. Hush-sh the water said, rush-hush, the wind passed over the top of the water, no other sound but the shaking of rushes and far away now it seemed the roar of the sea like a secret sea that had crept inside your head for ever.[23]

This passage concludes with yet another movement back to the peace and warmth that is associated with the children's parents, but this time the familiar form of escapism is not allowed to conclude the story. For when they arrive back at their home, they find that their cat is dead.

Where the first two stories discussed above end with a comfortable return to childhood, "Swans" seems, because of its disturbing conclusion, to be about the collapse of childhood and the beginning of adolescence. The lagoon of the first story has lost forever its grubby but pleasant treasures of seaweed and crabs, and is threatened by movement, suggesting change and disturbance. There are "murmurings and rustlings," the darkness threatens to "swell and fill the earth" and then seems to have changed to the threatening swans which move on the lagoon. The wind disturbs the rushes, and the sea of childhood is now a memory "crept inside your head forever." And there is the belief that the world of the adult is secret, unsuspected by the child but sensed by the adolescent who is poised between the private lagoon of childhood and the threatening sea of adult life. Death is much closer to the children of this story than to those of the earlier ones.

Other stories portray this threat in a less autobiographical way. An early parable, "Spirit," appears in this collection: it presents death as a blackbird which swoops from the sky on a sunny day to take the unsuspecting from their mundane activities. Later, in "The birds began to sing," blackbirds on a telegraph wire seem to be singing about something beyond ordinary human understanding; when their song ceases, the narrator is aware of darkness, "although the sun was shining."[24] In "Summer," a young boy's game of cricket is ended by rain from a dark sky and the loss of his cricket ball; and in "A Note on the Russian War," the narrator's childlike ability to imagine herself a native Russian suddenly gives way to an apprehension of the approach of war. Other stories are simply autobiographical, such as "My father's best suit," which recalls the poverty of her own childhood, or "The pictures," which is about escapist trips—

with a mother-figure, of course—to the cinema. The best of these childhood reminiscences is "My Cousins who could eat cooked turnips." When the children of this story visit their aunt's home, they are "visitors to an alien world,"[25] particularly aghast at their cousins' docile willingness to consume large quantities of cooked turnips at the dinner table, something which the visiting children would never do in their own home. Then, out of politeness, they indulge in the unspeakable rite themselves and are initiated into their cousins' way of life and become close friends.

Two stories stand out in *The Lagoon* as revealing at a relatively early stage something of the conflict between inner and outer worlds. In "Dossy," a little girl plays in the streets with a disreputable bigger and older girl called Dossy; the narration then shifts to a group of nuns who comment on "little Dossy Park," a motherless child who habitually plays alone. And in "Jan Godfrey" the narrator attempts to write about her boardinghouse roommate, Alison Hendry, but constantly lapses into an account of her mental hospital experiences. The point is that as she does so, for all her lamentations about wandering from her original intention of discussing the tall, quiet woman who sits knitting on the bed opposite, she is in fact discussing that very person: "My name is Alison Hendry."[26] Stories like these, and the imaginative "Note on the Russian War," represent an important development in Janet Frame's art, for they go beyond the mere pessimism and fear of the earlier tales of threatened childhood to create a positive alternative, a means of escape from the harsh and unpleasant world from which Winnie, the girl-narrator of "Keel and Kool," can see no escape. The means of escape lies within the self, the individual world of insight and imagination.

Some of the stories collected in *The Reservoir* belong properly to this early period in which Janet Frame was coming to terms with her own childhood. The title story of this volume again links images of water with the threat of adult life, but its tone is lighter and more pleasant than in the earlier stories. The young children of the family in this story are used to playing in the harmless local creek, but their parents' constant warnings not to visit the distant reservoir raise it to the level of a myth representing the boundaries of childhood and the beginnings of adult experience. The relationship of the reservoir to the tiny creek it feeds is depicted in a masterly manner, unobtrusively symbolizing the slow disturbance of the tranquil waters of childhood. Thus the children note that occasionally the creek becomes unusually full, sluggish, and turbid; this is when the overflow from the reservoir is increased, making the tiny creek unrecognizable. And the reservoir is credited with typically adult powers of adulteration, in a passage which underlines the tendency of society to meddle with the authentic power of nature.

Then, during a heat wave, the children decide to make their forbidden journey up the swollen creek to the reservoir. It is a long, tedious trip during which, as the afternoon wears on, some of the children begin to have misgivings; but when they reach their little heart of darkness it is to find, apparently, no horror at all. When they return home they pity what they think is their parents' fear of the reservoir; but its truly threatening nature, seen in retrospect, is subtly and indirectly revealed through the innocent narrator herself. On the way there the children see "huge trees that lived with their heads in the sky, and their mazed and linked roots rubbed bare of earth, like bones with the flesh cleaned from them."[27] They see threatening notices as well as a ferocious bull, and later briefly lose track of the creek only to find that it has changed in appearance when they see it again: "it had adopted the shape, depth, mood of foreign water, foaming in a way we did not recognize."[28] The pines around them make a crying sound, "a sound of speech at its loneliest level where the meaning is felt but never explained, and it goes on and on in a kind of despair."[29] There are other pines around the reservoir itself:

The fringe of young pines on the edge, like toy trees, subjected to the wind, sighed and told us their sad secrets. In the Reservoir there was an appearance of neatness which concealed a disarray too frightening to be acknowledged except, without any defense, in moments of deep sleep and dreaming. The little sparkling innocent waves shone now green, now gray, petticoats, lettuce leaves; the trees sighed, and told us to be quiet, hush-sh, as if something were sleeping and should not be disturbed—perhaps that was what the trees were always telling us, to hush-sh in case we disturbed something which must never be awakened?

What was it? Was it sleeping in the Reservoir? Was that why people were afraid of the Reservoir?[30]

The pathos of this story comes from its retrospective knowledge that the confidence of the innocently returning children is doomed; but it also draws a distinction between the tendency of the children's parents to shy away from all that the reservoir stands for, and the children's confidence. This story records one of the first cries for Safety which mark her fiction: it is not safe for the children to play near the reservoir because it carries a disturbing quality which the children, aided by their innocent imagination, can comprehend despite the fear the place instills in them. This is the ability, protective yet demanding, which adult society with the desperate craze for safety wishes to pluck from the child.

"Obstacles" is a similar story in the same collection. There is another puberty rite, this time involving the crossing of a water pipe which spans the creek at its most dangerous point, where it is "unfathomable, like Lake Waihola,"[31] and where a notice which once read "DANGER" now reads much more mysteriously, through the loss of a letter, "ANGER."[32] The children who cross this happy pipe of childhood become adults; significantly, the narrator is never able to do this.

The loss of childhood innocence with its protective and valuable powers is always to be the central tragedy of her fiction, as these early short stories make clear; and the culprits are always the adult world and the forces of destruction that are both associated with it and at the same time its greatest source of terror. Because this vision of the world has very personal origins, her best writing is always personal and frequently autobiographical, although, as Winston Rhodes points out, it would be wrong to assume that all of her work refers to herself.[33] Nevertheless, as these early stories show, a knowledge of her life will always increase our understanding of her fiction and poetry rather more than is the case with most other writers. In the subsequent chapters of this study, such a knowledge will be seen often to reduce the apparent complexity of her writing.

III   *Robin Hyde and* The Godwits Fly

During her years in hospital, Janet Frame read deeply in the literature of her own country as well as in that of the world,[34] but only one New Zealand novel, Robin Hyde's *The Godwits Fly*, published just before the outbreak of the Second World War, has had any traceable influence upon her own work. "Robin Hyde" was the pen name of Iris Wilkinson, an Auckland writer who committed suicide in England at the age of thirty-three, shortly after the publication of her novel. This was a remarkable piece of fiction for its time, for New Zealand was not noted for its production of sensitive,

inward-turning fiction like *The Godwits Fly*. It is an autobiographical account of the development of Iris Wilkinson's own artistic vision, along the lines of Joyce's *Portrait of the Artist,* a subject which
in itself would have recommended the novel to Janet Frame during
these crucial years. And much of its content would have seemed
strikingly familiar. It is narrated by its central figure, Eliza Hannay,
the second of the three daughters of an impoverished family struggling to survive in New Zealand between the two wars. Like the
younger Janet Frame, Eliza has a red bush of hair, is afflicted by her
constant awareness of her poverty during her school years, and can
look back to an early succession of rented homes. Augusta Hannay is
an imposing mother-figure, her husband John the struggling veteran of the Great War. There are a number of coincidences in the
lives of the two writers, too: both were remarkably intelligent and
sensitive to the point of suffering breakdown, for Iris Wilkinson had
attempted suicide and subsequently spent three years in Auckland
Mental Hospital, in an annex called The Lodge.

Her novel describes the loss of innocence in the child who grows
to adulthood, and examines the relationship between dream and
reality. Both of the Hannay parents show aspects of the failure of
youthful ideals, a failure that drives them increasingly apart from
each other. Augusta Hannay is a puritan, determined that poverty
will not corrupt her children, and sustained only by a long-held
desire to travel to England. She never gets there, for she is bowed
by poverty and the toil of motherhood; one of the most tragic moments of the novel occurs when she realizes that her ideal has
become a dream that will never be fulfilled and the source of her
frustrated battle with an inhospitable reality. Her husband, too, has
unfulfilled dreams: his wife does not return his love, so that he falls
back upon socialism as a means of spreading love and unity amongst
his fellows. But this, too, is a vain dream that lapses into lonely
futility. And the oldest child of the family, Carly, is protected from
reality by her mother and later by a fiancé who gives her the long-
term security of a prolonged engagement without the final benefit of
a wedding. Carly's one attempt to come to grips with reality is a
disastrous failure—she becomes a student nurse and witnesses the
birth of a deformed child—and she withdraws to the protection of
her mother.

Eliza's is the story of the slow dispersion of idealism into fantasy
and the growth of an inner voice. The touchstone of her innocent

idealism is the "glory hole," an aperture in the floor of a neighbor's house, which reveals nothing but darkness when she is shown it as a young child but which her child's imagination manages to fill with the possibility of fairies and enchantment. Typically, she is not allowed to search for these things in the glory hole for fear of dirtying her clothes, which her mother has cleaned for her. It is always the adult who thwarts the child's imaginative vision, and Augusta Hannay is an especially repressive force. Her husband, on the other hand, has estranged himself from his wife by his willingness to encourage Eliza's imagination through the free use of his own: he, in this case, destroys his own ideals by attempting to fulfill his daughter's.

As reality proves itself decreasingly in harmony with all the promise of the glory hole, the growing Eliza retreats further into dreams and fantasies, which occasionally have a nightmarish quality, and whose alternative is a kind of hallucinatory feeling of communion with nature. At the same time, the narrative voice of the novel breaks and the adolescent girl is depicted more poetically. The novel gains the elusiveness and suggestive imprecision of poetry as it progresses. Timothy, with whom Eliza later falls in love, is an idealized and ethereal figure more appropriate to poetical romance than to realistic fiction; it is the collapse of his relationship with Eliza that precipitates the greatest crisis in her life. Timothy travels overseas without her and soon dies; Eliza, confronted by a wintry existence after her godwit has flown, has a desultory love affair with a near-stranger, bears his child in Sydney, Australia, only to find that it is dead, and returns to New Zealand with the knowledge that one either submits to life or retreats from it into a dream which will finally destroy the dreamer. For the only ideal which can be converted into reality is the artistic ideal: art alone provides meaning and survives existence intact.

The Godwits Fly is certainly not original in what it says; many writers before and since have advised their readers to immerse themselves in the destructive element. But for all its desperation, the work has a curiously intimate quality, a tone which had no parallel in fiction at the time it was written and which could more properly have been sought in poetry. These attributes clearly attracted Janet Frame's attention, and the novel consequently leaves its mark on much of her fiction. Cherry Hankin has remarked on the similarity of its title to that of Janet Frame's first novel, *Owls Do Cry*;[35] the names, Timothy and Toby, are common to both books; Robin Hyde's ninth chapter is called "Reflections in the Water," while Janet Frame's second novel is *Faces in the Water*; the first chapter of Robin Hyde's novel is "The Glory Hole," while the first part of Janet Frame's is called "Talk of Treasure" and expands the imaginative touchstone of Eliza Hannay's life into the rubbish dump, a symbol which dominates and controls the entire later novel. The influence of Robin Hyde carries on into *The Edge of the Alphabet*, where Zoe Bryce's failed love affair, trip to England, and suicide there all echo the experience of Robin Hyde herself. Certainly, the insight Zoe Bryce gains before she dies is precisely the same as that which comes to Eliza Hannay at the end of *The Godwits Fly*, occurring too amidst quotations from Rilke's "Sonnets to Orpheus."

But beyond all these influences, the earlier novel helped establish a pattern that is visible in all Janet Frame's writing. Her characters may be divided into one of three groups represented in the Hannay family: like Eliza, they can be gifted with a knowledge of the power of the imagination when it is directed towards art; or like Augusta, they can establish a safe dream of order which will forever be threatened by reality; or like John, they can be slumped in the disillusionment which follows the realization that idealism is at an end and all dreams futile. But it is one of the triumphs of Janet Frame's art, as will be seen, that she is able to make these characters her own, and to establish them within a vision that is distinctive and individualistic.

III *The Last Twenty Years*

Janet Frame had left hospital by the summer of 1954–55 and was staying with her sister June and her family in Auckland. It was June who introduced her to the distinguished New Zealand writer, Frank Sargeson, at his home in Takapuna on the outskirts of Auckland. Later, Sargeson recalled that first meeting:

I knew about her and her sister turned up with her in a car one day and said this is Janet Frame . . . . You could see this girl had this marvellous intelligence. She was very shy, retiring, and I showed her the army hut and I said, "Well why not come and live in the hut?" and she did and she stayed about eighteen months.[36]

Sargeson's generosity did not stop here; soon he was another
"locksmith," arranging through an understanding doctor for her
support on a Social Security Benefit. After a short time, he
suggested that she should begin to write a full-length novel, and she
turned to this task later in 1955 and was occupied with it for a year.[37]
Owls Do Cry was published in 1957, when Janet Frame had left for
the Mediterranean. It was received with the kind of acclaim that is
reserved for a very special work: it was variously described as "the
most striking novel of our hundred years,"[38] as "an outstanding
literary event,"[39] and as containing "a lot of profound truths for
Everyman"[40]; even *Time* magazine found it exciting. Janet Frame
had become established overnight as a major New Zealand writer,
already showing that appeal for readers abroad which was to mark
her later fiction.

This success did not mean the end of her personal struggles,
however. While her novel was awaiting publication she was still
unknown; and the doctor who had helped her qualify for a Social
Security Benefit for eighteen months had begun to convince himself, as she recalls, that "nothing could be done for me, I would be
'better off' in hospital."[41] The doctor's certificates stopped coming,
and she had again to confront "this" world, spending a "nightmare
two weeks"[42] cleaning rooms at a huge Auckland hotel until she was
dismissed one afternoon, three and a half hours after all other maids
had gone home and with her work only half-finished. Again Frank
Sargeson stepped in, suggesting that she apply for a State Literary
Fund Grant to travel overseas. This was granted, with an extra
bursary of $300 for the writing of a new novel, and late in 1956 she
left New Zealand, not to return for seven years.

She spent the next period of her life in the Mediterranean area,
living on the island of Ibiza and later in Andorra. Then, in 1958, she
travelled to England, where she was based for the five years which
were to prove the most productive of her life. In London, she made
the friendship of another "locksmith," R. H. Cawley of the
Maudsley Institute, where she stayed for a time. It was he who
made her understand the importance of writing for her future. As
she recalls,

when the doctor had studied my history and difficulties, I was astonished
and grateful to hear him refute all previous commands—Why mix, why
conform? I think you need to write to survive. First write the story of your

years in hospital, then keep on writing. You've no money, no income? We
will arrange a National Assistance grant. There will be the usual personal
difficulties, depressions; but we will try to make them more endurable.[43]

A flood of books and stories followed Cawley's advice, many of them
dedicated to him; there was also what she has referred to as "a
novel-length autobiographical essay, *Towards Another Summer*,"[44]
which has not been published. She found the time and sense of
humor, too, to needle a few established institutions. While in New
Zealand she had sent poems to a rather self-conscious literary
magazine in London, pretending to be the daughter of a Polynesian
chief who had only recently come to civilization. The editor had
replied, saying that her poetry had shown considerable promise for
one with such a limited command of English. In London she repeated the ruse with different poems and the same editor, although
on this occasion she posed as a dark-skinned poet from the Carib-
bean. Again, the editor was enthusiastic, especially about the fresh-
ness of the poems, "a characteristic quality of writers like yourself,
whose native tongue is not English." The noble savage had arrived.[45]

Faces in the Water was praised for its more genuine poetic beauty
and its lyrical insights when it first appeared during these years; but
its function as a development of the first novel was not fully understood until the following year, when the third volume of the trilogy,
The Edge of the Alphabet, appeared. Indeed, the second novel was
taken for a documentary, as is shown by the fact that for some time
after its publication it was a compulsory text for all nursing staff at
New Zealand mental institutions.[46] Then came *Scented Gardens for
the Blind*, amongst the most complex and subtle novels to be written in English since the war; like the first volume of stories, it won
the Hubert Church Memorial Award for literature. In the same year
she collected the stories and parables from the decade before and
published them in two volumes, *The Reservoir* and *Snowman
Snowman*.

While in England, she had had a number of homes. After leaving
the Maudsley Institute, she lived in lodgings in Camberwell, sup-
plementing her National Assistance grant by working as an usher in
a cinema. Later she shifted to Camden Town, and also lived for a
while in a caravan on the property of a friend she shared with Frank
Sargeson, Miss E. P. Dawson of Itteringham in Norfolk.[47] But in

August 1963, Janet Frame's father died suddenly in Oamaru, upon
which she almost immediately set sail for New Zealand to help settle
the family estate, her mother having died eight years before.[48] In
1956, she had left New Zealand almost completely unknown; now,
her return was noticed by the public with that particular interest
New Zealanders have for their fellow countrymen who achieve distinction abroad. The bustle of being noticed and the demands this
made on an essentially shy person were expressed in a poem she
wrote a little later, which began,

> —How does the place strike you on your return?
> —It's too soon to feel or listen.
> This close-thrust microphone
> alters my heart-beat, the breath in my mouth
> to gales down the Buller Gorge
> uprooting the native trees
> —or platitudes—who can distinguish between these . . . .[49]

There were inquiries about her unfinished novel (this was *The
Adaptable Man*, which she had begun in England) and where she
would live to finish it. Eventually, having disposed of "Willow
Glen" (she had briefly contemplated living in it[50]), she settled in a
house on Evans Street, Opoho, Dunedin, which also occasioned a
poem:

> I came one day upon a cream-painted wooden house
> with a white bargeboard, a red roof, two gates,
> two kinds of japonica bushes, one gooseberry bush,
> one apple tree lately in blossom; and thus I counted
> my fortune in gates and flowers, even in the white
> bargeboard and the fallen roofbeam crying religiously to the carpenter,
> Raise me high! and in this part of the city that would be
> high indeed for here my head is level with hills and sky.[51]

Here, near the streets and cemetery in which she used to wander
twenty years before, she completed *The Adaptable Man*, which was
published in 1965.

During 1964, Janet Frame broadcast a series of radio talks on the
relationship between artist and society in New Zealand, which were
probably abstracted from *Towards Another Summer*. In these talks
she displayed an ambivalent attitude towards her own country,

showing an obvious love of its physical character and an awareness that the exiled writer runs the danger of withering at the roots, but also showing an awareness that, as she has said elsewhere, New Zealand society has no second floor and no staircase to reach one:[52]

At one time it seemed that our knowledge and understanding of the grown men and women of New Zealand would be enlarged less by fiction than by the records of the Psychology Department of the University. It seemed that the Teds, Freds and Harrys, the Marjories, Dorothys and Shirleys, would remain only as characters in a national fallacy: writers write on interesting themes. Few New Zealand writers describe grown men and women. Therefore the grown men and women are dull, faceless, lacking in individuality.

The loss of an expatriate writer is felt as a blow to literature, also to national morale. We keep asking defensively: Why don't you stay? What's wrong with us, what's wrong with your own country? Yet many writers are living and working now in this country; an exile is not missed greatly while many of his fellows choose to remain, to love and hate and write about themselves, the landscape, and Ted and Fred and Marjory. Yet though the balance of creative artists remains the same no matter what the population of a country may be, the methods of creation are not stable.

A few people may prefer kicking footballs, raising fat lambs, to kicking thoughts around and raising books. The need to shape a political or social ideal may be greater than the need to shape a poem or painting. Yet it is the writer, the painter, who identifies, names, captures the yacht sailing in Waitemata Harbour, rather than the yachtsman who sails it. Art is a process of capture, of possession. The complaint of an artist who feels he "doesn't *belong* in his native land" may mean that the task of getting the land and the people to belong to him is a lonely one when there seem to be so few attempting it. It costs less in suffering to enjoy the "gift of the sea" than to accept, name, possess it.[53]

Such thoughts as these are evident in the novels she wrote next, *A State of Siege* and *The Rainbirds*, both of which depict a society of blind men and women moving through a country whose savage beauty they refuse to confront directly.

The former novel has an interesting genesis which tends to destroy any suggestion that Janet Frame's art is born within herself and that it is without contact with exterior life. It came after she had rented a holiday cottage for a short stay on Waiheke Island, a resort not far from Auckland. There she made a number of discoveries of a literary nature: she found a copy of Frank Sargeson's *A Man and His Wife*; a critical book on the musician Richard Wagner in which she

found the phrase, "the room two inches behind the eyes" as a description of the imaginative faculties; and she also discovered that
the cottage had formerly belonged to Rebie Eleanor Rowlandson,
Sargeson's favorite teacher of many years before upon whom he had
modelled the spinster schoolteacher who appears early in *Memoirs
of a Peon*. Sargeson told Janet Frame the woman's story—that she
was related to the famous English artist of the same surname, that
she gave up teaching comparatively early to devote herself to music,
and that after living at the cottage for some time she had died in
great poverty. Janet Frame based the character of Malfred Signal on
her: in *A State of Siege* she is an art mistress from a southern town
who retires to a cottage on a northern island to become a genuine
artist, and fails.[54]

In 1964, Janet Frame was awarded the Burns Fellowship for the
following year. Given an Assistant Lecturer's salary, a study in the
Department of English, a typewriter, and reams of fresh paper, she
set about writing *The Rainbirds* (to be retitled *Yellow Flowers in the
Antipodean Room* when published in North America). She also became a familiar figure on campus, and on one occasion agreed to
address a few members of the university's literary club, only to find
when she arrived that the word had spread and that half the university crammed the room she was to speak in. She met this challenge
to her natural shyness by a simple expedient—she immediately and
silently left.[55]

An important development in her career occurred in 1967, when
she began her first extended visit to the United States. This was the
first of a series of stays at the Yaddo Foundation, an artists' colony in
Saratoga Springs, New York. The colony had been financed by
wealthy patrons of the arts in America and offered ideal surroundings for creative work. Each artist at the foundation had private
quarters, including a studio, and pleasantly rural surroundings. In
the evenings, for the first time in her life, she was able to mingle
exclusively with fellow artists—usually painters and musicians—
who had a similar disposition and outlook. Between bursts of creative activity during these years she travelled in other parts of the
United States and in Europe, as well as returning to New Zealand,
and in 1969 she spent some time at the McDowell Colony in Peterborough, New Hampshire, which was founded by the wife of the
composer Edward McDowell. Like the Yaddo Foundation, the

McDowell Colony offered peaceful seclusion, a wooded environment, and congenial company.[56]

During these cosmopolitan years she wrote *Intensive Care,* a novel whose range and scope were promised in *Scented Gardens for the Blind. Daughter Buffalo* was begun in the United States in 1971 and completed in New Zealand: it is a curious parable about the relationship between her public and private selves, her youth and her recent past, her New Zealand identity and her overseas identity; it is also a penetrating insight into the psychology of a nation whose lively bustle is attractive while its violence is appalling.[57] Perhaps a sign of her awareness of the tensions in public life can be seen in her decision at this time to change her surname to Clutha, the name of the river which lies to the south of Oamaru. The name she was born with connotes rigidity and fixity; to take the name of a river is to opt for fluidity, adaptability, and elusiveness. In 1972 she proved this adaptability by leaving her Dunedin home and the south of New Zealand and settling at Shakespeare Bay on the Whangaparoa Peninsula just north of Auckland, a "land of motor-mowers, circular saws and floor sanding machines, against a background of wonderful silence."[58]

Daughter Buffalo was awarded the Hubert Church Memorial Award, and late in 1973 she was awarded the Winn-Menton Scholarship for 1974. She travelled to France in that year and spent some months writing in the Katherine Mansfield room at Menton. On her return to New Zealand she shifted from the Whangaparoa Peninsula to Glenfield, a suburb of Auckland.

CHAPTER 3

In The Fox's Belly

I The Waimaru World

O wls Do Cry consists of two parts tied together by an epilogue. The division is chronological: the first part, subtitled "Talk of Treasure," describes a golden childhood that is becoming tarnished by time; the second part, "Twenty Years After," examines the lives of the Withers family after they have become adults. The epilogue is subtitled, "Anyone We Know?"

Bob and Amy Withers, the parents, are a struggling working-class couple. He is an unimaginative man who has worked as an engine driver all his life and become increasingly hardened in his beliefs and habits. His wife is a gentler figure, deferential to him but equally trapped by routines of which the most exciting is her daily baking, which she slides endlessly in and out of the oven as the novel progresses. Amy has minor literary pretensions which she satisfies by writing pseudonymous letters to the paper, although house and family take precedence over these activities. The oldest child of the Withers family is Francie, an adolescent poised on the brink of the adult world—she "had *come*, that was the word their mother used when she whispered about it in the bathroom."[1] At the beginning of the novel she is about to leave school. The second child is Daphne, who narrates the whole work; she is a sensitive, intro-spective girl who loves poetry and responds to her surroundings imaginatively. Their brother, Toby, is a slow-witted epileptic who relies heavily on his mother and sisters and is the most obviously "abnormal" member of the family. The youngest child is Teresa, nicknamed Chicks: she is little seen in the first section except as a tiny child who straggles behind the others.

"Talk of Treasure" is very familiar to anyone who has read the *Lagoon* stories. The poor families and ostracized children of those

56

stories are forerunners of the Withers family. Here is society's view
of Francie, for example:

> Francie Withers has a brother who's a shingle short. She couldn't bring
> the fuji silk for sewing, she had to bring ordinary boiling silk that you shoot
> peas through, because she's poor. You never see her mother dressed up.
> They haven't any clothes and Francie hasn't any shoes for changing to at
> drill time, and her pants are not *real* black Italian cloth.
> She hasn't a school blazer with a monogram.[2]

This is the adult world's view and these are the collective, un-
examined social values that the novel rejects. "Talk of Treasure" sets
out the alternative: the childhood vision of imaginative truth which
transforms the children's favorite playing ground, the town rubbish
dump. Here they find all those things that society discards because
their utilitarian value has gone—bedsprings and car tires and moldy
books—and that their innocent vision sees as a magic world in which
all rust is gold. They find a book of fairy stories and a volume of
Ernest Dowson's poetry, the former described with a careful dif-
ferentiation between its value and its use:

> The book smelt, and it too had been eaten by worms which still lived in its
> yellow pages, and it was dusted over with ashes, and it had been thrown
> away because it did not anymore speak the right language, and the people
> could not read it because they could not find the way to its world. It had
> curly writing on the cover, saying, The Brothers Grimm. It spoke of Cin-
> derella and her ugly sisters with their cut-off heel, and the blood flowing
> back, the snow colour of every bean flower.[3]

For the children, the rubbish dump is a fairy land that is attractive
to the imagination; for adults, it is a place from which smells and
germs might be brought home. Time is always the greatest enemy,
with its "old old shuffle of decay,"[4] turning imaginative children into
unimaginative adults: "Talk of Treasure" is crammed with images of
time threatening children with adolescence, and adolescents with
adulthood. There is the mantel clock into whose interior Bob and
Amy cram the bills which measure out their lives (later in the novel,
they need four clocks to take all the bills and to accommodate all the
time they have wasted). And there are calendars which also attract
bills and which somehow "contrive in hanging there to collect all the
days and months of the year, numbering them, like convicts, in case
they escape."[5]

Francie, of all the Withers children, is most threatened by time, for as an adolescent she is in the process of losing her childhood vision and assuming the impaired sight of the adult. In some ways she is eager to enter adult life, but only those parts which have been sufficiently romanticized to disguise their prosaic squalor. Thus her adolescent friendship with a spotty local youth becomes translated into the stuff of which celluloid dreams are made, although she later discovers that the boy's father is not the noted brain surgeon she had thought but a workman in a park. Along with her aberrant liking for aspects of the adult experience, Francie retains some remnants of the truthful vision of childhood: she returns to the dump occasionally, drawn by the treasure there, and when she is briefly employed as a maid in the house of a wealthy neighboring family she has sufficient insight to perceive the unhappiness of its mistress. But when Mr. Withers finds the girl a job in the local woollen mills, she begins to feel that society is closing in upon her. Both she and Daphne see the mill as a prison employed by society to drive individuality from the young; the increasing tension of impending imprisonment becomes focused upon an event which occurs one Saturday when Francie takes the other children to the rubbish dump, falls into a fire there, and is burned to death.

The second section of *Owls Do Cry*, "Twenty Years After," is subdivided into three parts, each of which in turn examines the surviving Withers children in adulthood. Toby still lives at home twenty years after the death of Francie, and although he suffers less from his epileptic fits he is still regarded as an oddity by the rest of society. Nevertheless, he has become a fairly successful businessman of an independent sort: he is a specialist in destruction, knocking down an old hotel under contract and selling scrap metal from the rubbish dump for profit. But success brings him only money, and he remains a lonely and alienated figure on the outskirts of "normal" life. In a poignant scene in this subsection, he visits a childhood sweetheart before her wedding day to give her a gift and to express, in his idiosyncratic but accurate manner, both his own loneliness and an awareness that the girl is about to enter a life of crippling routine in which all that is good and valuable from her childhood will be betrayed. For Toby is both caught up by the utilitarian ethics of the society he lives in and aware of its limitations, especially when he dreams that Daphne scolds him for making a profit from the rubbish dump. This subsection ends with a joyless celebration of Christmas in which no arid routine is forgotten and at whose conclusion Amy Withers realizes that she has long forsaken the healing gifts of childhood.

Chicks, who has reverted to her given name of Teresa in her subsection of Part Two, has managed to transcend her humble background almost completely. Her story is given by means of extracts from a diary she keeps, which Toby surreptitiously reads when he visits her well-equipped North Island home. Her acceptance of the shallow values of society is almost total: she has married Timothy Harlow, the boy with whom Francie had been friendly at the time of her death, and he has become a successful businessman who is able to provide his family with many material comforts and his wife with the means to make several forays into the upper reaches of society. "What more can one ask of life," she writes without perception in her diary, "than to be popular and sought after."[6]

One of her "targets" is a wealthy society doctor and his wife, the Bessicks. After a stifling evening of entertainment in which they listen to Beethoven's Fifth Sympony while Chicks sways "backward and forward" with what she hopes is an "intelligent expression" on her face,[7] she is congratulating herself on her success when she reads that Dr. Bessick has just murdered his wife. This is disturbing for Chicks but not so disturbing that she can understand its full significance for herself. Her hopeless crassness is revealed in her response to the plight of Daphne, who is not in a mental hospital: one of her letters to Chicks has the words "Help help help" scrawled along the bottom[8]; Chicks does not see that Daphne is crying to be rescued from the threat of a brain operation, but thinks rather that she wants to be rescued from insanity by having the operation. She decides to present her older sister with her old steam iron when normality returns to her, since all people need a material basis on which to begin their return to life. Toby, half "dead" and half "alive," can see that his younger sister is almost completely lost. And at the end of this subsection, the Harlows' loss becomes utter, as they return to Waimaru to live in a house that has been built over the rubbish dump of childhood.

The final section of "Twenty Years After" is reserved for the narrator, Daphne, in the mental hospital. In this part, complex themes emerge in which the issues of "normality" and "abnormality" are examined in the light of private and public values; these will be discussed fully later in this chapter. These themes are directed into the struggle of Daphne to avoid electric shock treatment and the leucotomy which will physically remove her imaginative faculties from her. Near the end of this section she is visited by her brother and newly widowed father, Toby suffering an epileptic fit in the waiting room of the hospital and making utterances which frighten his father and the other visitors there. When Bob confronts Daphne, he is overwhelmed by the sight of her shaven head, which has been prepared for the brain operation, and weeps for his dead daughter. After his departure, the operation occurs, Daphne is returned to society with her mind cut down to safe proportions, and the book she is narrating suddenly ceases.

The epilogue, "Anyone We Know?," is devised to universalize the themes of *Owls Do Cry* and extend their significance beyond the Withers family. It depicts the manager of the local mill and his wife who are sunning themselves on the glass-screened verandah of their home on a Saturday morning while he reads aloud items from the local newspaper. Each item refers to an anonymous figure who resembles one of the characters in the novel, but an italicized line after each points specifically to the character involved, turning the epilogue into a series of epitaphs which show that all of society is withered, that the Withers family is not alone but representative. An anonymous social security clerk is reported guilty of embezzlement, his wife committing suicide from shame; the reference is to Fay Crudge, Toby's former childhood sweetheart, and the man she married. A murder is reported in the paper—a society figure has been killed by her husband—and reference is made to Timothy and Teresa Harlow. A nameless vagrant is arrested; it is obviously Toby, although once more "the paper said another name."[9] A former inmate of a mental hospital has been promoted in the woollen mill, her acceptability in society confirmed by the presentation of a watch in which the jewels of childhood are finally trapped in the circle of time. It is both Daphne and anyone. Her father is depicted at the conclusion of the novel, not as anyone but specifically as himself, a drooling old man mindlessly sunning himself outside the geriatric hospital in which he will die. On this resoundingly empty note, the novel ends.

II *Narration*

It is a little misleading to depict *Owls Do Cry* in summary form, for any reader who is familiar with the novel will rightly feel that it seems far more conventional in outline than it actually is. Nevertheless, it is useful to be reminded that the novel can be described in such a way, for the author's concern to make a formal statement rather than a lyrical outburst is made evident in this reminder. Yet it is this lyrical "inwardness" which distinguishes the novel and knits its parts together by means of a series of italicized passages of considerably poetic beauty uttered by Daphne from the "dead room." This is the room in the mental hospital in which the leucotomy will eventually rob her of the imagination from which the poetry comes, and from which she can see past, present, and future in the events she recounts. Thus, a sort of counterpoint operates throughout the work, in which narrative passages of the kind that helped provide the summary above alternate with densely symbolic lyrics in which Daphne walks, as she says,

> *like Theseus or an ashman*
> *in the labyrinth, with our memories unwound on threads of*
> *silk or fire; and after slaying by what power the minotaurs of*
> *our yesterday we return again and again to the birth of the*
> *thread, the Where.*[10]

Along these threads may be found childhood, *"the boy in the fox's belly"* who is *"locked in the suffocating belly of memory."*[11] And so primacy is given to the poetical voice in this novel, an inevitable development of Janet Frame's regard for Rilke and his belief that the poet is prophet and poetry the voice of imaginative truth. Great significance lies in the lyrics of *Owls Do Cry,* for they must be seen to contain truths about existence and to represent a preferable mode of utterance to prose, the language of the everyday.

There are many examples on the basis of which such a judgment might be made. The novel begins with a passage reminiscent of Blake's "Songs of Innocence," with references to a happy pipe of childhood and many lush pastoral images. But the process of decay threatens all—carrot seeds shrivel instead of sprouting, young beans are eaten by black insects, wind comes from the cold south, and all these provoke the question,

what use the green river, the gold place, if time and death pinned
human in the pocket of my land not rest from taking underground the
green all-willowed and white rose and bean flower and morning-mist
picnic of song in pepper-pot breast of thrush?[12]

This imaginative vision of time is followed by a passage which anticipates the shabby Christmas the novel depicts, referring to "vol-
uminous, dyspeptic Santa Claus" and "a mound of snow at the door
of Christmas" irrevocably piled up by the south wind of time.[13]

The second lyrical passage follows the narrative chapters in which
the reader is introduced to the Withers family and the children's
love of the rubbish dump with the "gold tickle of toi-toi around its
edges."[14] This lyric evokes darkness and rain and the flaying of
blue-gum trees by the wind; all these are shown to be direct threats
to the Withers children. The malevolent feeling of threat becomes
focused on Francie in particular, since the narrating Daphne has
foreknowledge of her fate, and she can see the significance of Francie's role in the school play in which she takes the part of Joan of Arc:

Oh, Francie, Francie was Joan of Arc in the play, wearing a helmet
and breastplate of silver cardboard. She was burned, she was burned
at the stake.[15]

This symbolically predicted event then occurs within the next narrative chapter. The third passage of lyrical utterance follows, setting
forth the aim of unstitching the child of memory from the womb of
time. Here, too, there is set up an important group of images, in
which the entire Withers family are likened to birds in a storm
which sweeps them from their home:

Francie, come in you naughty bird
the rain is pouring down
What would your mother say
if you stay there and drown?
You are a very naughty bird,
You do not think of me,
I'm sure I do not care,
said the sparrow on the tree.
Francie, come in you naughty bird, the rain is pouring down,
the fire is pouring down.[16]

The imagery of the lost birds continues through the remainder of the novel. It has occurred when Bob Withers hears of Francie's death and looks "the way a fowl looks when the rest of the fowls have been put in for the night; and the realization of their going has overtaken the last fowl; and she panics."[17] And at this time the other members of the family come home, but

not to warmth. Driven inside to outerness, as if the moment they passed through the door of knowing, they came not to warm nests, but dropped down to dark . . . and there was Bob waiting to be driven inside to share the darkness of their complete knowing, and not wanting to go, and being scared, like the lost fowl.[18]

Later, Toby watches ducks take refuge in the Withers's garden at the beginning of the shooting season and thinks of "the Withers island with its huddled Bob and Amy and Toby and its wild ducks crying out, this morning, beneath the winter clouds."[19] He remembers too his mother's warning when he was a child, and fears that he, like the chicks, may be swallowed whole by eels. This identification lies within the disturbing utterance he makes in the waiting room of the mental hospital:

Yes, the winter is hanging on, its teeth are indrawn like the teeth of an eel and that is why it is hanging on. Whatever it swallows will never escape from the black coil of winter.[20]

Teresa is the "littlest chicken,"[21] as her nickname suggests, and Toby sees Fay Chalklin, the girl he visits, as a threatened bird; in an interesting inversion of the metaphor, Daphne sees her father as one of the unthinking duckshooters who drive the birds to seek refuge.

This lyric, it can be seen, "contains" the imagery of the novel in a condensed form; but it is merely the best example of a process which goes on in all of Daphne's poetic passages. The fourth lyrical passage concludes "Talk of Treasure" and, with Daphne now in the "dead room," sets about the process of tracing the thread of memory. Now the happy pipe of childhood becomes the breathing tube forced into the throat of the patient undergoing electric shock treatment, and this grim knowledge of decay continues as "Twenty Years After" begins, with Daphne's vision of Toby, living

in a half-world, a microscopic place of
bitten oranges like blighted sunfall, where neither the
wind blowing the way forward nor the way back, articulate
with ripe fruit of night could feed or make you whole.[22]

An even greater significance becomes attached to Daphne's lyrics
from this point on, for they incarnate throughout Part Two the
vision and speech which the Withers children possess but must
conceal in order to survive unmolested in society. The juxtaposition
of lyrical and prose narratives provides a constant reminder of the
imaginative dimension, of the magical within the ordinary.

As a modernistic technique, the lyrical passages of *Owls Do Cry*
are familiar enough, with their suspension of time in order that all
events may be scrutinized fully. But the device becomes especially
Janet Frame's own because the passages are the touchstone of the
novel, expressing and embodying a truth not uttered in prosaic
statements but incarnated in the sensitive reader's mind by the
poetic celebration of the beauty and terror of the natural world. All
the members of the Withers family show some sort of awareness of
this imaginative world, as has already been seen; but a brief analysis
of the imagery involved will reveal further points: that instead of
existing independently, the Withers children are disguised forms of
the narrating Daphne, and more generally, that the Withers family
is conceived as one being.

All of them share the terrifying vision of themselves and others as
birds caught without shelter in a storm. Daphne and Francie are
always aware of the rainstorms brought by the north wind and of the
snowstorms which come from the mountains to the south; they both
fear

an opposite world of snow, no colour, that would creep nearer, first in a
breath of south wind, then in a storm they could not see or understand, that
would cover them with flakes, like lace . . . and they would struggle and cry
out, and nothing would save them.[23]

In the mental hospital, Daphne imagines that she is trapped in a hut
on the icy slopes of the Remarkables, a mountain range in the south
of New Zealand. Teresa, amid her comfortable suburban existence,
recalls her childhood in Waimaru in exactly the same sort of imagery: "Down in the south you feel all the time a kind of formidable
background, like a block of grey shadow, of a continent of ice,

Antarctica in the wings. The dark there is more frightening and less friendly, you are trapped in it as in a tomb, and the stone of ice will not roll away."[24]

If the novel is seen to revolve about a single central sensibility which has adopted similar personae, it comes to resemble many of the earlier stories collected in *The Lagoon* or *The Reservoir*, where a young child saw the placid lagoon of childhood ruffled by storms and the darkness of the world began to gather. Certainly, the Withers family is seen by all its members as being in a state of siege. The children listen to Bob complaining of the harshness of the world and then hear his decision to send Francie to work in the woollen mill; they fear that the house will collapse

and the world in one stride would walk in and take possession of them, holding them tight in its hand of rock and lava, as if they were insects, and they would have to struggle and kick and fight to escape and make their way. And each time they made their way and the world had dropped them for a while to a peaceful hiding place, it would again seize them with a burning one of its million hands, and the struggle would begin again and again and go on and on and never finish.[25]

This passage is worth quoting in full because it so perfectly sums up the feeling not only of the novel as a whole but of all the fiction Janet Frame has written.

In this work, the threats and complexities of life which confront the Withers children become condensed into two paired symbols which have great meaning for Francie and Daphne. These are the woollen mill and the mental hospital, the one merely an image of the other, since both are noted to have a siren and both use wool—the hospital for therapy, the mill for profit. In a nineteenth-century vision of work at the mill, Francie, Daphne, and Toby all believe that the mill girls become branded on the brow by leather straps, a stigma which resembles the brand of leucotomy impressed upon the patients at the mental hospital. The mill is a metaphor too for all kinds of adult employment which blind by excluding the sunlight of reality and scar with a binding leather strap of subservience. It threatens to entangle Francie forever in its wool till she drowns "in red and gold and blue the way a swimmer struggles with seaweed, outside the flags, in Friendly Bay or the world, and is pulled under."[26] Her father is drowned in toil and unpaid bills—the opposite side of the metaphor—and seems to the children to be trying "to

pick and unpick something inside himself that every year of being
alive had knitted, with the pattern, the purl and plain of time gone
muddled and different from the dream neatness."[27]

The mill's meaning is clear enough to Toby, for all his other
shortcomings, and brings him closer to his older sisters. To Fay
Crudge he speaks with the sensitivity and insight of Daphne herself,
telling her "you *have* got the mark, Fay. I saw it there. We all carry
some kind of mark like that because we are all branded in our lives,
as I was."[28] The mark which differentiates him from others is his
epilepsy: like the children in the *Lagoon* stories and like Daphne
too, he is threatened by a dark object in the sky, for his fits come as
"a dark cloak . . . thrown over his head."[29] Symbolically, Toby lies
halfway between Chicks, with her almost complete commitment to
the values of "normal" society, and Daphne, with her commitment
to the agonizing gifts and insights which come from the "dead
room." Like Chicks, he struggles against his gifts, seeing only the
pain and none of the value of the imagination; but like Daphne, his
true place is in "the quiet and lonely night, with a room of its own
but no window that the stars . . . may look through."[30]

The death of Francie, the novel's most significant incident, sees
Toby undergo an experience which allies him to Daphne and all that
she represents, for the brother and sister experience a moment of
communion and commitment. Sitting in the Harlows' living room
while waiting to be taken home after the tragedy, Daphne watches a
"tall gold flower"[31] grow from the seedcake Mrs. Harlow has given
them. This is the point at which Daphne commits herself to the
world of childhood imagination, the logic of fairy tales in which
flowers *ought* to grow from seedcakes: it is a rejection of the adult
world which has burnt the adolescent Francie. Toby sits next to her
on the sofa and his response is similar: because the sofa looks to him
like a giant, over-stuffed hedgehog, he suddenly imagines that a
giant hedgehog squeezes through the door "after him, its quills on
fire."[32] Since Toby's commitment to the imaginative world is ambiguous, his vision lapses into an epileptic attack, the sort of thing
that can be understood by the Harlows.

It is clear, then, that a system of images exists, beneath the
realism of the book, to tie Daphne to her brother; an equally strong
link draws her close to Francie, who is seen quite consistently as
Daphne projected into the future by a couple of years (as when she
sees that Francie "had pink bulges where Daphne had mere tittie

dots"[33]). At times the girls are so close as to be one; at others Daphne knows that "Francie was secret," on the far side of adolescence where childhood is renounced and the childhood self "captured forever."[34] Francie's death in the rubbish-tip fire, with the ring of gold toi-toi about its perimeter, symbolizes what society will do to Daphne in the mental hospital. The fire burns the children's treasure, which adult society sees as worthless, and burns the child-Francie too; in the hospital, the fire becomes figurative, represented by the fire of the feared electric shock treatment (E. C. T.) which society uses to burn the "childish" imagination from Daphne and her kind. Imagery, again, draws the children's experiences together: here is the description of Daphne being prepared for electric shock treatment:

She climbs a suspended shadow of mountain and finds on its summit a golden hollow, her own size, for lying in. How well it fits, carved for her comfort, by each year of her life, changed to rain and wind from the north, or the south, bringing snow.[35]

Later, Daphne in her "dead room" imagines "all the Francies being burnt for ever in a toi-toi hollow of mind," making it clearer still that Francie's death is a symbol for the death of Daphne's childhood imagination in the dead room.[36] And in her early days in the hospital, she envisages all the patients who suffer her own fate as being in a frozen wasteland, and thinks of them being wheeled to the toi-toi dump instead of to the electric shock machine or the leucotomy operation, to be burned and scattered about as society's waste.

It is not difficult to acknowledge that the Withers family, and especially the children, form an intense image of innocence beset by a shocking reality; theirs is a composite experience ranging from the prosaic and nervously unimaginative Bob to the intensely symbolical experience of Francie. In all of the family the narrating Daphne makes her Orphic presence felt, invading the privacy of each and turning them into various expressions of her own experience. It is a process that occurs in the later novels too, where the "dismemberment" of Daphne, which Jeanne Delbaere-Garant has mentioned,[37] produces narrators and subsidiary characters alike.

The Withers "self" is blockaded at every point: by mill and hospital, by rain from the north and snowstorms from the mountains to the south, by marshes infested with shooters, by creeks infested with eels and flowing into a sea infested with gray nurse sharks (joined, in the minds of the children, by the school nurse). Of these, the mill and the hospital represent society and its limited values, and although they are as implacably opposed to the Withers family as is any other element of predatory nature, the society the mill and the hospital stand for is caught curiously between the two. Its aim is to regulate as much of life as it can and to ignore those aspects of life that are too powerful to be controlled by anything. Thus, it is itself preyed upon by nature, yet at the same time directs the power of nature—electricity, for example—to control the gifted outsider like Daphne. Society's blindness and its ways are vigorously attacked in *Owls Do Cry*.

III   *Society*

The attack on society is focused, of course, on the little town of Waimaru, a barely disguised version of Oamaru; but the criticism is general, and meant to apply to all of New Zealand, if not modern Western society in its more suburban forms. "Waimaru was a respectable town with the population increasing so quickly that the Mayor kept being forced to call special meetings of the borough council."[38] This kind of dry and often ironic social comment is typical; here, killed by kindness, is the town described in its full glory:

> You should read a booklet that you may buy for five shillings and sixpence, reduced at sale time to five shillings, increased at Christmas to six shillings. This booklet will tell you the important things about the town and show you photographs—the town clock saying ten to three (the correct position of the hands for driving, says the local traffic inspector); the begonia house at the Gardens, and a perplexed-looking little man who must be the curator, holding a begonia plant in flower; the roses in the rose arch and the ferns in the fernery; also a photograph of the Freezing Works, the outside with its own garden and fancy flower beds, and the inside with rows of pegged pigs with their tiny trotters thrust out stiff; of the Woollen Mills, the chocolate factory, the flour mill—all meaning prosperity and wealth and a fat filled land . . . .[39]

This town is safe and necessarily boring; but the description goes on to picture "the foreshore with its long sweep of furious and hungry water . . . where you cannot bathe without fear," reminding the reader that there is no escape from predatory nature,[40] and also suggesting that the safer life becomes, the less well attuned human beings will be to threats from uncontrollable nature.

The proximity of such threats to monotonous suburban existence is shown very clearly in the sequence describing the death of Francie. This moment, whose symbolic importance has been suggested above, is preceded by descriptions of a society lax with Saturday afternoon boredom:

> Over the hedge from the Withers the lawnmower spitting out grass and the smell in the air and the green stain on old Bill Flett's boots and on Phyllis Flett's hands, playing with the grass, fistful, and smelling it with no one to throw it at, only big brothers away where?[41]
>
> No lawnmower now, it must be nearly afternoon tea time.
>
> The Withers children dangling doing nothing, caught in the scruff of the neck by afternoon; looking through the fence at the Fletts who are Catholic dogs and stink like frogs and eat no meat on Fri-i-i-i-day.[42]
>
> It wasn't far for the Withers children to go. Over the hill and down and then along to Cross Street. All the way there were people working in their gardens, mowing the lawn or digging; and ladies, on little rubber mats, kneeling over primrose plants and pansies. And all the way there were houses with lace curtains looped in front, and ornaments, dogs and frogs looking out of the window and being so surprised, perhaps, to see Francie, Toby, Daphne, Chicks on their way to the rubbish dump to look for treasure.[43]

On the way there they confront an image of their future experience—a hedgehog that has been crushed the night before while crossing the apparently safe and man-made road. The death of the Withers child amid apparent safety in the man-made rubbish dump crushes the entire Withers family shortly afterward. *Owls Do Cry* is full of sequences like this one, where society's rituals are carefully observed against the threatening world which surrounds them. Toby's visit to Fay Chalklin on the eve of her marriage to Albert Crudge is one of these, a masterly description of middle-class marriage rites juxtaposed with Toby's rare moment of truth and imagination, a vision of threat.

Society casts its values in the form of theories and statements and rules that have little to do with life; and this "knowledge" is imprinted upon its young at schools before they are let loose on the world. Here is the sum of Francie's knowledge as she prepares to leave school:

She could count up to thirty in French. She could make puff pastry, dabbing the butter carefully before each fold. She could cook sago, lemon or pink with cochineal, that swelled in cooking from dirty little grains, same, same, dusty and bagged in paper, to lemon or pink pearls. She knew that a drop of iodine on a slice of banana will blacken the fruit, and prove starch; that water is H_2O; that a man called Shakespeare, in a wood near Athens, contrived a moonlit dream.[44]

Francie has spent years in an institution whose sole purpose, it seems, has been to drive imagination from the young, and "in all her knowing, she had not learned of the time of living" and wishes that she had "some kind of treasure inside her, to help her; if only grown-ups could tell what is treasure and not treasure."[45] Toby, although he follows false lights in the first years of his manhood, is never more truthful than when he disclaims knowledge. Talking to Fay Chalklin and seeing that she is doomed, he says, "I don't know much, not how to spell anyway," but goes on to indicate that he nonetheless possesses valuable gifts of imagination and insight that he has only partly suppressed during his school years.[46] His dream of Daphne in which she tells him that his pursuit of money as treasure is false and that the mind alone is the path to true treasure is a dream he cannot articulate but can only sense—true understanding, unlike formal "knowledge," cannot be set out neatly.

The opposition of imaginative knowledge to society's knowledge is seen again when Daphne is in the mental hospital. There, her doctor, who has written her case history and its particulars in a ledgerlike volume as if she were some entry in a bookkeeping exercise, *knows* that a leucotomy will be the best treatment for Daphne. On the other hand, Daphne herself knows his worth and what he stands for, and is therefore superior to him:

They are frauds, for the real how and where and who and why are in the circle of toi-toi, with the beautiful ledger writing and the book thrown away that told of Tom Thumb sitting in the horse's ear; and the sun shining through the sacrificial fire, to make real diamonds and gold. And we sat, didn't we, Toby, Chicks and Francie, as the world sits in the morning, unafraid, touching how and why and where, the wonder currency that I take with me, slipped in the lining of my heart, to hide it because I know. And Toby carries it backward and forward across continents and seas and does not understand it though it glitters and strikes part of the fire in him;

and Chicks is afraid, and covers it with a washing-machine and refrigerator, and a space-heater behind glass.[47]

Such vision is obviously that of a superior mind, and the difference between Daphne and other people is typified in the response to the ledgers she finds at the rubbish dump. She finds them magical and valuable because they contain beautiful writing; but Toby values them because they represent a connection with money; the doctor values them because patients are profit and loss in his world; and Fay Chalklin values them because her future husband is one of those who fills ledgers with figures.

Society, the novel states, rules on all its members as if they belonged to a ledger, with a huge number in the profit column and a few like Daphne on the other side, awaiting forcible transference. Bob Withers and his son ought to belong with Daphne, but habit and blind fear keep them with the mass. Of his children, Bob says, "they can't tell what's rubbish from what isn't rubbish"[48]; he, on the other hand, knows his rubbish. For security he clings to his radio, because "the radio *knew*, and its telling, in a human voice, gave comfort to Bob and Amy and Toby Withers." "Every day he liked to hear the weather report . . . he felt that nowadays it was the thing to be *told*, and have everything worked out for you. Hearing the weather report made Bob feel safe . . . ."[49] Bob also relies on the "sick yellow treasure" of the newspaper (the color recalling that of the discarded volume of fairy stories at the dump), which Toby hides in order to exercise power over him; they both rely equally on its daily "drug-drop of . . . sick magic."[50] As Bob ages, retires, and loses his wife, these anchors prove weak before the advance of death; his habits are exposed as a shell and he finds that he knows nothing of value. He becomes his own ghost, wandering about the railway yards in which he has spent his working life.

"Knowledge" and "truth" are issues which involve an evaluation of language, it need hardly be stated, and the latter category, it has been seen, is served by the poetical voice of Daphne. Its reverse, cliché and predictable patterns of speech, is the language used by society to disseminate its false knowledge. To understand one mode of language is to become deaf to the other: the adults who discarded the book of fairy tales and consigned it to the dump did so because it "did not any more speak the right language, and the people could

not read it because they could not find a way to its world."[51] At his
worst, Toby endlessly illustrates the inadequacy of the language of
everyday as he spouts his unconsidered clichés:

I'd like to give you some money Dad, but I've got to get going in life, and
money's something to hang on to, otherwise you sink. When have *I* had a
start in life? I've got commitments.[52]

Bob, too, is ruled by prosaic language and the slogans which wrap
thought and experience into unquestioned bundles of "knowledge."
In one of his more insightful moments, Toby sees that he might
commit himself so utterly to society that he will become "a whirling
spiritless machine that makes the same speech day after day till its
life ends."[53] The reader might be forgiven for interpreting this as a
description of Bob.

IV   *Daphne's Section*

The battle between the true and the imaginative on the one side
and the false and the dull on the other reaches its pitch in Daphne's
section of *Owls Do Cry,* where Daphne is seen as a young woman in
the mental hospital. Here, on the battleground of "normal" and
"abnormal," the main threats are the electric shock treatment and
the leucotomy operation by which society will extinguish her truth-
seeing imagination and return her to the "normal" life that has been
so brilliantly devalued throughout the novel. It is wise to point out
here that Janet Frame does not subscribe to the literary fallacy
wherein insanity becomes a gift vouchsafing great insights and understanding, or to the more general belief that a definable condition
under that name exists; the mental hospital, just like the woollen
mill, is a *symbol* for the dehumanizing processes and imprisoning
principles of adult society. Daphne's gifts are far from taking the
form of arcane wisdom: they are readily understandable to the sensitive reader, for they are uttered in the language of innocence and
the imagination.

It is the author's self-imposed task in this penultimate section of
the novel, in fact, to demonstrate the worth and honesty of Daphne's language by example, and to show by contrast the limitations of
any society that chooses to deny such qualities. So, in the hospital,
people are found to be adjudged "normal" or not according to the
degree to which they suppress within themselves their natural gifts

of childlike imagination and innocence. Such gifts are the property of all, it is emphasized, and here is found the germ of the second novel, which asks whose faces are reflected in the water in which Daphne finds herself; the answer is that *all* faces are found in the water, but that the blind will never be able to see that this is so. Daphne, therefore, must bring to them the world of the poetical mind, and these pages become filled with the unsuppressed language of metaphor in a prolonged celebration of all that is authentic and true in life—the dangerous, the threatening, the malevolent, and the beautiful. The imagery returns to that of the childhood of the Withers children, evoking icy winds and frozen mountains, hunted birds and savage beasts. And the reader's response to this section is a measure of his or her worth: if he or she dismisses Daphne's lyrical language as fanciful and valueless, the reader is revealed as belonging to the world of the prosaic, unimaginative, and inauthentic; if Daphne's language is accepted and sympathized with, then the reader has learned to understand the imaginative world of the novel. Daphne's episode, thus, is a crucial test of both writer and reader.

In its opening lines, the reader is shown how the mental hospital appears to the truth-seeing Daphne. It seems to her like the Remarkable Mountains she noticed as a child, a place of freezing wind and snow:

The Remarkables are mountains.
But half-imagined only; with the patients fastening their dream upon the picture and creating beyond the yellow and blue cloud their frozen slope of thought whose blizzard, emerging from the stillness, cut from snow-block of day-after-day dreaming, will blow like swans or arrows flying from the yellow and blue cloud's mouth to whip or sing in the demented night of four walls and the dead bulb of milk behind wire; and the eyes of the world from hour to hour staring through, amazed at the white storm and not knowing why.[54]

In this vision of the world around her, Daphne sees the staff of the mental hospital as a tribe that lives on the icy mountain; metaphorically, this has great power, conveying the chill horror of the institution far more fully than would a literal description. Nurses and doctors terrify her by their impersonality and their inability to understand her, and therefore *become* terrifying objects, often de-

picted as silent insects with long, waving feelers. Daphne reacts
according to the logic of the poetic mind, as when she escapes from
her bed to show that there is nothing wrong with her, after she has
heard a nurse say that she is too "ill" to understand what people say.
It is they who are too sick to understand her, and in protest she
reverts to a silence which they interpret as proof of her mental
sickness. But her own thoughts and judgments of those who "care"
for her will reassure the reader that she is healthy and wise:

They are mad. They are frauds. They are thieves who sneak through the
night and day of their lives, exchanging their counterfeit whys and hows and
wheres, like fake diamonds and gold, to zip them inside their leather human
brain till the next raid and violence of exchanging, when they jingle their
clay and glass baubles, untouched by sun, in their hands, and cry out,
    —Who'll buy our answers, genuine treasure, who'll buy?[55]

Their treasure is counterfeit, of course, whether it be explanations
or a form of behavior inculcated in the patients.
    Daphne's behavior is independent and thoroughly charming, as
when she is informed of the death of her mother. This incident
pits "normal" against "abnormal" in a most illuminating way. It
begins with the dance the staff has arranged for patients in the
misguided belief that it is preparing them to adjust to the ways of
society, a belief similar in kind to Chicks's confidence that her gift of
a second-hand iron will help bring Daphne back to her senses, and
also involves sessions in which female patients are taught how to use
cosmetics. The dance is a dreadful affair, with the band members
constantly drinking to maintain their confidence and the patients
being bullied into dancing, whirling about the floor in an animal-like
stampede. What the evening lacks, Daphne perceives, is magic, and
the metaphor which begins to dominate her mind comes straight
from the remembered book of fairy stories from the childhood
dump: she is Cinderella. But there is no glass slipper in this prosaic
world, and the dance ends at ten o'clock with the stripping of the
patients' fine clothes and the quitting of a ballroom that is left
"empty and stuffy and smelling of tobacco"[56]; the nurses, Daphne
thinks, would not fit any magic slipper, for they would need to "hack
their heel of reason till the blood flowed" and their hidden imagination was bared.[57] The following day, news reaches the staff that Mrs.

Withers has died, and they summon Daphne to tell her, fearful of a violent or unpredictable reaction. Expecting mad grief, they are surprised when Daphne serenely dances upon hearing of her mother's death; but her understanding of death surpasses theirs, and she dances because midnight has come. She is hauled away by the amazed and angry staff (leaving her glass slipper behind, she notices), having demonstrated, to those who can see, that society has lost much by suppressing its spontaneous innocence.

A similar incident occurs at the Christmas party held in the mental hospital, another celebration arranged to remind patients of the "normal" world outside. Santa Claus is reluctantly portrayed by a sweating man growing increasingly irritable in the hot Antipodean Christmas weather as he distributes identical packages of soap and scent. Daphne receives one package and then holds out her hand for more; she is hustled away to her room for her greediness, although it is clear that she has seen through the dismal proceedings and is asking not for more soap but for the gift of magic the occasion lacks. And since the mental hospital is a microcosm of the world surrounding it, society outside has an equally dull Christmas. Back at home, Bob and Amy and Toby have a funereal time, all sensing in different ways that they have robbed themselves of some quality which could have made living joyous all the year round.

In her wisdom and insight into others, Daphne is clearly superior to all others in the novel. There is some irony, therefore, in her relationship with one of the nurses at the hospital, Flora Norris, who is in an authoritative position over her and yet, Daphne can see, is essentially still a lost child. The woman has lived her entire working life in the hospital, until she is like a frightened inmate when beyond its walls; like Bob Withers, she fears retirement as a limbo from which the only escape may be to commit herself to the hospital once more as a patient. A typical member of society, she has progressively held back within herself the very gifts which could have made her whole without extraneous roles and status, and blindly helps to inflict upon Daphne the disaster which will remove those gifts from her.

This fear of life in its rawest forms, a fear which amounts to a basic uncertainty about the final worth of society's values, is seen again when Bob and Toby visit Daphne in the hospital near the end of the novel. The hospital is beyond the bounds of the safe little town of

Waimaru; and this is the haggard, lunar landscape that Toby sees through the windows of the train in which they make their journey there:

the whirl of stripped willows and dead leaves and ancient logs, trapped and bearded, rising from the dark pool and swamp; and broken fences dragged with cattle-hair and lumps of earth and river-stained sheep's wool; and crumbling farm-houses, eyeless, with their door open upon a yellow blotched throat of corridor lined with chains of decayed rosebuds and lilies. There seemed no people in the outside world, only great fearful white and red and grey ghosts of cattle prancing upon a shrivelled earth, and harnessed and blinkered draught-horses, elephantine, waiting to plough, unguided, the furow of nothing that the luminous train moved through on ribbons of iron; and the startled pallor of sheep, their panic and muffle of driven grey cloud.[58]

Toby, half a child and half a man, can confront the world outside the train window because he has gifts like Daphne's. But his father shrinks from the world, chattering volubly to his son about the operation the doctors have proposed for his daughter and revealing, as he speaks, his utter ignorance of her plight:

We've talked this over before. Your mother would have approved. The doctor said this brain operation was the only chance of making Daphne into a normal human being, a useful citizen, able to vote and take part in normal life, without getting any of these strange fancies that she has now.[59]

The remainder of his visit serves to show the precariousness of these safe, orderly phrases, for once in the hospital he has a nagging fear that somehow he belongs there. Like Flora Norris, he feels that he could become lost and then imprisoned within the institution; this is an unconscious acknowledgment that there is hidden within his mind somewhere exactly those qualities that have condemned his daughter to the hospital. Other visitors in the waiting room see this in both Bob and Toby ("It must be in the family," thinks one woman, completely unaware of the irony of her thought[60]) because they look and behave so oddly. Toby, who is about to have one of his fits, disgraces himself and his father with his startling but imaginative reply to a lady's remark that the winter is hanging on. He replies,

Yes, the winter is hanging on, its teeth are indrawn like the teeth of an eel and that is why it is hanging on. Whatever it swallows will never escape from the black coil of winter.[61]

Nothing could be in starker contrast to the vapidity of the woman's observation, and nothing could better expose its dishonesty. Bob's slight defenses are collapsed, too (for they consist of little other than routine and slogans), and he is led like a helpless child to see Daphne. He finds that her head has been shaven in readiness for the operation, and breaks down weeping for his dead daughter, Francie. But he cannot understand the language of metaphor, and does not realize that Daphne too is about to "die," as a result of the operation he has agreed she should have. And when he returns to the waiting room he swathes himself in comforting deceit as soon as he can, telling his son that Daphne's hairstyle is like her younger sister's. Daphne is left alone in her "dead room," awaiting the operation that is the book's central tragedy, knowing that she will "die tomorrow when snow falls criss-cross to darn the believed crevice of my world."[62]

V *Conclusions*

While there is no mistaking the author of *Owls Do Cry* for anyone but the person who wrote the *Lagoon* stories, the development between the two works is enormous. Robert T. Robertson has pointed out the similarities between the two works, showing the continuity of imagery and the deepening seriousness of purpose which lies behind the writing of the novel.[63] But the early stories are miniatures which contain little to suggest that their author would soon be able to plot, control, and orchestrate such a complex and substantial work of fiction. Obviously, these years saw considerable self-scrutiny and artistic self-discipline by Janet Frame, and the result is a work of art which has been widely recognized in the years since its publication, and which probably has been subjected to more group discussions, sophomore essays, and critical speculation than any other Australasian work since the war.

It is, however, an open-ended work, in the sense that its conclusion does not fully resolve all the themes that have appeared in it. Daphne's section, structurally a part of "Twenty Years After," is a beginning and not an end, for it engenders a completely new metaphor for the discussion of the gifted individual's place in society. Toby, situated exactly on the dividing line between "normality" and "abnormality," is far too important a figure to be dealt with in one novel alone, for he symbolizes all those figures in Janet Frame's world who have not successfully crushed their own innocence. And the influence of Rilke's "Sonnets to Orpheus" is important too, with its encouragement of continuous creative effort and the metamorphosis of central characters, and its concern with the relationship between life and art. Thus Janet Frame had no shortage of material, aims, or motivation when she had written *Owls Do Cry*; her next novels were implicit in it, and *Faces in the Water* is a sequel, not a fresh start.

CHAPTER 4

The Withers Trilogy

I Fact or Fiction?

Faces in the Water presents immediate problems. It is obviously a slighter work than the first novel, lacking its range and artistic intensity. Joan Stevens has described it as "merely a documentary," a thinly disguised record of the author's own experiences,[1] and probably the experiences of Istina Mavet recall things that happened to Janet Frame during her years in hospital. But, as Winston Rhodes has pointed out, a purely autobiographical approach to her fiction can be dangerous; he warns that despite "a clear indication in *Faces in the Water* ('None of the characters, including Istina Mavet, portrays a living person'), it is deceptively easy to assume that 'I traded my safety for the glass beads of fantasy' is uttered by Janet Frame herself, and that 'the glass beads of fantasy' refers obliquely to her impressive but frequently bewildering use of imagery and verbal pyrotechnics."[2] On the other hand, if the work is accepted as being primarily fictional, it is still difficult to sense its focus, to know where it is weighted. Why, for example, is the apparent narrative element of the book—Istina Mavet's deepening illness and eventual recovery—so muted towards the end, and why are we never told quite why her recovery is so sudden? Is this in fact the subject of the novel?

An answer can be found in another of Winston Rhodes's comments on the art of Janet Frame. He has drawn attention to what he describes as her "gift for parabolic utterance and the remarkable ability she displays in developing, diversifying and coordinating associated parables, whether these are limited to a phrase, repeated in a refrain or expanded in such a way that they give rise to further parables, ultimately achieving what might be called a parabolic unity."[3] The work of Janet Frame written overseas between 1960 and 1964 is such a unity, reaching back to *Owls Do Cry* and forward to later works, but with a density of its own. Ideas and themes overlap, metaphors expand and change, characters from stories reappear under different names in novels, and so on. This is to say, simply, that there is no understanding a novel, poem, or story by Janet Frame without placing it in the context of *all* the novels, poems, and stories. Each work is enriched by others. The following chapters will deal with these works chronologically, although there is no strict need for them to do so; and the parabolic, contextual approach advocated by Winston Rhodes will be used. Thus, it will be seen that in many cases the stories collected in *The Reservoir* and *Snowman, Snowman* will help the reader to understand the novels written during the same period.

Faces in the Water, then, must be understood as more than a documentary but as less than a novel; it gains stature only on being located in the center of a trilogy concluded by *The Edge of the Alphabet.* Robert T. Robertson has been alone among critics so far to assume that the first three novels of Janet Frame were intended to be read in this way, as an expression of the problem of the artist's relationship to life—a problem confronting Janet Frame herself at this time. [4] *Faces in the Water* extends and develops Daphne's section of *Owls Do Cry,* while the third novel transfers attention to Daphne's brother, Toby, and his Orphic quest for the gift of artistic utterance. Janet Frame's fourth novel, *Scented Gardens for the Blind,* published in 1963, is quite distinct from the trilogy in form and theme, as if the trilogy enabled the author to rid herself of many artistic problems.

Istina Mavet's story is much like that of Daphne Withers. The first third of *Faces in the Water* sees Istina in Cliffhaven mental hospital, whose name provides the subtitle of the section. Her stay begins in Ward Four, whose occupants can be as apparently normal as Mrs. Everett and Mrs. Pilling, two long-term patients whose behavior cannot be distinguished from that of any member of the world Istina has just left. But, typically, Istina finds a dark threat within this relative peace—the threat of electric shock treatment, which so disturbed Daphne Withers and which all patients see as a punishment and not as therapy. Shock treatment threatens to destroy what she knows is her true self, and she describes the experience as a collapse into darkness from which she rises again in a disembodied form. The conviction that she has been torn away from herself allows her to describe her own illness quite coolly for much of the novel, for her "other" self seems to belong to someone else.

Part One of the novel skims the surface of mental illness, preparing the reader for the horrors of the later sections by subtle and indirect methods. While at Cliffhaven, for example, Istina Mavet dreams of herself as a mental patient: she envisages a queue of terrified women, who were waiting for shock treatment the day before, as if they had been transformed into travellers in a train from whose windows they peer fearfully; amongst them, indistinguishable from the rest, is herself. Throughout this first part, Istina is in this situation, seeing but not participating. She sees Ward Two, where the incurable patients live, as a race apart; their briefly glimpsed faces make her wonder, "Why were they so changed from people that you see walking and talking in the streets of the World?"[5]

This part concludes optimistically, with Istina returning to the "normal" world on probation. But Part Two, "Treecroft," which forms the center of the book, finds her in the home of her sister, once more unable to deal with the world and without a sense of identity—"burgled of body and hung in the sky like a woman of straw."[6] Her descriptions of the outside world are far more desolating and forbidding than were her descriptions of Cliffhaven. She mentions "derelict apple trees, blighted and scabbed with lichen," "the menacing hawks gently sliding down the wind, biding their time in the sky," and a "big, rocking and sighing fir-tree that was under sentence of death."[7] In contrast to this, Ward Seven at Treecroft, the new hospital she goes to, closely resembles the pleasant conditions of Ward Four at Cliffhaven, a resemblance that is made more intense when Istina decides that Mrs. Hill, a trusted long-term patient, is just like Mrs. Pilling from Cliffhaven. But the peacefulness of her new surroundings makes her uneasy, and she wonders whether they are "a subaqueous condition of the mind which gave the fearful shapes drowned there the rhythmic distortion of peace."[8]

This metaphor of deeply concealed threat dominates the Treecroft section of the novel. Electric shock treatment, always discreetly administered behind screens at Cliffhaven, is now conducted in a new and terrifying setting, a ward named "Four Five and One," where incurable patients are kept in squalid and desolate surroundings. This ward corresponds to Ward Two at Cliffhaven, appearing to Istina, as she huddles in the relatively secure company of patients recovering from nervous breakdowns, to be deeply horrifying and a threat specifically to her. This apprehension is realized indirectly when a Ward Seven patient, after a quarrel over precedence at a bath, is hauled struggling by nurses through a mysterious door in the bathroom and returned much later as a bloated corpse from Ward Four Five and One. Istina begins to feel

increasingly like a guest who is given every hospitality in a country mansion yet who finds in unexpected moments a trace of a mysterious presence; sliding panels; secret tappings; and at last surprises the host and hostess in clandestine conversations and plottings which mention of poison, torture, and death.[9]

Yet there is another level which exists below Ward Four Five and One: this is a decrepit, decaying building known by the euphemistic name of Lawn Lodge. Describing it early in her stay at Treecroft, Istina Mavet little realizes that during the nadir of her life she will be a patient there. But soon her descent has begun—she is sent to Four Five and One with its patients who are "automatons geared to a pitch of excitement they could not understand and fearful lest whatever or whoever controlled them should tire of giving them distraction, and let them run down like broken toys and have to find in their own selves a way of overcoming the desolation in which they lived."[10] Under the threat of the brutally administered electric shock treatment, Istina herself becomes less and less controllable, and quite suddenly finds that she has been consigned to Lawn Lodge. This is the refractory ward that she glimpsed earlier, where a hundred screaming and fighting women surround her, some so violent that they are encased from neck to knee in heavy straight jackets. And soon Istina too is one of this inhuman horde, slithering under the table to wet the floor like an animal and fighting with any woman who comes near her. When her Aunt Rose, a regular visitor, gives her a pink cretonne bag with a drawstring, Istina feels that she has been given life membership in Lawn Lodge—*all* the patients there have similar little bags in which they keep their jealously guarded personal possessions. "I belonged now," she acknowledges, "to the raging mass of people and the dead lying, like rests in music, upon the ground."[11]

Astonishingly enough, this central part of *Faces in the Water* concludes with nearly the optimism of the first part. After the passage of a great period of time, Istina is returned without explanation to Ward Seven, and begins the third part of the novel (called "Cliffhaven") in the company of her sister and family once more. But after only six weeks she is back at Cliffhaven, again unable to cope with the loneliness and desolation of the outside world. Her return is a great step backward for her, into the unchanged company of Mrs. Pilling and Mrs. Everett; but this time she is to experience the depths of Cliffhaven as she experienced the depths of Treecroft. Soon she is amongst the strange menagerie of Ward Two, which she glimpsed so long before when she had been a patient for only a short time.

This final part of the novel is twice the length of either of the other parts, as if to emphasize the tragic monotony of existence in Cliffhaven. Life in Ward Two contains routines that are familiar rather than strange: there are regular visits by a troupe of middle-aged ladies who radiate a nervous goodwill and a barely concealed terror that they will be accidentally locked up forever as patients; there is a grotesque annual dance in which patients enjoy frenzied, lumbering waltzes; there is the annual sports day, as well as an unusual celebration of the coronation of the Queen of England. From time to time, the cheapness of life in this ward is transmitted with great power and economy, as in this single sentence:

Some days later Susan and I went to the city for an X-ray, and Susan was found to have tuberculosis, and was put in one of the small rooms down the corridor next to Margaret and to Eva who woke one morning, vomited, and died, and her mother, a small woman with bandy legs and wearing a grey coat, came to collect her things.[12]

One day Istina manages to escape from this existence, but at the local railway station she finds herself ringing the Cliffhaven staff on the telephone and asking meekly to be taken back. For, despite the anguish and boredom of living there, Cliffhaven is her life, and no other way of life is possible for her. Like the bird in Franz Kafka's famous aphorism, she must fly in search of a cage.

Desperate, she tries to commit suicide, and gains the reputation of a problem patient when her attempt fails. A group of doctors and patients begins to tell her of a new operation that will make her "normal" by the surgical removal of part of her brain—this is the

leucotomy operation which extinguished the mind of Daphne Withers. Terrified at this prospect, Istina appeals to a sympathetic doctor, who prevents the operation from taking place and has her transferred back to Ward Four. He encourages her to read, and under his
influence she begins to recover steadily; her release from Cliffhaven
coincides with the opening of a new bowling green at the hospital,
an ironic reminder that the hospital is but a version of the everyday
world.

II *Form*

The theme of this carefully formed novel is announced in its
opening paragraph, where the reader is shown a society deliberately
blinding itself to the fullness of existence:

> They have said we owe allegiance to Safety, that he is our Red-Cross God
> who will provide us with ointment and bandages for our wounds and re-
> move the foreign ideas, the glass beads of fantasy, the bent hairpins of
> unreason embedded in our minds. On all the doors which lead to and from
> the world they have posted warning notices and lists of safety measures to
> be taken in extreme emergency. Lightning, isolation in the snows of the
> Antarctic, snake-bite, riots, earthquakes. Never sleep in the snow. Hide the
> scissors. Beware of strangers. Lost in a foreign land take your time from the
> sun and your position from the creeks flowing towards the sea. Don't strug-
> gle if you would be rescued from drowning. Suck the snake-bite from the
> wound. When the earth opens and the chimneys topple, run out beneath
> the sky. But for the final day of destruction, when "those that look from the
> windows shall be darkened" they have provided no slogan. The streets
> throng with people who panic, looking to the left and the right, covering the
> scissors, sucking poison from a wound they cannot find . . . .[13]

The point being made here is to be insisted upon throughout the
later novels: that society has devised numerous methods by which to
regulate its life and protect itself from the hazards of existence, and
in the process has become numb before those parts of life which give
authenticity and strength. One of these regulatory methods is the
establishment of mental hospitals in which a division is enforced
between the "sane" and the "insane." Istina Mavet's chilling visions
of hawk, rain, snow, and wind are disturbingly unsafe and threatening to a society which likes to pretend that such things do not exist.
But for Istina, who sees all things truly, hospitals are not the strictly
exclusive domains their administrators think them; they are merely

a microcosm of the world outside (a fact Daphne Withers also acknowledged), and in them the staff must constantly work to differentiate themselves from the patients.

The metaphor which expresses this division throughout *Faces in the Water* is created in Daphne's section of *Owls Do Cry*. There, not long after her arrival at the hospital, she notices the "slippery brown mirror that was spread like a floor," which is being buffed by a large electric polisher.[14] The more its surface becomes like a mirror, the more it becomes like the lagoon of the first stories, as the title of the novel seems to suggest. Thus the floor polisher marks the division between the "normal" world above the floor and the terrifying, deathlike world below its surface.

It is not surprising that Istina associates the polisher with the electric shock machine, for the latter also asserts a division between two worlds, trying to shock the patients into the "normal" world and away from the depths which await Istina in the novel.

But there is more to this metaphor—the surface of the lagoonlike floor mingles both staff and patients in its reflection. The fact that there is *no* division in the world, that "normality" is merely a word, is evident in this passage from near the end of the novel, when Istina is listening to a patient who is playing the piano:

Listening to her one experienced a deep uneasiness, as of having avoided an urgent responsibility, like someone who walking at night along the banks of a stream catches a glimpse in the water of a white face or a moving limb and turns quickly away refusing to help or to search for help. We all see the faces in the water. We smother our memory of them, even our belief in their reality, and become calm people of the world; or we can neither forget nor help them; sometimes by a trick of circumstance or a dream or a hostile neighbourhood of light we see our own face.[15]

All people belong to the lagoon, and only self-deception will allow them to believe otherwise. A half-conscious awareness of this truth causes the nervous women who make furtive charitable visits to the hospital to fear that they will remain there; the trusted long-term patients, Mrs. Pilling and Mrs. Hill, are indistinguishable from any suburban housewife; and the opening of a bowling green at the hospital is merely acknowledgment of its duplication of the outside world. Patients are much like visitors, who are "the ones to be pitied, as emotion could still write fitting signals on their faces and they had not learned to apply the mask of nothingness; their faces

showed fear, loneliness, exasperation, resignation, sympathy; looking from visitor to patient you could not tell immediately which was
which."[16]

This is what Istina Mavet learns as the book progresses: that all
people in society possess the same faculties which they suppress or
express in varying degrees, and that "normality" is a concept but not
a fact. In her first spell in hospital, she is unaware of this truth, as
the name of the hospital would seem to suggest—only the blind find
a haven on the cliff—and she feels that a vast difference lies between
herself and the lost, "dead" people in Ward Two. At Treecroft, she
finds herself returned to similar surroundings but this time plunges
deep into the waters of self-knowledge, exploring the depths which
lie within herself and, she comes to understand, within all others.
With this understanding comes the knowledge that the vision of life
as a united whole is a source of artistic inspiration, a truth which
needs to be celebrated in poetry. For the hospital is the underworld, the home of the dead that Orpheus visited, and through its
levels Daphne too must descend. Death lurks in her name ("Mavet"
is a transliteration of the Hebrew word for death, while "Istina"
contains the meaning, "truth"[17]), and she becomes both Orpheus
and Eurydice, the seeker and the lost woman sought. The truth she
finds in the underworld is the same truth that Rilke found in the
"Sonnets to Orpheus": that death cannot be separated from life (as
the "insane" cannot be divided from the "sane"), and that to understand the unity of all things, including life and death, is to achieve
the status of poet. Thus, when she returns to Cliffhaven, she is
equipped with a new wisdom which enables her to see the cliff as
well as the haven; and the entire concluding sequence, with its
constant references to the outside world, provides an almost parodic
image of everyday life with its stifling routines that can be escaped
only through literature.

The dominant figure in this last section is Sister Bridge, with
whom Istina develops an important relationship resembling Daphne's with the two nurses, Flora Norris and Sister Dulling, in the first
novel. Daphne and Istina both see the nurses who are in charge of
them as individuals who cling to the values of society in order to
repress their own imaginations. Sister Bridge fascinates Istina, because she seems at times to have "discarded words as a means of
communication and put her meaning across in some other way."[18]
Living at the edge of the alphabet, Sister Bridge nevertheless erects

defenses as well as bridges, and Istina angers and frightens her by showing that she knows that such defenses exist. In fact, she thinks of the nurse as her other self:

sometimes it seemed as if we shared a dreadful secret; sometimes I had the fantastic idea that we were two hawks in the sky, as distant from each other as opposing winds, who had both swooped at a precise moment upon the same corpse and on beginning to scavenge it had found it to be composed of decaying parts of our two selves.[19]

This disturbing image could never be revealed to Sister Bridge, Istina knows, for the nurse "sprayed all fantasy with contempt in order to conceal herself from it and escape its danger."[20] But when Istina runs away from Cliffhaven and then asks to be returned there, she finds a moment of communion with the older woman when the latter points out the small, tumbledown house in which she lives, and Istina senses the desolate loneliness of her life there. But the moment passes, Sister Bridge becomes authoritative once more, and so disappoints Istina that she knocks her down.

Sister Bridge, like most people, has the opportunity to recognize her own face in the water, but she turns in fear towards the institutions and discipline which help to avoid this chance. Thus she wants Istina to have the leucotomy operation in order that the imagination which conceives such strange notions as that quoted above may be extinguished, and Safety reign unchallenged. A similar authoritarianism can be seen in the staff's attitude towards the books which are Istina's means to final recovery. Seeing a mobile library full of books on the grounds of the hospital, she finds herself unable to resist the temptation to creep in and pore over them. But the hospital chaplain orders her out, for he is one who "sees the land of meaning, and one path to it, and the so-called 'normal' people travelling swiftly and in comfort to the land."[21] But she knows that his view "does not include the shipwrecked people who arrive by devious, lonely routes, and the many who dwell in the land in the beginning."[22] Books represent the world of the imagination and are the property of the gifted outsider rather than of impersonal social institutions. Knowing this, Istina recalls the lending library of her childhood years and the giant skeleton of a moa, a flightless bird once indigenous to New Zealand but now extinct; as a girl, she constantly associated the wired skeleton and its brooding presence with the letters that are joined together to form "secret presences" in the library.[23] "So it was for her own protection that the librarian hid behind a grille and pinned notices on the wall," she observes,[24] for the librarian fears the power of language and imagination which Istina herself feeds upon, and which becomes the source of her regeneration.

III   The Edge of the Alphabet

The last novel of the Withers trilogy was completed within a year of the second, suggesting a unity of inspiration and theme. Certainly, although Daphne-Istina is no longer the focus of the work, her brother, Toby, plays a central part as he did in the first novel. But there is a new form of narration here, with two figures being interposed between reader and novel. The first is Thora Pattern, who remains a voice outside the action and is largely reminiscent of the narrating Daphne; the second is Peter Heron, a travelling salesman and former artist who is purported to have found the manuscript of the novel amongst Thora Pattern's papers after her death and submitted them to the publisher. The novel, it is announced at the beginning, will be a voyage of discovery undertaken through three people: Toby Withers, Zoe Bryce, a spinster ex-schoolteacher from the English Midlands who has come to New Zealand on a working holiday to forget a brief and half-imagined love affair; and Pat Keenan, an Irish bus driver who has come to New Zealand to visit his sister.

The three parts of the novel are dominated in turn by each character, although the divisions are not as strict as in the first novel, and here all characters have a part to play in all sections. Part One, "A Home There," is dominated by Toby Withers and his decision to leave his father and his home in Waimaru to travel overseas to England. Toby undertakes this as an act of communion with his late mother, with whom he is in the habit of holding long, imaginary conversations. She had always been proud of her English ancestry, and as a result Toby imagines that his proposed journey will lead him to discover his true identity. As before, he is seen as a complete misfit in New Zealand society, unable to endure the company of his pathetic, cliché-spouting father, yet also unable to avoid dreams of settling into the very society of which his father is typical. He enjoys a completely imaginary love affair with a local girl, Evelina Festing, the daughter of an elderly invalid whom he regularly visits; this is a repetition of his earlier passion for Fay Chalklin. Although the girl has been engaged to another man for some time, Toby presents her, in a humiliating scene, with a pair of greenstone earrings as a token of their engagement. Afterwards, he wears the rejected gift on his watchchain as a symbol of his dashed dream, although it is no talisman against revivals of the dream, for he constantly imagines himself to be happily married to the woman and unobtrusively settled with her in society "out the North Road in a new house, roughcast with a flat roof painted your favourite colour,"[25] and imagines the pair of them as the happy couple depicted in an advertisement for a house paint. But when he travels with his father to Wellington to catch the S.S. *Matua* for England, staying overnight with his Aunt Norma, both men reveal their awkwardness when actually caught within the society of Toby's dreams. Proven to be essentially at odds with the world, he leaves on his "affliction of dream called Overseas."[26]

Near the end of the first part of the novel, Toby meets Pat Keenan, the Irishman who is to be his cabinmate throughout the journey. They meet as the ship is departing from Wellington; significantly, Pat is holding a streamer which has not been caught by anyone on the dock, for "At the edge of the alphabet all streamers are torn or trail into strangeness,"[27] and Pat Keenan essentially belongs to the outer reaches of society. Much of Part Two, "The Lost Traveller's Dream of Speech," which describes the *Matua*'s journey to England, is described from Pat Keenan's point of view. He plainly belongs to Sister Bridge's kind, a follower of ritual who represses his imagination and seeks identity in his passport, insurance card, and the contents of his wallet. Zoe Bryce appears for the first time in this section, as a passenger returning from a working holiday in New Zealand. She and Toby feel kinship, sharing in their respective pasts shattered, half-imagined love affairs; seeing her, he is seized by an inexplicable feeling that she might write the book about the Lost Tribe of Manapouri[28] that he hopes to write in London. This ambition is yet another of Toby's futile dreams—he can barely write a word—and when the boat reaches Pitcairn Island and he finds himself enjoying the hospitality of the natives, he is bewildered to find that they too vanish like a dream.

For Zoe Bryce, the voyage has involved the most important experience of her life, one which takes her beyond any depth of alienation or height of self-knowledge that Toby Withers could achieve.

While ill with seasickness in the ship's hospital, she is suddenly and
inexplicably kissed by an anonymous crew member who then dashes
out of her life and the novel. This kiss—her first from a man—
obsesses and alters her, and her mind changes it into a symbolic act.
One of its effects is to prevent the likelihood of her ever achieving
communion with Toby, although some kind of relationship seems
imminent throughout Part Two. But despite the apparent similarities between Zoe and Toby, they are not truly partners, as
becomes apparent at a shipboard party where, labelled "Orpheus"
and seeking Eurydice, he finds that Zoe has been labelled "Minnie
Mouse."

Part Three, "The Silver Forest," is primarily devoted to Zoe
Bryce, but also tells the stories of all three travellers on their arrival
in London. Pat Keenan falls into his former groove, returning to his
Clapham boardinghouse and the reassuring company of his old landlady, Ma Crane, who is as meanly repressive as he. Toby lives in a
tenement with a couple of Irishmen and seeks employment of any
sort after his disappointing discovery that Piccadilly Circus contains
no ringmasters or caged animals. For diversion he pretends to hold
up a bank, using a gun that is actually a cigarette lighter. But soon
he has a job as a cinema commissionaire, from which he wanders
home every night to nurse a huge sore that has grown on his arm,
and to continue his desultory attempts to write his book about the
Lost Tribe. In time, he realizes that he will never be able to put his
meaning into words—or even decide finally what his meaning
is—and abandons the unlikely project.

Zoe's London experience, which is very similar to Toby's, is described in this last section. Outwardly, she falls under the stiflingly
regulatory influence of Pat Keenan, who persuades her to live in a
room at Ma Crane's boardinghouse. Inwardly, she is still deeply
disturbed by memories of her kiss. Instead of returning to the respectable but futile occupation of schoolteaching, she takes a menial
job as a maid in a hotel, claiming to be devoted to private research,
although this of course is quite imaginary. At the hotel she finds
herself an alien among aliens, the women she works with representing society's outcasts; she changes her job and becomes an usherette
in a cinema called The Palace—an occupation which draws her
closer, symbolically, to Toby. Throughout this section, as during the
middle section, she and Toby come close to each other; but they
never meaningfully communicate. When he visits her boarding-

house she is out, and when they do meet they simply have nothing significant to say to each other. Toby's physical decline continues, and soon, with some imagined prompting from his dead mother, he begins to consider returning to New Zealand.

Almost all that remains of the novel belongs to Zoe. Still considering the significance of her kiss, she has determined to shape a permanent monument to the love that has been revealed to her in that magical encounter. This monument, she decides, will endure the depredations of winter and all that is menacing in the world. Soon she feels herself being guided towards the moment of its creation by an elderly homosexual called Lawrence who introduces her to the company of numerous artists and their followers, of whom the most gifted is Peter Heron. While sitting by the Serpentine with this group one day, Zoe makes a miniature silver forest from discarded cigarette papers, producing an object whose beauty and originality win considerable admiration. Feeling fulfillment for the first time in her life, Zoe gives the silver forest to a tart named Zara, then returns to Ma Crane's boardinghouse, where she commits suicide. Peter Heron, on hearing the news, destroys all his paintings and becomes a hire-purchase salesman. The novel ends with Pat Keenan in a new job that involves selling blank sheets of paper at a stationery shop, and Toby back in New Zealand living with his Aunt Cora, who is slowly dying of a disease that is turning her bones to chalk. In the last paragraph of the novel, Thora Pattern provides a metaphor which describes the novel's characters as caged yellow birds caught in the trite pleasures of mirrors, treadmills, and useless toys.

IV   *Form and Narration*

The Edge of the Alphabet is the most "typical," because the most strictly paradigmatic, of all Janet Frame's novels. Its form brings together the technique of the first two novels, with the narrator of *Owls Do Cry*, Daphne Withers, being replaced by the obviously named Thora Pattern. The central section of the novel, describing the journey from New Zealand to England, again crosses the surface of the spoiled lagoon of *Faces in the Water* and hauls aboard the *Matua* many of the themes discussed there. The whole novel is dominated by the voice of Thora Pattern (as the first two were dominated by Daphne Withers and Istina Mavet), the voice of truth, sensitivity, insight, knowledge, and death—of all things contained within Janet Frame's vision of authenticity. Thora states that she lives at the edge of the alphabet, beyond the ordered communication which the very term, "alphabet," suggests; there, she finds "no safeguard against the dead" where

words like plants either grow poisonous tall and hollow about the rusted knives and empty drums of meaning, or, like people exposed to a deathly weather, shed their fleshy confusion and show luminous, knitted with force and permanence . . . .[29]

Her most specific reference to herself occurs in Chapter 21, when she appears as a figure who resembles the people she writes about, living in a boardinghouse where "the child practises the piano in the front room,"[30] the landlord checks invoices, the upstairs lodger lies dreaming in bed. She projects herself imaginatively into the lives of these and other people, in a manner which recalls the epilogue to the first novel, making the same point that imagination dwells in all people.

In this novel, Thora Pattern is very much an extension of Daphne Withers, differing only in that she has less to do and more to say. That development is important, for it gives increased objectivity and a greater resonance of meaning. The interspersed lyrics which came to be associated with Daphne are used here again, set apart from the prose narrative, and, as with the first novel, expressing theme and meaning with pungence and frequent wit. Here, for example, the wordless strength of nature is suggested:

An October warmed by frost,
the children sucking pink slabs of glacial earth,
the running stitch of snow in the sky
to mend
birthsprout
the hamster his cheek lined with fat, wordless.
Conferences
the rusting resorts this October birched with memory the switch
from the green trees where the birds were plump and sleek
of paradise and ample morning shadows
the day served for light to feed on
now October scraps of leaves and light
the starved shapes creeping up the evening walls
around corners

the tall skeleton transparent
while sleeps the tortoise his back marked muted mapped
   with boundaries . . . .[31]

Daphne Withers was capable of this degree and kind of narrative intrusion; with Thora Pattern, Janet Frame develops the technique further. Thora Pattern has a great deal to say, imposing her pattern far more often than earlier narrators were apt to do, and she frequently "melts" impersonal third-person narration into a curious mixture of the first person and the third that is highly personal and extremely direct. She frequently "enters" both Toby and Zoe, and, although less frequently, she speaks "within" Pat Keenan, making pronouncements which thrust the vision of truth before the reader in a way that constantly underlines the inauthentic lives of these characters. When Toby, for example, is locked within the humdrum dullness of life in New Zealand before his trip overseas, Thora Pattern suddenly speaks from the edge of the alphabet: "Is it a waste of light out here, in the natural dark, with the mauling sea so close?"[32] The fragility of Aunt Norma's comfortable home, the precariousness of her ordered way of life, become exposed immediately to Toby as his half-alive imagination is quickened again.

The routine life of Pat Keenan is similarly assailed by Thora Pattern's voice, through those dreams that are the refuge of the imagination in the strongly repressed individual. In Chapter 10, after urging Toby to take a greater part in the social life of the *Matua* (one is reminded of those who urged Janet Frame herself to "mix, adapt, conform"), Pat has a dream of truth prompted by an earlier glance at his bedside statuette of Our Lady; in his dream, he finds himself "walking in a lonely place, near the edge, among weeds and rusty tin-cans and derelict words and people"[33]—it is Thora Pattern's natural home, the bedrock of all existence, the edge of the alphabet. Zoe Bryce's relationship with the edge of the alphabet is also asserted by Thora Pattern, who often indicates the origin of her narrative voice by the typographical means of setting shorter statements alone against the margin of the page, at the very limit of the conventions by which novels communicate.

The narrative voice of *The Edge of the Alphabet* is distinguished by its dire message. Daphne Withers and Istina Mavet had little to say that was reassuring; but the vision of Thora Pattern is truly apocalyptic, cast in images of the immediate and the probable. This is an aspect of the author's increasing ability to generalize, a development that occurs during the course of the Withers trilogy, and it produces a vision that is painfully familiar to us:

It is raining and raining and I will die. The buildings topple, slide with the bruised and broken leaves into the earth, folded deep. The yellow glare in the sky is the striped mantle of tigers, licked cool, healed by the darting tongues of frost. Yet winter, age, loneliness, have come leaping with seventy claws unleashed from summer, youth, and the gentle conditions of love, to stripe our lives with death, to set fire to our cage.[34]

Here, the personal and the general are interwoven; by the end of the novel, the personal element has been transcended and the scenes described are postapocalyptic:

Outside, all the buildings have toppled. Men in white suits, as if for tennis, prance about the debris in search of the last victims. The woman next door, blinded, has found a pot of white-wash which trickles down the window-pane . . . but the sun, the merry-go-round sun bearing the full blame and journeying of the flat immovable earth, blares its music while the painted horses rise and fall under the tall streamered poles of light.[35]

The last twenty pages or so of this novel represent a distinct development in Janet Frame's work, for they express the tragic view of life and history that the next novel, *Scented Gardens for the Blind*, will set out fully.

V   *Characters*

The three main characters through whom Thora Pattern makes her "voyage of discovery" provide a range of types beneath which are subsumed all kinds of people Janet Frame has depicted so far. Pat Keenan is the easiest target for the criticism the work makes, for his repressive narrowness is portrayed in detail. Our first view of him, confusedly clutching the streamer which has no one at the other end, reveals his essential loneliness to everyone but himself. His literary prototype may be seen in a short story called "The Advocate" in *The Reservoir*, which sketches a man whose gregariousness and desire to help others is equalled only by their hatred of him. Pat Keenan is prey to misgivings about himself only when dreaming; while awake he is a creature of habit and a speaker of slogans. On the single occasion when he wonders about his essential identity, he rapidly reassures himself with a glance at the documents society has provided him with. Inevitably, he strongly supports everything in society which regulates, his job as a bus driver involving endless repetition and a flimsy form of communication. He allies himself with all agents of authority, and his recreations range from sharing drivelling conversations and cups of tea with his landlady to reporting prostitutes to the police. He also attempts to control the lives of others—particularly Zoe's—by subjecting them to the slogans which keep society buoyant. According to Pat, Zoe needs to think of a pension, for "the most important thing in the world is to lay a little by," "to invest in security,"[36] and he advises Toby and Zoe to "leave their jobs and 'invest' in something 'safe and clean.' "[37] Toby, according to Pat Keenan, has only one problem: a lack of "proper meals"[38]; while Zoe's life would suddenly become meaningful, in his view, if she stopped working as an usherette and resumed her old career as a school-teacher ("He said the word 'school-teacher' with the same reverence that he used for saying 'doctor,' 'police,' 'authorities' "[39]). At times he is possessed by a vision of life in a state of wonderful order and cleanliness:

when he came to train the beams of his love upon that part of the world around him which he desired for himself, he formed, out of some topographical fantasy, a landscape of canals, of deep slits of prejudice where his love could not penetrate; a bizarre land- and seascape which he could not possess. Swans flew there, and leprechauns kept their neat clean houses, and Our Lady in a blue silk dress watched over everything; but there were few human beings unless Pat himself could plant them there, digging holes for them in the earth where they lived helpless to fend for themselves, relying (Pat knew and rejoiced) upon his devoted care.[40]

But Zoe is not a plant: she wishes strongly enough to live her own life that she is able to survive his attempts to live it for her, and he is left to expose his essential blankness through his last job as a salesman of white paper.

Where Pat Keenan finds himself nagged by truth in his dreams, Toby Withers finds dreams a refuge from truth. His dream of living in suburban anonymity with Evelina Festing is replaced by his "affliction of dream called Overseas," to which is related the mission of writing a novel about the Lost Tribe. Sometimes he dreams that he is a tree or "an entire forest, with the Lost Tribe inhabiting him."[41] But although his illiteracy is an admirable qualification for a resident at the edge of the alphabet, he will never write anything on the kind of paper Pat Keenan sells. In fact, all Toby's dreams dissolve: his dream of fame in New Zealand after success in London, his dream of Piccadilly Circus as a stage for acrobats and clowns, the dream about his past which concludes his journey on the *Matua*. It is inevitable that he should find a job that associates him with a cinema in London, for films are the refuge of avoiders of truth. His Overseas quest fails because he allows himself to abandon his writing project—his imaginative life—instead of cherishing it as a means of establishing his difference from Pat Keenan and his kind. When his attempt to communicate with Zoe comes to nothing, he begins to acknowledge the inauthenticity of his life in a series of mirror images (he wonders whether he is in a fun fair), and at the end of the novel he is back in New Zealand, doomed to live out his life safely and inauthentically, in mirrors.

It has been seen that Toby is very closely linked with Zoe Bryce. At times, they seem to be aspects of one sensibility—as the Withers family seemed to stand for the single sensibility of the narrator— rather than two different characters. Thus Toby senses that Zoe might write his book about the Lost Tribe before he does, and they both find jobs connected to cinemas. Zoe is the most important character in the novel, largely by virtue of the creation of the little silver forest of twisted cigarette papers; the central incident of the novel involves her curious experience aboard the *Matua*, when the mysterious crewman dashes into the ship's hospital to kiss her. Improbable as this incident may seem, it is extremely significant. The kiss brings a moment of love to this loveless woman and awakens in her a new imaginative vision which often expresses itself richly and in a lyrical manner which surprises those who have known Zoe as an unimaginative and slightly repressive schoolteacher. It is a "tiny, precious berry from the one branch of a huge tree in a forest where the trees are numberless,"[42] and "talk of truth was the first sign that *It* was going to happen."[43] Later, she sees the kiss as a communication from beyond the alphabet of language and feels urged to begin creating works of art:

The wall of dream is punctured like a sieve and the strange other world pours in upon me in a way that never happened before. I am concerned with an intensity of making—yet I make nothing. The kiss is the core of my life . . . I need to walk in that forest . . . I need to build a house, a tower, under and through the silver leaves into the sky.[44]

The reader may better understand why such a small act is weighted with such significance if attention is drawn to another companion story to the novel. This is "An Incident in Mid-Ocean" from *The Reservoir*, in which a woman who is a prototype of Zoe Bryce wins the friendship of a young schoolboy, grows to love him, and destroys all by kissing him quite innocently one day. Society is shocked that the woman should molest the child, and the woman has lost the only thing she has ever been able to love. The title of the story is revealing, connecting it not only with Zoe Bryce but with the water imagery of earlier fiction. What the kiss makes Zoe understand is that restrictions and boundaries and conventions are a betrayal of life; she senses and then grows to see with increasing clarity the forest of life—the forest which Toby wishes to write about, with its tribe of lost human beings. In that forest, humans uninhibitedly mingle in a joyous celebration of life, and innocent love is never conceived as molestation. Having seen life as a wonderful unity, Zoe achieves the status of artist, requiring only to make some work of art to celebrate the natural world in the manner advocated by Rilke. By making a beautiful object from discarded cigarette foil she creates from the mundane, making something worthwhile and permanent from the ashes of her former life. After such fulfillment, it is difficult to think of her suicide as an admission of failure.

VI *Dream and Reality*

In Chapter 30, Toby recalls his last visit to Central Otago, the hinterland of his home town, when the river there had been diverted and its bed—rumored to be solid gold—exposed. Large crowds gather upon the exposed bed in search of gold, but one man stays far longer than any others and drowns when the river is returned to its course. This small parable stands for the larger experience of the novel which contains it: all three of the main characters are dreamers who, to a certain degree, find themselves unable to face reality. Pat has his dream of order and control, Toby his paired dreams of settling into society and writing about the Lost Tribe, and Zoe her dream of finding comfort and fulfillment in New Zealand after the collapse of her fleeting love affair in England. Only by prolonged suppression of the imagination can Pat preserve his dream; Toby abandons his after taking the wrong course, as he did in the first novel, in this case attempting to articulate an experience which lies beyond the alphabet.

Zoe's dream lies in ashes by the time she leaves New Zealand on board the *Matua*. The middle section of the novel, where she makes her first appearance, is reminiscent of *Faces in the Water*, employing the same metaphor of reflection and dwelling again on the relationship of "this" world to "that." On the water, the main characters of the novel find themselves tested in ways they are unused to: Pat Keenan is disturbed by his dreams, and Toby and Zoe find they must choose which mode of life they will adopt, a decision that will determine whether they will spend the rest of their lives caught in their dreams or in an authentic relationship with the whole of existence. The shipboard social evening in which Toby finds himself labelled "Orpheus" and Zoe "Minnie Mouse" tells the reader much about their respective decisions. At first glance, Toby seems to suit his label: as his "affair" with Evelina Festing showed, he is a lonely man who needs a woman to love. It is hard, initially, to understand why Zoe Bryce cannot be his Eurydice; but in fact he lacks the strength of character and the gifts to become her partner, and is much more suited to be a partner to a figure from the popular subculture. Each needs something the other lacks; as a result, their relationship is unsatisfactory, promising much but expressing itself in missed meetings and periods spent together without any communication whatever. Toby becomes a sort of debased Orpheus-figure, one who has betrayed his gifts: his underworld is London, whose barrenness he has no music to alter. Instead of being fruitfully dismembered as Orpheus was, he remains whole but mysteriously infected as if his suppressed powers were festering within him, and he leaves London loveless and defeated, still enshrouded by his dream.

And so it is Zoe Bryce alone who discovers truth in *The Edge of the Alphabet* and who performs the task that Toby—in a parabolic recollection of some dwarfs who lived near him in his childhood— describes as plucking jewels from the ashes of burnt dreams. Zoe's life has been a series of burnt dreams, but her kiss in mid-ocean rescues her by revealing the existence of the forest of life in its entirety. This vision redeems her life entirely, for it makes it the stuff from which she may form the silver forest of art and stands for a world which may be entered only through her own death.

VII   *The Withers Trilogy*

It is now quite clear that Janet Frame's first three novels are linked in theme and tone, and particularly by a system of images which still persists in the fourth novel, *Scented Gardens for the Blind*. But these three novels also cohere in that they trace the fortunes of the Withers family as well as the generation of the artist from the ordinary and extraordinary experiences of life. Here too the influence of Robin Hyde's novel, *The Godwits Fly*, may be seen to provide coherence and form. In Daphne and Francie Withers, Istina Mavet, Thora Pattern and Zoe Bryce there is a progression from the childlike innocence of the young Eliza Hannay through her darkening vision as she loses her own child and lover to her final insights, which resemble those of Zoe Bryce. But where Robin Hyde has compacted a prolonged experience of personal artistic evolution into a single novel, Janet Frame has more wisely allowed it to develop within a trilogy, exploring each stage of development by attributing it to a different character. Thus, the childhood years of Eliza Hannay stand behind the whole span of Janet Frame's first novel, the modest image of the glory hole becoming, in the hands of the surer artist, the governing symbol of the treasure-laden rubbish dump; Eliza's disillusioned trip to the wasteland of Sydney is paralleled by Istina's descent into the underworld of the mental hospital; and the last novel of the trilogy explores themes which are like those set out late in *The Godwits Fly*—of dream and disillusionment and artistic achievement. In all aspects, Janet Frame's work is more fully achieved, more rounded, and more deeply searching.

The trilogy may also be seen as an extended parable of the author's own growth to artistic status, and thus prepares the way for the novels which lie beyond it. The myth of Orpheus is central to this parable, beginning in the painful loss of childhood and reaching consummation in the troubled transition from civilian into poet. Francie, a symbolic other version of Daphne, is swept underground as Eurydice was; slowly, Daphne learns what Orpheus learned, that the girl is not sacrificed but has become a means of understanding life and its relationship to death. Daphne and her avatar, Istina

Mavet, wander the underworld for years to discover this truth. The metamorphoses of Daphne in the early fiction have been summed up by Jeanne Delbaere-Garant in this way:

Orpheus is the common denominator. Each of the different versions of Daphne possesses some of his features. Like him Istina wanders in the country of the dead. Thora imposes order on the confusion of the world, Vera turns the shelter into a temple and rescues language from complete annihilation. Like him they have visited the country of Eurydice and have come back alienated from the society of mankind and aware that the dead are as much part of their lives as the living. Like him—torn to pieces by the fierce Maenads—they have limbs loosely attached or are split into fragments of themselves—unifying and holding together by their very dispersion.[45]

The truth that Istina finds at Cliffhaven and Treecroft is that the dead and the living belong together, just as "normal" and "abnormal" people really belong together simply as human beings. Her emergence at the end of the novel does not represent a return to "normal" life: it is the fusing of the knowledge of the underworld with everyday life. Thus Orpheus "links Janet Frame herself with Rilke and Ovid and all the poets of the past whom she has assimilated and those whose voice is part of her own," as Jeanne Delbaere-Garant has said.[46] The inevitable result of Istina's sojourn in hospital is her elevation to the status of poet and pattern-maker; and thus she becomes Thora Pattern, the "author" of *The Edge of the Alphabet*, in which Toby Withers and Zoe Bryce demonstrate the failure and the triumph of art.

Both Jeanne Delbaere-Garant and Winston Rhodes have emphasized in their studies of these early novels the coherence of theme and imagery which results from the creation of several works in a single, prolonged eruption of creative energy. That the first four novels are nevertheless not a tetralogy is evident in the autobiographical coherence of the first three and their reliance on a mutating narrator. The Withers trilogy sees the working out, often with difficulty, of the artist's correct position in life; *Scented Gardens for the Blind* is a *celebration* of the relationship between art and life, a work of confidence and wit whose tone is different from that of the trilogy, and which marks a significant development in her art.

CHAPTER 5

The Burning Snowman

I Necessary Silence

THE unity of Janet Frame's fiction during the early 1960's, sensed by Winston Rhodes, is nowhere better illustrated than in the relationship of the long parable "Snowman, Snowman" and the better-known novel *Scented Gardens for the Blind*, which were published in the same year. The former work, buried within the collection of short pieces to which it lends its name, is almost unknown to many readers who are well acquainted with the second, a work that is not quite twice the length of the story. Yet the two read like aspects of a whole, and it could certainly be argued that the novel would be both enriched and made more readily intelligible by the inclusion of supplementary passages from "Snowman, Snowman." As it is, the latter remains as a sort of ghostly presence behind the story of Vera Glace.

Scented Gardens for the Blind is a remarkably nonexpository work, its inwardness not fully revealed till the last chapter but nevertheless presenting difficulties long before its conclusion, to the reader who likes his narrative to be straightforward. Since parts of the novel take the form of apparently straightforward narrative, it might be as well to grasp these small threads as the only means by which something of the essential nature of the novel can be represented. Unlike the preceding novels, it has no internal divisions into parts, instead developing organically through sixteen brief chapters. Its first narrator is Vera Glace, who portrays herself as a sensitive mother stricken with worry at the predicament of her daughter, Erlene, who broods in an adjacent room, deprived of the power of speech. Imagining a phonetician's diagram of the human head, Vera announces to herself her belief that the words formed there are ordered and meaningful:

101

The speech will be clear, beautiful, the words pleasurably patterned like daisy-chains, with biting-links, with the smell of the earth and the sun and the juice of man.[1]

But this is no ordinary speech that Vera Glace wishes for: it is a part of a desire evident throughout the novel for a new language of authenticity "which is understood by no one and nothing, and which causes a smokescreen of fear to cloud the mind, as defence against the strangeness."[2] Ordinary speech, she knows, is valueless: "On and on, saying nothing, the tattered bargain-price words, the great red-flagged sale of trivialities, the shut-down sell-out of the mind."[3] The opening chapter also reminds the reader of a couple of important notions already familiar from the earlier novels: that the sun and its light are truth, and that the narrator is a voyager through the lives of others, "my own, Edward's, Erlene's, and my father's."[4]

In the second chapter the reader becomes immersed in the lyrical imagination of Erlene, locked in her lonely room and holding imaginary conversations with "Uncle Black Beetle," a children's story figure she has concocted complete with carpenter's apron and a fixed place on her windowsill. The third chapter presents Edward Glace, her father, in a process of flitting from character to character which Janet Frame maintains throughout the book. Edward Glace is a genealogist with a particular interest in tracking down members of the Strang family: for eleven years he has lived in England apart from his family, concerned only with the Strangs and his hobby of playing with toy soldiers.

Chapter 8, the pivotal part of the novel, contains Erlene's first confrontation with the ridiculous Dr. Clapper, a psychiatrist whom the girl's mother has called in as part of her campaign to get the child to speak. The meeting is disastrous, for the psychiatrist is an insensitive fool who is too garrulous and fatuous to see how unsuccessful his efforts are. Meanwhile, back in England, Erlene's father has managed to trace and meet Georgina Strang, one of the living generation of the family to whom his researches have led him. But he finds himself disappointed by her dull, unimaginative way of life and particularly by her inability to mourn her recently deceased husband, Lyndon, in any authentic way or even to understand what is involved in her loss. When a letter from Vera tells him of Erlene's refusal to speak, Edward decides to fly back to New Zealand, convinced of the importance of making the girl speak and hearing what she has to say; for, like his wife, Edward believes that Erlene verges on the brink of an utterance of the greatest importance for mankind.

In Chapter 11, Erlene has the conversation with Uncle Black Beetle which provides some of the most explicit statements to be found in the novel. Uncle Black Beetle tells her that death is the common denominator of all stories, and provides a parable which illustrates this proposition. He tells the story of Albert the Dung-Beetle, who lets himself wither and his family die as he waits to fulfill his dream of getting a giant ball of dung. When, after many years, his dream is fulfilled, he is crushed to death while trying to roll the ball into his own home. At the end of this story, Uncle Black Beetle appears to turn into Dr. Clapper, who is his opposite in every way—a threatening reminder to the girl that her refuge in dream is being eroded. Edward meanwhile is being forced to confront an unpleasant truth too, for in the penultimate chapter of the novel he meets another living member of the Strang family, Clara, who lives in Dunedin, and finds her to be worse than Georgina, her English relative. Clara Strang has adopted three small orphaned boys whom she is teaching to read and write while coldly thrusting down upon them all the limited and limiting values of society. But in the last chapter, the illusion which has sustained the novel for fifteen chapters is removed as it is revealed that Vera Glace is a former librarian who has spent thirty years sitting silently in a mental hospital, her only companion another elderly patient called Clara Strang, who has been her devoted nurse throughout this time. Vera Glace is about to break her long silence: Dr. Clapper listens to the first utterance, which, he finds, consists of primitive grunts. "Out of ancient rock and marshland," the novel concludes, "out of ice and stone."[5]

II *Form and Theme*

Summarizing a novel in this way is as little satisfactory as summarizing a poem; but the taut, organic development of *Scented Gardens for the Blind,* so unusual in a novel, allows it to set out its theme more subtly and effectively than does the more rigidly segmented novel it follows. It is possible to sense more easily here the basic ideas which have developed during the earlier fiction, and also to feel that in this work they have matured. The novel's dominant metaphor is set out in the epigraph:

We want those who are blind to be able to appreciate what lies around them; therefore we have planted these specially scented gardens.[6]

The speaker here is the anonymous "Mayor of the City," and the passage could have been culled from any newspaper report of any civic ceremony. The metaphor of blindness established here initially seems at odds with the attributes established for each character. The doggedly mute Vera Glace and her "daughter," Erlene, live at the edge of the alphabet where sight should presumably be true and unhindered, and blindness would seem to be the least likely of their characteristics.

But at the edge of the alphabet, exposed to truth in life and the overwhelming fullness of experience, one yearns for blindness as a respite. Winston Rhodes has shown how the parabolic method signals this to the reader: he links the novel to "The Red-Currant Bush, the Black-Currant Bush, the Gooseberry Bush, the African Thorn Hedge, and the Garden Gate Who Was Once the Head of an Iron Bedstead," a fantasy in the *Snowman, Snowman* collection that is not very much longer than its title. The objects referred to reside on the shady side of a garden and must debate how to receive more light and warmth:

They must persuade the sun to rise in the west, but "are faced with the principle of an indisputable fact." Their discussion ranges from the proposal that they should deny that the sun rises in the east to a plan whereby everything in the garden is blinded—"Then no-one can contradict us when we say that the sun is rising in the west." In parabolic form the evasions of reality are delightfully described in terms of shade and sunlight.[7]

It has already been well established that sunlight is a powerful image for the light of unrelenting truth in Janet Frame's art; it lights all things impartially and, short of death itself, is the most undeniable thing in existence. To accept its light is to accept the truth of existence, while only complete and determined blindness will exclude its light and permit us to accept falsehoods, such as a convention that the sun rises in the west. A second such parable in *Snowman, Snowman* refers specifically to man's blindness when faced with reality: this is called "The Mythmaker's Office," and satirizes the habit of devising bureaucratic myths to counter unpalatable truths. The "Minister of Mythmaking" has established a rule that the sun must never be referred to; when this fails to win popularity, he bans all references to death, which becomes "relegated to a Resistance Movement, a Black Market, and furtive shovellings on the outskirts of the city."[8] What Janet Frame is saying here, of course, is that society really does blind itself to things it cannot face, anesthetizing itself against death just as Georgina Strang does. When Vera Glace imagines what it would be like to be blind, she finds the idea comforting, for

The sun is all love and murder, judgment, the perpetual raid of conscience, paratrooping light which opens like snow-blossom in the downward drift of death. Wherever I turn—the golden cymbals of judgment, the summoning of the torturers, the inquisitors of light.[9]

The price of authentic life in the world of Janet Frame is the painfulness of truth, the confrontation with unmediated experience which brings both pain and advantage, love and murder. But despite her longings to blind her eyes to this vision, Vera Glace is not blind. The blind, as Winston Rhodes has said, are

those of us for whom "specially scented gardens" have been planted because we obstinately prefer darkness and illusion to the truths of existence. Not only may we retreat through the help of scented gardens, but by choosing to live in a world of shadows and appearances or in a labyrinth of words and meaningless phrases. "Some turn to the future, others to the past, others remain in a perpetual historic present."[10]

And Vera Glace lives authentically, in that uncomfortable world beyond the alphabet, where only the imagination protects.

All this is fairly familiar, for the Withers trilogy also explored the degrees to which humans express or repress their faculties of honesty and imagination. As it was before, the place of trial in this novel is the mental hospital, where society's agents in their white coats repeatedly urge the nonconformist to "mix, adapt, conform." But this novel takes the blindness of such figures and examines it as a literal phenomenon. For example, Vera Glace recalls a childhood visit to the beach, where she admired a lighthouse set up to protect humans from the marauding sea. But its electricity is man-made, and like the electricity of electric shock treatment, it can betray as well as serve: inevitably, the lighthouse keeper is soon conveyed from the lighthouse, raving mad. A further childhood memory illustrates why humans need electricity and its false light: Vera recalls her primitive childhood home where candles provided the only illumination and the overwhelming darkness seemed to conceal terrifying dogs and huddled beggars. The girl's parents clung to their candles

and their bodies were insignificant compared with their giant, grotesque shadows striding up the wall and across the ceiling, capturing in their journey the lesser immobile shadows of furniture which nevertheless could change swiftly; everything depended on the movement of the lamp or candle.[11]

Such man-made methods of lighting the world are all fictions by which reality can be turned away as man tries to blind himself to the truths he does not wish to see. His efforts are frantic and eager; Edward Glace, for example, fearing that his sight is failing through overwork and visiting an eye specialist, secretly wishes that he may lose his vision altogether; and he finds comfort in the waiting room by listening to background music from a program with the moronic title "Light and Bright." But in *Scented Gardens for the Blind,* light destroys those who fail to confront it, the scented garden emits toxic fumes, and all dreams destroy the dreamer, as the sad little parable of Albert Dung-Beetle shows.

Although the novel treats blindness as a literal condition, it continues the trilogy's work of illustrating society's figurative blindness, setting out many events that are inauthentic and showing many people who live inauthentically, according to private dreams or public fictions. Teaching, for example, comes under attack again; Vera asserts that teaching is "cheating and dishonest" because it uses a "topped and tailed language."[12] A parallel story of this period, "A Sense of Proportion,"[13] takes up this theme, showing the inflexibility of an art mistress who makes her pupils shade their model objects according to a rigid set of rules. In the novel, this figure is developed to form two teachers Vera remembers from her childhood schooldays, Miss Walters and Miss Galloway. The former lives a life of barren punctuality and dismisses the despair of Arnold's "Dover Beach" with sad cries of hope and joy; the latter blushes when discussing copulative verbs and conceals during class readings those passages which Dr. Bowdler should have dealt with. These women suppress their true imagination, as does another character, Vera Glace's father, whose instinct to make his life orderly is always attacked by the disorderly intrusions of his half-suppressed imagination. He has always been fascinated by the gardening trousers of his son-in-law, Edward, not because he is a fetishist but because Edward claims to have bought them in Arabia. The old man spends weeks in torment, shambling into the house repeatedly to peer at the exotic pants and then furtively slipping outside again to his perfectly ordered vegetable garden. Erlene, his granddaughter, asks him to take her to Arabia, a proposition so frightening to him, however, that he reacts violently. First-hand experience is difficult to predict or to control, and most people, like Vera's father, revert to mirrors, spectacles, and maps to keep all experience at a remove where it is safe. And so the "Arabian" trousers are cut up for polishing rags, and the old man can lie in bed comforted by the meretricious warmth of his electric blanket.

Like Erlene and Vera's father, Edward Glace is a figment of the imagination; but for all this, he is the most-worked character in the novel. As is suggested by his mirrorlike spectacles and watery, half-blind eyes, he has a strong desire for order which manifests itself in the control he exercises over the battles he sets out on his living room floor and in his pursuit of the Strangs through generation after disordered generation. Battles are confusing for participants, while the human family also spawns in a confusingly chaotic way over centuries during which it leaves few records of its activities. The reason for Edward's interest in two such disorderly processes is suggested in the following passage, where his desire to bring order and control to them is evident:

Edward lived, as he wished to fight with his plastic armies, by remote control. Also he liked power; he liked to be able to make the awards now, to judge *personally*. The Strangs haunted him. They persisted about him, their voices echoing, whispering. They were an ordinary family—he had been particular about tracing the lineage of an "ordinary family" because he was aware that families, so described, share the common nightmare, put poison in one another's food, bed, and brain, and make love with the taste of death in their mouth, breathing it in their partner's face or trying to get rid of it by first swallowing little green tablets coloured like silkworm dung. An ordinary family, in the chain-gang of the human race, linked in the ordinary way with doom.[14]

Edward's desire for order is not only the result of a dislike of disorder, however. In his two obsessive activities he has sensed an
important truth which he must dig from the past, clean, and recon-
struct. And the reader too must do a share of analysis and assembling, for the Strangs in their ordinariness do not at first seem to
warrant pronouncements of doom, nor Edward's claim that in studying them he is studying the world.

Nevertheless, for all the dullness of the living representatives of
the Strang family, Edward Glace's confrontations with them are
vitally important. Both incidents resemble others from earlier fiction featuring similarly disapproved figures, although Georgina
Strang in London and Clara Strang in Dunedin are dignified by the
significant weight of past which is conferred upon them both. Certainly their suburban values are noticeable: both attempt to deny
kinship with a condemned murderer of the same surname, and
Georgina Strang seems to Edward to be the "kind of person who
could say, I will cry now, I will laugh now, and who would prepare
her surroundings carefully . . . before she could enjoy her outburst."[15] Although a coarser woman, Clara Strang shows the same
values, with her unhappy and frightened foster children who have
been beaten into orderly behavior and branded with the task of
learning to read and write. The two women, this novel states, are
the end result of generation upon generation of human procreation.

For truly, the Strangs stand as representatives of all humans in
Janet Frame's fictional world. Edward's aim in studying them, and
the truth he is attempting to reveal from within their experience,
are indicated here:

He only wanted to fulfil a small ambition, to make a complete, beautiful
chronicle of one family which had persisted over the centuries in spite of
war, disease, and other catastrophes which have visited mankind. To Edward the important fact of each war, plague, earthquake, famine was not the
number killed, but the realization that at one moment during the disaster
two people were giving expression of their love for each other, were lying
nakedly giving and receiving, in spite of deceits, disgusts, errors, calami-
tous misunderstandings, with that ultimate generosity and gratitude which
create in the human mind among tenements of despair, enough believing-
space and praising-space for a God.[16]

This astonishing realization animates the whole novel: that through
centuries of violence and disaster men can still love women "with

the taste of death" in their mouths[17] and can still reproduce their kind. Edward's obsession with genealogy and his love of miniature battlefields are merely images for his insight into the nature of human history, in which love mingles with death and the act of continuing the species is itself a battle. That humans should be able to do both things together is not ridiculous or tragic but marvellous, and convincing proof that some ultimate purpose and meaning exist to life.

Edward's way of expressing and defining his insights is rather halting and prosaic, because of the almost mathematical nature of his hobbies and his limited mind and speech. But by the end of the novel he seems to Erlene to have become fused with Uncle Black Beetle, a process which transfers the reader's attention to an alternative mode of understanding that the novel establishes through this tiny fairy-tale figure.

III *The Language of Communion*

All novels deceive by pretending to create life on their pages; *Scented Gardens for the Blind* rejoices in the illusions and delusions it creates, and in its clever concealment of them. But helpful clues and signals are planted here and there to aid the reader in his quest for understanding; and perhaps the most helpful of these occurs in Chapter 8 when Uncle Black Beetle remarks that his literary cousin who lives in a dictionary emerges from a hole between *trichotomy* and *trick*. Winston Rhodes has discussed the significance of this remark. "Despite her 'tragic vision' so stressed by reviewers," he states, "Janet Frame's sense of humour is never far below the surface and the wanderings of this literary cousin through the world of words becomes a moving as well as a ludicrous commentary on the human situation."[18] Uncle Black Beetle's literary cousin, Rhodes continues, resembles the reader of this novel wandering among words in search of meaning and finding special significance in two words. For the "trick" of *Scented Gardens for the Blind* is its prolonged delusion of the reader which conceals the "trichotomy" into which Vera Glace has divided herself. Until the reader understands that he too is, colloquially speaking, "in a hole," like the literary cousin caught in the alphabetically arranged dictionary, until the reader himself moves towards the edge of the alphabet, both the novel and the world of everyday language it deprecates will remain confusing.

Throughout the Withers trilogy Janet Frame showed a concern
for the need for human love and communion between individuals,
and for the need for everyone to recognize his or her own face in the
water. The tragedy of Zoe Bryce, for example, was that she attempted to communicate her need to give love in a world that could
not understand her language. In the world of Vera Glace there is an
even greater concern with the possibility that human beings may
contain a latent capacity to communicate in a new way, from beyond
the alphabet. Sensing that the marvel of human survival points to a
purpose in life, Edward Glace begins to believe that this purpose
involves achieving communion in such a way that humans will
mingle with one another as if under water, with all barriers and
boundaries dissolved:

> The dream of Edward's life was the time when the human race would reach
> the sea, when it would not be important who was Georgina Strang and who
> was Vera Glace, or who was anybody, there would be no Strang family, no
> names, and none of the guilt arising from the denial of essence and
> name . . . .
> Galleons, old caves where the drowned look in windows with the weed
> floating across their eyes, the dead kept under by the hand of the water
> which moves softly, powerfully, and how the parched dead spring to the
> surface, light, white merry bones which form a rocking-chair for the sun to
> laze in and pay the rent to the landlord dead, the invisible flesh changed
> into salt and shells and singing fish . . . .[19]

It was made clear in *Faces in the Water*—from which this passage
might well have been taken, so familiar is the tone and imagery—
that the ideal communion envisaged here is to be brought about by
the free expression of love. But this ideal, as Vera Glace realizes, is
unlikely to be fulfilled: "each person's life contains one message
which never reaches its destination" because a language of communion is lacking in a society which utters its mindless slogans from
deep *within* the alphabet.[20]
    Thematically, the novel is constantly devoted to the problem of
finding this language which will "saw through the bars, the mile-
wide walls"[21] created through everyday language such as is seen in
some letters Edward reads in Chapter 9. These have been written
by various members of the Strang family at the time of Lyndon
Strang's death, and are masterpieces of cliché and euphemism. It is
his confrontation with their barrenness that prompts Edward to

travel to New Zealand and persuade his daughter to speak; for the Strangs, he comes to realize, have not yet learned to speak, and must be cared for until some descendant speaks the language of authenticity:

> Perhaps some time in the future the written and spoken words of this ordinary family will touch like lances upon the skin of those nearest to them, will draw blood from the selected wound, will penetrate and unfold the flower closed upon its own heart; but sun and lances are so old, and dead, and this is tomorrow, it is the time of the flash in the sky, the deep burn of words which destroy all power to create, the time of a first-degree language so articulate that the vision of it results in physical blindness, and those who have spoken one word of it are struck dumb and forbidden ever to speak again.[22]

The Strangs and the Glaces have developed side by side, the former away from genuine communication and towards the evolution of nuclear weapons, the ultimate form of violence, while the latter have developed away from violence and towards the possibility of communion through language. Thus, the most crucial point of the novel is the moment at which Erlene speaks, and two possible modes of utterance are envisaged for her. In one, she may speak

> as an ancestral voice, the voice of the beast, that would make her father tremble with fear and clutch protectively at his carefully compiled generations; that would make her mother hurry to find the little pink wax balls to stop her ears from the true sound rising at last from ice and marshland, ancient rock and stone, the ultimate denial of cities and people and rich stores of language skimmed century after century from the settled civilizations of human beings.[23]

But there is another language she may utter:

> not mere animal cries, demands for food, warmth, love, nor human pleas for forgiveness, salvation, peace of mind, but the speech which arranges the dance and pattern of the most complicated ideas and feelings of man in relation to truth; truth; it, the center, the circus, the crack of the whip, the feeding-time of the spirit; then the great striped tigers leaping unharmed through the fire. It is something to hope for.[24]

Erlene's final utterance is spoken in fact by her mute "creator," Vera Glace; when she speaks, there is no doubt that her statement belongs to the first of these categories, and not the ideal second:

"Ug-g-Ug. Ohhh g. Ugg."
Out of ancient rock and marshland; out of ice and stone.[25]

This is not a language at all, but it is the only statement that could arise from the situation set out in *Scented Gardens for the Blind*. Mankind in this novel is seen as irrevocably marching the path towards violence and destruction, its failure of language degenerated finally into an antilanguage of hurled nuclear weapons and individual bestiality. This is why the novel ends with the nuclear destruction of Britain which leaves the rest of the world "still numb with fear, tasting people-ash in their mouth and trying to whitewash the fallen skies"[26] and the land returned to the ancient rock and marsh from which it began. For, in order that the ideal communion hinted at above be fulfilled, the slate must be wiped clean and a return to primitive origins be made. The chance that a new language might be formed without such destruction, a language which might even avert such destruction, is gone; for the road to destruction has signposts which point only ahead.

Thus, the conclusion of this novel is not as pessimistic as it at first appears to be. It envisages a holocaust that is nevertheless a purgation of all that is bad, accumulated from years of habit and ignorance. And it sees the possibility that a truly human voice may rise for the first time, out of the ashes of destruction.

IV   *The Snowman's Story*

In this novel, Janet Frame tests the ability of her readers to practise what she preaches—to respond to her fiction poetically and imaginatively and to learn in doing so the advantages of the language of poetry and the imagination. Failure to make this response—to identify with the literary cousin of Uncle Black Beetle—leaves the novel bewildering and senseless. Success admits the reader to the vivid imagination of Erlene and the beetle whose images do so much to enrich the meaning of the novel. Compare, for example, the sketchiness of Edward Glace's limited understanding of his task in life with the pungency of Uncle Black Beetle's knowledge: where the former merely handles his lead soldiers, the latter refers to "the soldiers passing in twos and threes, with iron bands round their foreheads and little sachets of diseases and lavender flowers tied to their waist, and their teeth cleaned with white ash."[27] Always, the comparison between the language of everyday and the language of poetry reveals the immediacy of communication which the latter brings and the frustrating poverty of the former.

The "successful" reader of this difficult and challenging novel becomes a sort of graduate, complete with a key which can unlock other novels by a recognition that, in the art of Janet Frame, metaphor is truth. It is an understanding that applies to all her other works, but it would be wrong to assume that it leads the reader to Uncle Black Beetle alone. Vera Glace's "trick" of dividing herself into three is not the only one in the novel, as all who have identified themselves with the literary beetle will soon acknowledge. A further "trick" relates to Vera Glace's own name, which Joan Stevens has described as the "true mirror" in which Vera's imaginary selves are reflected.[28] But as well as being a true mirror, Vera Glace is a false one. By continuing to investigate the possibility of further meanings in her name through the puns that obviously reside in it, one will consider the "truth" about "Glace," which suggests both "ice" and (as something to be seen through) "window." Thus, Vera Glace suggests truth, transparency, and iciness, a combination of qualities which cannot help but make the reader think of a contemporaneous work with the title "Snowman, Snowman." It will become clear that this subtle signposting is intentional on the part of the author and that the two works in fact belong together.

A brief synopsis—again, barely possible because of the informality of the work—will begin to make this evident. "Snowman, Snowman" is a long fable narrated by a snowman who considers himself to be both human and immortal. Gradually, with the passage of winter and the approach of the thawing sun of spring, he begins to realize that he is mortal. The snowman has been built in the garden of a family called Dincer, by their daughter, Rosemary, and there he conducts long conversations with the Perpetual Snowflake, an immortal crystal of ice which lies on one of the windowsills of the Dincers' house. Like Erlene Glace in this respect, the Snowman resembles her too in his mute immobility, which obliges him to become the observer of a pageant of people and events already familiar to the reader of Janet Frame's fiction. Harry Dincer, for example, is a telephonist who cannot communicate (a similar figure appears in a story of this period called "How Can I Get in Touch With Persia?"[29]). His limitations are compared with the freedom of a group of twelve-year-old boys who enjoy a preadolescent language of communion. Another family, known simply as Ken,

Myra, and Phyllis, are exposed in their drab, monotonous existence, particularly by the women's liberal use of cosmetics in their attempts to conceal their plainness and by their fondness for consumer goods. Their neighbors are a West Indian family, a young couple who conceal their baby from the world for several weeks until they have taught it how to look at the bare, snow-covered world according to conventional values.

A fourth family is described in greater detail by the Snowman. This family is dominated by its mother-in-law, a Mrs. Wilbur, who is herself an image of all that is bad in suburban life:

The mother-in-law is the head of the house because she wears a purple hat and a blue apron and sweeps their share of the pavement and carefully closes the gate when the postman and the milkman have left it open. She makes strangled cries to children in danger in the street. Her face is almost overshadowed now by the thrusting bone-shape which will command it when it is a mean-nosed skeleton with dark worked-out mines for eyes. It is strange to think that she resembles most of the other middle-aged women in the street, yet they are not related, but all possess domineering bones impatient to be rid of the tired webbing flesh with its yellow-ochre tint which appeared gradually as the cloudy colors of time were poured into the smooth golden morning mixture . . . .[30]

Mrs. Wilbur and her daughter and son-in-law lead a life of highly conventional ritual, sunk in anonymity and obsessed with Safety, but their abnormality—the stain that all people have and try to conceal—appears in the aptly named grandson, Mark, a seven-year-old who attends a special school and needs to be carried everywhere. But, as the Perpetual Snowflake tells the Snowman, the boy's father is carried by his car, while all people are sustained by dreams. This universal mark can also be the stain of death, as is seen in the Snowman's observation of the Inchman family, whose mother has recently died. The intrusion of death into this orderly family leads to chaos: Mr. Inchman falls from his daily habits and wanders bareheaded in the snow, his son drives his car about on pointless errands, and no one knows quite what to do with Mrs. Inchman's clothes and possessions. The Perpetual Snowflake remarks,

In this part of the world, Snowman, dying is meant to be a discreet matter like taking tea but the untidiness of death makes itself visible in the clothes of the bereaved, in the daily routine—yesterday's milk not opened or even collected, the television silent, the beds unmade. In spite of people's desire for death to be a neat occasion—what is neater than dying?—there are always slovenly obtrusions which mar the effect.[31]

After the loss of his mother, Robert Inchman becomes increasingly aware of "prowling death" and locks his doors and windows at night as if a wild animal were outside. He turns for refuge to a book of science fiction, but his unconscious obsession with death and disorder begins to interfere with the words he is reading: "Dr. Merriman smiled. My God, he thought. He knew and the others in the room knew. The holtrime, the wentwail, the sturgescene had . . . ."[32]

Shortly after this move towards the edge of the alphabet, the real—or imagined—death of Rosemary Dincer occurs. Slipping in the snow, she is apparently run over by a heavy truck. Her death is not quite literal—it is never explained whether the Snowman has fantasized it or not—and as a result it becomes a symbol of death in life. The incident yields six pages of unrelieved conversation from the crowds which gather helplessly around her body and chatter their orderly, futile phrases at one another. The girl's death, whether actual or not, is a sign of the gradual demise of the Snowman, upon whom the first sunshine of spring has fallen. One of his eyes (a lump of coal) tumbles out and his arm falls off; confronting death, he falls back upon the comforts of falsehood when a piece of newspaper blows across his head and conceals the reality of the sun with its comforting print and a reassuring picture of the sun with a smiling face. But the hawks of truth will always come out of the sky—although, since this is a story in the mode of a fairy tale, the task is delegated to a blackbird, which swoops down and pecks a hole in the newspaper. The process of melting is resumed, the newspaper is dislodged, and the Snowman finally sinks into the earth.

V *The Story and the Novel*

The similarities between the story and the novel are numerous. There is an obvious link between the image of the mute, gifted girl talking to the beetle on her windowsill and the Snowman talking to the snowflake on his. The desire to discern the skull beneath the grubby skin of suburbia is common to both works, too, and often the imagery overlaps from one to another, as when Robert Inchman finds that his dead mother's clothes resemble the discarded armor of a beetle. But "Snowman, Snowman" is a denser work, a parable of the human condition, made up of brilliantly compressed images which fuse into an intense symbol of the experiences set out in the novel. The first echo of the novel occurs early in the story when the newly made Snowman, rejoicing in his sense of immortality, thinks of the snowflakes of which he is formed as "lost armies . . . para-trooping in clouds of silk,"[33] an image used by Vera Glace when she describes the sun as "all love and murder, judgement, the perpetual raid of conscience, paratrooping light which opens like a snow-blossom in the downward drift of death."[34] The Snowman, then, although he thinks himself immortal because already "half a man," is an image of the light-filled sun and is made of the stuff of death, not life. Not only does he consist of murdering light, but he is formed from the sea, as the opening paragraph of the story states. Thus, three of the most powerful images of authenticity in Janet Frame's art combine to freeze the Snowman into a symbol: the shark-filled, marauding sea, the freezing winds of the south which lift the mois-ture into the sky, and the murderous sunlight which enables the crystals to become visible. And the Snowman's "coal-black, pine-forest eyes,"[35] the two lumps of coal, recall the dark trees of the earliest stories.

Thus weighted with meaning, the Snowman stands as a symbol for all the major characters of Janet Frame's fiction—and especially for the self-aware, sensitive Vera Glace. What the Snowman sees and experiences is an illumination of her role in *Scented Gardens for the Blind.* In the guise of Erlene, Vera listens to Uncle Black Bee-tle's intimations of mortality; the Perpetual Snowflake assures the Snowman that he too will die, as the result of the very sunlight which gave him his initial existence. His task is to see truly, to understand that "Trees, cars, streets, people, they are but the dark print upon the white page of snow," to learn to "read the page itself, as men read books, passing beyond the visible obstructions of print to draw forth the invisible words with the warmth of their passionate breathing."[36]

This in fact is exactly what the reader has learned to do in seeing the metaphoric truth of Vera Glace's name and passing "behind" the printed words of the novel she dominates to the snow-filled and symbolic world of the Snowman, where truth lives in parable. Here we learn of the loss of innocence and of the need to acknowledge the sovereignty of death in order to live authentically. These ideas are dramatized in an incident which occurs just after Christmas when the Snowman sees another snowman laden with Christmas-tree tinsel and baubles that are lit, melting the snowman and leaving a grey ash where it stood. All characters in Janet Frame's world are burning snowmen, destroyed by the truth which they are nevertheless compelled to seek, and which reduces their dreams to ashes.

The story also delineates the vision of truth in a further way, for the snow which makes the Snowman also covers "Trees, cars, streets, people,"[37] obliterating the careful divisions by which people regulate and order their lives. It freezes a clock, for example, and time waits while workmen repair it. The Snowman notices that while children frolic in the snow, adults worry about which boundaries they are transgressing; and the Perpetual Snowflake remarks that people even die by numbers: "Ron Smith, forty-four, suffered a heart attack. Peter Lyon, seventeen, was in collision with a van driven by Herbert Kelly, fifty-five. It is a kind of code, a time-attention and bribery."[38] This method of living puts society at a remove from experience, the Snowflake says, because it refuses to acknowledge individuality; people begin to look alike, as both works often point out. We have stethoscopes to examine the beat of the heart, but we have no device which will look into the heart of the individual and record "the storms, the sudden darknesses and flashes of lightning, the commotions of the unseen life."[39] People realize themselves remotely, in commodities and things: when Rosemary Dincer is not allowed out with a young man because her parents think her too young, they comfort her with a box of chocolates. But in the snow, these trite certainties and the frail boundaries by which people regulate their lives are removed, "recognition is wounded," and Rosemary is slain beneath the truck.[40]

Edward Glace's role in *Scented Gardens for the Blind* is made clearer, too, if the story of the Snowman is related to it. There is no point in the novel at which the link between his two obsessions, genealogy and toy soldiers, is made explicit. The passages the reader might have expected there are instead to be found in "Snowman, Snowman," where the two fields of interest become one. Here, people are said to owe their desperation and violence to "the growth of centuries" which has entangled them in the habit as in a noxious weed which they are afraid to eradicate because in clearing the confusion between being and being . . . they face each other set in an unbearable clearing of light and proper original shade, with the sky naked in its truth . . . . Or they kill on impulse because, loving too much, they isolate the act of love and thus extend it to encompass the memorable loneliness of death. [41]

Killing is a habit ingrained in each generation, and when one is confronted by a mother and son, one will "feel a sense of uneasiness, of the massing of hidden determined forces which will destroy every obstacle in order to retain their right-of-way within the deep genetic groove."[42] In this view, the act of copulation by which the human race reproduces itself becomes an act of cannibalism in which men and women devour each other in the name of love. So used are humans to these brutalities that

Language wanes . . . . Feelings wane. Death comes to be no more than a disappointment, and grief over events must be strictly rationed and the size of the ration is controlled by distance in time and space—the attentions of the heart are measured by the pacing of the feet and the movements of the hands of the clock. The massacre of a race of people is only on the level of a disappointment if it is beyond the range of the stay-at-home feet controlled by the stay-at-home heart beating in time with the familiar clock. When a man puts his telescope to his snow-blinded eye he can see streams of oil flowing and fields of wheat trampled by cloud-shadows driven by the wind, but he can't see the tiny distant ration of his own Care. But no, wait, what is that fluttering speck in his snow-blinded eye? It is a fly, disappointment and death, Care and Love crawling close to his own skin, the source of their lifeblood. Why should they travel to face the flood and the earthquake, the dark camp where the children's bones push soft as mushrooms through their flesh . . . . [43]

This terrifyingly true vision of the twentieth century as the culmination of aeons of careless evolution is the property of the shorter work, and must be reserved for those readers who fulfill some of the novel's desire for a more poetic language of communion. For only they, through their understanding that metaphor is the language of truth, will be admitted "through" *Scented Gardens for the Blind* to the fantastic world of the Snowman, where these truths are set out.

VI *Conclusions*

If these two works are treated in the manner argued for above, as a single work cleverly drawn together by their author, they may be seen to represent the major single development of Janet Frame's fiction so far. The critical response to the earlier fiction, although it properly admired her skill and unusual technique, always drew attention to the restricted range of the work. Of the first novel, for example, Lawrence Jones suggests that there is experience that is "intense but incomplete,"[44] and the remainder of the Withers trilogy, with its task of finding a creative voice, can hardly be said to alter these limitations. But with the two works dealt with in this chapter, all such criticism must be extinguished. The sudden expansion of the range of her fiction at this point has been noted by Winston Rhodes, who describes Erlene Glace as being "confounded by the enigma of a world in which the wonder and infinite possibilities of life are constantly shattered by its horror and cruelty," and goes on to mention the novel's

evolutionary theme of the long struggle of human beings to emerge from darkness into light, how they have used and wasted their gift of language, nurtured and abandoned great aspirations, and destroyed themselves and others during "their movement forward in time with their accumulation of energy and being."[45]

From this novel on, the referents of Janet Frame's fiction will be supplied increasingly in words such as "evolution," "life," "world," and "aspiration," and less in terms such as "self" and "mind." As Stanley Edgar Hyman has noted, there is a moral probity in *Scented Gardens for the Blind* which distinguishes it from a hundred other novels of its time[46]: this seriousness continues throughout Janet Frame's subsequent writing.

It is at this point in the development of her art, too, that some of the major themes of the later fiction are born as ideas, from the visual metaphors of *A State of Siege* to the theme of care that is at the center of *Intensive Care*. *The Adaptable Man*, a novel which works in the same range as *Scented Gardens for the Blind* and "Snowman, Snowman" but is perhaps of even greater virtuosity and skill, is an inevitable extension of these two works, as a clarification of their achievements will suggest. Vera Glace's story tells of the impoverishment of language and the imagination by the brutalizing instincts of generations of human beings; it ends with guarded optimism, for the destruction of Britain leads to the purged utterance of the novel's central figure. But the "trick" of the novel is also revealed as the reader scrambles safely, like Uncle Black Beetle's

literary cousin, from amongst its words: Vera Glace is a
"trichotomy" of characters, her name a signpost which points towards the story which is, in fact, the remainder of the novel. And
once within "Snowman, Snowman," we find that Uncle Black Beetle
and his magic are not dead at all and that his world of childhood
fantasy lives on in the conversations of the Snowman and the
Snowflake. Only those who have been converted to the language
advocated by the novel, in which metaphor yields truth, are admitted to the story, where the meanings of the novel are compressed in
the snow-covered setting of the Snowman's world.

It would be difficult to argue, after all this, that Janet Frame's
attitude towards the conventional novel is at all respectful. It has
been seen that one of her thematic concerns at this point in her
artistic development is that humans should learn to mingle beyond
enumerations, linguistic conventions, and measurements. This
preference for an area of experience found beyond the rim of language of the everyday sort obliges her to move away from the formal
conventions of plot, characterization, and so on, which are the leg-
acy of traditional fiction. It might be said that one function of the
novel that has been the subject of this chapter is to direct the
reader's attention away from itself, rather than to draw its reader in,
as most fiction attempts to do. Certainly, the conventions of sequence, orderly development, and conclusion are rendered useless
by a novel which overflows its own apparent boundaries and, like its
own central character, mingles with other versions of itself. This
process, in which the limits of fiction are constantly being tested and
expanded, develops into open warfare in *The Adaptable Man*.

CHAPTER 6

The Adaptable Novel

I *Necessary Voices*

AT the time of its writing, *The Adaptable Man* was Janet Frame's longest and most ambitious novel. She divided it very precisely into four sections, with a prologue of five pages to introduce some ideas familiar from earlier fiction; for instance, the idea of the novelist as a kind of witch who concocts characters, and that of the irrepressible growth of imagination and individuality from under the "crash helmet" society uses to suppress these qualities. The themes of generation and migration, which first came into the open in the imaginary world of Vera Glace, are mentioned here, and the fourteen major characters of the book are introduced, including "I, the earth," a surprising but nevertheless central figure.[1]

Part One (entitled "These Photographs Are Underexposed. Please Will You Intensify Them?") begins with a long and sensitive evocation of the Suffolk countryside around Little Burgelstatham, the tiny English village in which the novel is set. It then moves to the figure of Botti Julio, an Italian exiled to Andorra, who has been contracted to work on a farm in Little Burgelstatham. Botti is a stateless citizen, dispossessed by one of the twentieth century's many wars; as soon as he arrives in the nearby village of Murston he is mysteriously murdered and left in a pool in which he is assumed to have drowned. The novel then turns towards the Reverend Aisley Maude, a gentle clergyman who has come to Little Burgelstatham to recover from quiescent tuberculosis at the home of his brother, Russell, and sister-in-law, Greta. Aisley has recently been bereaved of his beautiful, dynamic wife, Katherine, and as a consequence has lost his faith in God. His sojourn in the Suffolk countryside is, he likes to think, a pilgrimage to Northumbria, the home of his beloved St. Cuthbert, whose reclusive and authentic quest for God he wants

121

to emulate, aiding his contemplation by reading Anglo-Saxon poetry and that vastly more modern work, the King James Bible.

Muriel Baldry is briefly mentioned at this point in the novel, at a "home movie" evening during which her husband, Vic, is interminably showing their neighbors slides of their honeymoon trip around the world (both she and Vic have been married before and their honeymoon is a recent one). The remainder of Part One continues in the same manner—as a series of slides. Alwyn Maude, a twenty-year-old student at Manchester University and the only son of Russell and Greta, is seen to be inscrutable and threatening, like the lonely scarecrows which witnessed the murder of Botti Julio. Alwyn is determinedly free in his behavior, sleeping with his girl friend Jenny Sparling in a room at Clematis Cottage that is next to Aisley's and thus causing the unworldly clergyman endless embarrassment. Just as Aisley has insight into Alwyn, Alwyn has insight into others; both nephew and uncle share a knowledge that civilization is frail, Alwyn providing a parable about a tent that is waterproof until touched, as humans touch everything. He also notices that an affluent neighbor, Beatrice Sapley, is protected by a similar "tent," "dark and smoothly cellophaned in the usual affluent afterbirth. She was safe enough. One could, of course, remove her transparent covering."[2] Appropriately, the woman's "hard and bright" photograph appears frequently in fashionable newspapers.[3]

Russell Maude, a determinedly old-fashioned dentist renowned for possessing one of the most out-of-date surgeries in the country, is a keen collector of stamps. Not surprisingly, his marriage to Greta has decayed into a lifeless routine. She is one of the central figures of *The Adaptable Man* and is shown in this section to be far more sensitive to the failure of her marriage than is Russell, and sympathetic too towards her son, especially to his desire to become a novelist. In addition to these initial "snapshots" of the novel's characters, Janet Frame also "photographs" a group of villagers. They include the seventy-four-year-old Bert Whattling, a pensioner whose memories stretch back to the nineteenth century and whose daily habits are just beginning to be threatened by changes in bus timetables and by the demolition of cottages which have long been familiar landmarks in his life. His closest friend is Ruby Unwin, a widow of eighty-five, who is living out her last years as a tenant in the farmhouse her husband used to own. She is determinedly active as the novel begins, although her recurring fantasies about meeting the Duchess of Rutland suggest a certain amount of senility. Her son Lex and his wife Dot (who is a "foreigner" from London) are forced to support themselves by running a milk round instead of by working the family farm, whose passage from generation to generation has been halted by the refusal of Lex's father to leave it to him in his will.

Also mentioned in this first section is the minor and satirized figure of Unity Foreman, a London journalist who writes a newsletter for a magazine called *Cornstalk* from the bucolic setting of her London flat. Part One ends with the revelation of a fact that Aisley Maude and possibly the reader as well have been aware of for some time—that Alwyn is the murderer of Botti Julio.

Part Two is subtitled "Maplestone's Chart," a reference to the gardening guide Greta Maude uses to help control the pests in her beloved garden. This part of the book further develops the theme adumbrated by the subtitle of Part One: the "snapshots" of the characters seen there here become "intensified" by further exploration and interaction. Jenny Sparling, for example, is shown disapprovingly when she remarks that "Skin's not a very efficient hedge. People do *invade*"[4]; although she mingles with Alwyn as frequently as possible in their bedroom, the act is merely physical and not the communion aspired to in the earlier fiction. Jenny senses in Alwyn "a sinister element which frightened her, with a fear that lay . . . close to her bones."[5] Alwyn steadily becomes the dominant figure of *The Adaptable Man*. His happy childhood is remembered along with the memory of a picture of a monstrously deformed child that he had once glimpsed in a magazine; increasingly, Alwyn identifies himself with this child and with the inhuman scarecrows who witnessed the murder of Botti Julio.

The histories of other characters are also explored. It is revealed that Greta was once a nurse, a career she had chosen because she wanted to confront life and death in "neat, clean surroundings."[6] Her first love was for a handsome young doctor who later was killed in the war, thereby robbing Greta of her dream of living in a fashionable London suburb with a husband who had a fashionable London practice. Instead, she met and married Russell, a man who seemed uniformed even when naked. With him she has subsided into a dull existence relieved only by the orderliness of her garden and the vividness of her son. In Part Two, her growing physical attraction to her son becomes evident, in preparation for the surprising event that ends this section of *The Adaptable Man*.

We also learn here more about Aisley Maude, and especially about his rigid inability to adapt to the new age. He spends much of his convalescence looking back upon his former self almost with incredulity, at the rules and formality which seemed to stifle genuine faith. He recalls his early years as a parson and his growing misgivings then at the dislocation between the act of belief and the mundane doings of the "cure of souls." Faced with the shabby reality of parsonical poverty and jumble sales, Aisley soon found that he "went to earth, like a fox,"[7] burrowing into the past. His marriage to the vivacious, forward-looking Katherine, outwardly appearing to be marvellously complementary, a fruitful joining together of the conservative and the progressive, was for him a complete disaster—he recalls finding to his horror a newspaper description of himself as "that up-to-date clergyman who, with his model-type wife are doing so much to transform the Church from a medieval white elephant to a bang-on, space-age tiger."[8] But habit dies hard with Aisley Maude, and he cannot resist even during convalescence the steady entering of births, deaths, and marriages in his "Memory Tickler," using red and black inks for the appropriate entries.

Vic and Muriel Baldry are explored in greater detail in the second part of this novel, too. They are the Maudes' neighbors, and to them is tied some of the basic imagery of the novel. Muriel Baldry wishes to remain in her home in Little Burgelstatham, and anticipates the illumination there of a Venini chandelier which she has inherited and which, when installed in a strengthened ceiling, will be connected to electric power as soon as that comes to the backward village. Her husband, Vic, wishes to emigrate to Australia, however, "pursuing . . . an idea"[9] which is embodied in the drawings and photographs he has brought back from his honeymoon there. Of these drawings, the most disturbing—particularly to Muriel—shows the Australian explorers, Burke and Wills, as parched scarecrows under the relentless Antipodean sun.

Just as Part One ended unexpectedly with the revelation of the identity of Botti Julio's murderer, when the reader might reasonably have expected that fact to be concealed, Part Two ends with another unexpected act involving Alwyn. Coming one day into his mother's potting shed, he finds her sleeping there and thinks her dead. When she suddenly wakes up, they are both shaken from their usual composure and the incestuous act which has been incipient in this section of the novel occurs between them.

Part Three of *The Adaptable Man* is called "Red Ink, Black Ink," and after the strange events of the first half of the novel is markedly different in tone. It begins with five parodies of fictional modes, from the Romantic through the Realistic to the contemporary. This literary emphasis continues, for the theme of this section, set against the decline of the English summer into autumn, is the poetic impulse of each character, and there are frequent references to the poet Keats. Greta announces that Stephen Spender was always her favorite poet, although Jenny Sparling is cruel enough to point out that his summer is now declining into autumn too. Aisley prefers St. Cuthbert and Wordsworth, and the conversation concludes with Alwyn's sudden announcement that he will marry Jenny that night and travel with her to Spain, where he will begin his career as a novelist.

Meanwhile, Muriel Baldry's coveted chandelier—her own "poem", since it has taken possession of her imagination—arrives at her home, disappointingly grey in color, like "wasted snow."[10] In a curious incident, she shows Greta and Aisley the half-unpacked chandelier and a large rat bursts out from within the crate. The need to control vermin with poison becomes linked with a need that both Muriel and Greta feel, to deny that they read poetry. This incident, linking dream and disillusionment to art, foreshadows events that occur throughout Part Three as autumn declines into winter: for example, old Mrs. Unwin watches a silver pie dish burn to ashes and later realizes that her silver hair has turned to the color of ash as well.

Part Three ends, like the earlier sections, with decisive developments. Ruby Unwin dies, Jenny and Alwyn marry secretly at Durham, and Greta tells a surprised Russell—an infrequent visitor of the marital bed—that she is pregnant. Aisley has so many events to record in his "Memory Tickler" that he runs out of his colored inks; but he retains sufficient acumen to sense that Alwyn is the father of Greta's child as well as being a murderer. Russell, meanwhile, has been sufficiently shocked out of his cast-iron routines to travel alone to London for a few days; there he spends most of his time at the airport staring in fascination at the planes.

The final part of *The Adaptable Man* is called "The Chandelier."

In it the fundamental theme of the novel becomes intense, bringing together the irresistible force of Progress and the immovable object of Tradition. "Overspill," the chilling term used to describe the relentless march of suburban population from London into the countryside around Little Burgelstatham, is mentioned for the first time. Part Four is a winter section, and sees Aisley's decision to spend the remainder of his life in solitude, seeking God in nature as St. Cuthbert did; this follows his visit to a harvest festival service at the local church, in which the Reverend Timothy Pillow preaches to a congregation consisting of his wife, his sister-in-law, and a dog. Shortly after this, Alwyn suddenly returns from Spain, to announce that he has become a journalist instead of a novelist and that his wife is expecting their first child.

The novel concludes with the dinner Muriel Baldry has arranged to celebrate the illumination of her Venini chandelier, now attached to the ceiling of her dining room and fed with newly arrived electricity. The moment of illumination is the moment of death: the chandelier crashes down, killing Muriel, Greta, and Aisley, and maiming Vic Baldry, who remains paralyzed for the rest of his life, forced to view the world through a cracked mirror.

II   A Setting for Speech

The Adaptable Man reads in many parts like a traditional novel about English country life and could possibly be described as Janet Frame's tribute to Thomas Hardy, whose work she read as a young girl. But why is it the only one of her novels to be set entirely in England? Certainly, parts of earlier novels were set in London and a later one is set partly in the United States. But these settings bear a relationship of some sort to her native country; the rural England of *The Adaptable Man* does not seem to do so.

The answer to this question can be found by returning to some of the themes which began to be worked out in the preceding novel. Winston Rhodes has mentioned the "evolutionary theme of the long struggle of human beings to emerge from darkness into light, how they have used and wasted their gift of language," and has suggested that this wastage results in the generations of war and cruelty which, in Janet Frame's view, have reached a climax during this century. Turning to a fresh exploration of these themes, she needed to commit herself to a far richer tradition than that available—for example—to Edward Glace upon his return to New Zealand, a

country where significant European settlement did not begin until
the 1840's. But in Little Burgelstatham, "surrounded by the pre-
served earliest dreams and activities of the human mind,"[11] with
walking relics of the past in Ruby Unwin, Bert Whattling, and Olly
Drew, Janet Frame has found a setting that enables her to explore
most vividly the themes of her earlier fiction, particularly the theme
of the past and the language which has evolved from it.

In the first of many virtuoso passages in this remarkably well-
written novel, she peels away the years from the Suffolk of the
present and suggests the original land that lay there:

> Say the names, then, to yourself.
> Little Burgelstatham (a burgel was originally a burial place of the
> heathen). Tydd. Lakenthorpe. Murston. Segham. Colsea. Withigford. Say
> the names again and again, and soon there's no weetbox-coloured railway
> station . . . . There's no village store . . . . There's no Clematis Cottage . . .
> nothing but a dream of earliest praise, of sea-flooded inlets, lakes, marshes,
> sedge, willows and those birds, half-hidden, which walk tall, camouflaged as
> reeds, and sound, morning and evening, their lonely cries; water, birds,
> and now and again the soft rustle and wash and splash of the men, the
> Southfolk, guiding their boats through the inland seas.[12]

Man evolves and his language evolves with him, the latter toward a
degenerated speech which no longer communicates. In the beginning was the word; and at the earliest moments of the English
language the word was transparent in meaning:

> if you are imaginative and curious enough you will learn that Little
> Burgelstatham is in that part of Great Britain where the place-names are
> more memories than names—memories of water, well and ocean, govern-
> ment by *Things.* One ought to be afraid, to be surrounded by a world-mass
> of *things,* to learn the derivation of our enjoyment, menace, and master,
> how the *Thing* was the judicial and legislative assembly of the Scandinavian
> nations, how it met on an island, a promontory, was derived in its name
> from the Old Norse *tinga* to speak, and is etymological brother to *think.*
> Discuss, judge, think, speak.[13]

Here is a case where the word is the *Thing* it refers to; and Little
Burgelstatham is similarly located at the edge of the alphabet because there words and things are very closely linked in the way that
enabled the Snowman to be glimpsed "through" the name of Vera
Glace: in this rural setting, word and sense come close to melting

into one, and language is most nearly a window to the world. At Little Burgelstatham, for example, sprouting plants are said to "speak."[14]

In this novel rural history is very greatly valued because it preserves an authentic language whose patterns reflect the business of individual survival. Its opposite is the New Town, which no one can satisfactorily name and which is built in the country by the end of the novel. Both Bert Whattling and Olly Drew, who in their natural slowness are said to resemble trees, possess something ideal and true; as Aisley Maude pores over his Anglo-Saxon poetry and the thought of his idolized St. Cuthbert, he realizes that both stand for a lost state of being, a "dream of ancient praise" that must be regained and that is proper to the place in which he is staying. The names of plants are beyond the recollection of a man with such a reactionary attitude to language; typically, Greta knows them all, with the result that "no plant had ever spoken to her . . . she was not the imaginative kind of person to whom plants revealed their 'secrets' . . . she knew no *encounters* with them."[15] Attempting to control her environment by so much naming and poisoning, Greta Maude is at odds with the essentially authentic nature of Little Burgelstatham.

There are other reasons, less forceful than those outlined above, for the rural English setting of *The Adaptable Man*. *Scented Gardens for the Blind* was a winter novel, it will be remembered; one of the most important things about its successor is that it *becomes* a winter novel, in the same way that Keats's "Ode to Autumn" becomes a poem about winter. Keats is never far from the author's mind in this novel: one of the interruptions to the dull orderliness of Muriel Baldry's life is a recollection of an afternoon spent in the company of a minor poet, drinking a wine that Keats liked; and Unity Foreman's bogus letters contain many echoes and images from the Autumn Ode. Poetry, the language of metaphor, truth, and imagination, is vitally important to the work of Janet Frame, quite obviously; in this novel, a sensitivity to Keats in particular and to poetry in general is a sign that certain characters are sensitive to the meaning of key events which occur in the novel. Keats's "Ode to Autumn," after all, tells of decay in the moment of fruition, states (as Istina Mavet says in *Faces in the Water*) that "it was always winter," and points toward that last understanding which all the characters in the novel must reach.

III   *The Reality of the Age*

To look back upon Little Burgelstatham in the manner just outlined is to see it as a place of cheering integrity. But authenticity has
its price, and Botti Julio is the first to pay it; his mangled language-
manual phrases mark him as a foreigner in the little rural community because they are so deeply committed to the center of the
alphabet. The scenario for Botti's murder is a curious and haunting
one: it occurs in the pitch darkness of an unlit country lane in the
presence of scarecrows which crackle like flame over his murdered
body. To understand how the place can have both the rural integrity
that Aisley Maude senses there and this lethal quality, it must be
recalled that it is a part of the twentieth century, that "age which can
be symbolized by an immense sewer where the dead are drained
discreetly away, vanishing in turquoise transparent seas where the
population is encouraged to bathe in cleanliness and safety. It is an
Age of Safety, but Safety from poorly perceived and falsely identified dangers."[16] Aisley thinks of the twentieth century as an age
which "swarmed with youth entwining and copulating with the
shameless abandon of troops who kill and die . . . on a permanent
battlefield, who possess all the force, the power to destroy."[17] In a
rapacious age such as this, Little Burgelstatham is a pleasant and
threatened anachronism.

Its inhabitants are therefore ambiguous, superficially civilized—
like any twentieth-century figure—but savage within. Many of the
characters are portrayed in a manner that makes this subtly evident.
Alwyn "knows" that Russell himself has made the perforations on his
stamps by biting them, that Greta herself is the pest who ravages
her vegetable garden, that his own scars come not from a childhood
accident but from a vicious attack by Jenny. He thinks of his father
and uncle crawling "mumbling, through concentration camps and
extermination posts" without "knowledge or understanding of their
surroundings."[18] Man in the twentieth century tries to protect himself from the wrong dangers, largely dangers he has created himself.
"Only someone living at the beginning of the world of civilization
could say with truth and dignity—I'm not safe, I'm in deadly
danger.—Why?—Because the sun disappears each night and the
world grows dark."[19]

In these passages lies perhaps the clearest statement of Janet

Frame's mature thought that has been achieved so far. The rural countryside is close to the past: it "has always been a drowned place," according to Aisley Maude, as he thinks of monsters in the sea[20]; it is a place where danger is authentic danger springing out of nature itself and where "an *intelligent* scale of perils" exists.[21] Its darkness is a genuine, primitive threat, against which Botti Julio's degenerated language, half understood and half without meaning, is no protection. What threatens him is represented by the scarecrows, symbols of twentieth-century man, the flame of electricity with its man-made danger. And the murderer, Alwyn, is linked by imagery to the scarecrows and to the skeletons of Burke and Wills bleached to truth under the fierce Australian sun.

So the novel sets up its tensions between the old and the new. There will be no simple answer: the new is clearly not approved, but the old has its limitations, principally in its failure to withstand the pressures of the new. The central problem is how to adapt to the new age and what qualities are required to do so. Each character has a solution slightly different from the next.

IV   *Disturbed Dreamers*

One of the limitations of Janet Frame's fiction written during the early 1960's might be said to involve a certain stiffness of characterization that occurs from time to time. Where autobiographical links can be traced, as with the Withers family, characters can be convincing and "real." Elsewhere, as perhaps with Pat Keenan or Edward Glace, the symbolic function of a character often obscures his verisimilitude. But as the burden of the novels becomes increasingly humanitarian the need for fictional characters who are complete human beings and not merely clothed ideas also increases. *The Adaptable Man* is a triumphant fulfillment of that need: every character is convincingly drawn and lingers in the memory; each is obviously born from external observation and not preconception. Their outward behavior is consistent with their inward life, which develops from experience and not doctrine.

So "true" are these characters that it is sometimes a little difficult to see that they belong to patterned groups. The first of these groups, although it is not obtrusive, is made up of the rustics—Bert Whattling, Ruby Unwin, and Olly Drew. These are the most obviously tragic figures in the novel, seeming to grow out of the countryside itself and to be a part of its seasons and rhythms, their existence threatened by "progress." Bert Whattling, a pleasant, comic figure, is confused by changes in the bus timetable and almost swept from his bicycle by the slipstream of large trucks which rush past him. Although he can cope with the exigencies of village life, "Danger seemed not as simple as it used to be,"[22] and highways with their lethal traffic seem to him another example of the suicidal streak in modern man. Old Ruby Unwin, striving to play an active part in the daily routines of the farm on which she is now only a tenant, feels that she and her house are decaying together. Her sense of loss is shared by her son, Lex, with his dreary suburban milk-delivery round and his bitterness at failing to inherit a farm that had been in his family for generations.

The second—and largest—group of characters in *The Adaptable Man* is made up of the older Maudes and the Baldrys. Although the novel is propelled largely by its interest in their affairs, these characters lack the approval the author confers upon the elderly rural figures. For the Maudes and the Baldrys are all dreamers of some sort whose fatal flaw is their inability to reconcile themselves either wholly to the past or wholly to the future. Instead, they create orderly dreams somewhere between the two, and become escapers from the two realities of the novel. Of these characters, Aisley Maude is the most intelligent and introspective, and he alone achieves something close to true adaptability in his decision to spend his last years in monastic retreat, although the fall of the chandelier crushes that possibility.

Aisley is by nature "an ecclesiastical dinosaur,"[23] with "the Maude characteristic of unfashionableness, the subversive denial of 'the times.' "[24] The fashionable Katherine has made him, to all appearances, a perfect wife, but she has led him in the wrong direction, to a position where God is an easily accepted and unquestioned part of a garden party at a vicarage. But after Katherine's sudden and unexpected death, "the picture was blurred . . . God had moved . . . the steadfast landmark . . . had become an unidentifiable shadow,"[25] and Aisley's sufferings become inward, with his "unfashionable" tuberculosis, a disease which makes a shadow on his lung. His convalescence with his brother's family at Clematis Cottage allows him to ponder on the direction his life ought to take in the future, and particularly on the role his devotion to St. Cuthbert ought to play in it:

At times, now, when he looks from his window at the pleasantly rural scene he is not the Reverend Aisley Maude, he is—St. Cuthbert himself, saying his prayers in the sea while his astonished fellow-monks follow him, watching while the two seals come out of the deep water to warm him 'mid heora flyce.'

. . . he has whittled away the world, the world, the people, the land, the time, and because simplicity itself must have an end, he has arrived at himself, close to the first fluid world, the sea; he is an inhabitant of an island, gazing through the grille of loneliness at the few curious observers—the sea, the marsh birds, two seals; he re-enacts the life of St. Cuthbert. He wonders if, in this first simplicity, there is room for God to return to the picture.[26]

Aisley is nevertheless an ambiguous character, like his relatives and the Baldrys. On the one hand, he is sensitive to the language of poetry, both Anglo-Saxon and that of the King James Bible (he thinks the language of the Revised Version debased, fit only for the twentieth century). But despite the desire for a language of integrity in which words will finally reveal God to him, he persists in keeping his "Memory Tickler," with its orderly lists of events. The turning point for him comes when he meets the Reverend Timothy Pillow and his sparse congregation at the Harvest Festival service: Pillow's career had begun brilliantly, he discovers, but now he has a nagging wife, tedious bus trips about his parish, and the task of getting Approved School boys to weed out the nettles in his churchyard. In confronting Pillow, Aisley is confronting himself, and is reinforced in his decision to spend the rest of his life in solitude. There,

Perhaps in the peace he must find when he had abandoned the twentieth century and the future and had settled in his own carefully chosen time and place, his own existence would be possession enough, and the opportunity it would give him to stare, stare, stare at the meaning of being . . . .

He would be Man returned to stone, to communion with stone and sea and the first forms of life.[27]

Aisley's older brother, Russell, would never be capable of such a decision, for he is one of the "Great Dull."[28] Instead of examining his beliefs and actions, he examines his stamps, in which he can control and order experience and place it safely at a remove. The tiny mirror with which he inspects human teeth in his ancient surgery at Murston performs much the same function of distancing and removal; and as his son points out, Russell examines the decaying teeth of others while Aisley probes his own tubercular interior. But there is a connection of another sort between Russell and Aisley, for Russell's dentistry, like Aisley's passion for Anglo-Saxon, takes him back to primitive speech: "teeth from a million years past are still talking,"[29] and in one sense he is arranging a message for the future. But he is simply baffled by the present, and his trip to London Airport could be that of a Victorian, so confused does he find himself.

Of all the Maude family, Greta is perhaps the most obsessed by the need for order, as her control over her garden and her constant use of Maplestone's Chart would suggest. She is, typically, the holder of a lost dream: dull Russell has replaced lost Christopher, and she consoles herself by trying to create order in what remains of her life. Christopher had been a dream of fashionable order in London; her garden is a rural dream of order. The characterization of Greta Maude could be taken as evidence of the maturity Janet Frame has reached at this stage of her writing. Human beings are not simply a list of shortcomings: they are subtly ambiguous, and their good and their bad points intermingle. Greta, like all others in *The Adaptable Man*, is a full and convincing character because for all her limitations she does possess understanding and insight. She understands her own son as sensitively as Aisley understands him, knowing his aims to be unusual and ambitious and realizing that his affair with Jenny Sparling is merely a substitute for a love of all life. It is Greta who becomes desperate when she sees her own courtship with Russell being repeated by her son and Jenny, for she fears a senseless generic duplication of her own futility. And it is she who desperately wishes that the younger generation *cared* more, for care alone might end the senseless and destructive repetition of generations. Alwyn's lack of care, his mother perceives, will prevent him from ever writing his novel, for writers must care about people. Aisley, too, with his superior knowledge, realizes that Alwyn was careless of the life of Botti Julio; and Greta's willingness to couple with her own son, whatever other motives may be seen in the act, might be interpreted as a desire to deflect at least momentarily the onward flow of blind generations.

Vic and Muriel Baldry remain as slightly less central figures. They are both obviously dreamers, and knowing the fate of dreamers in the world of Janet Frame, the worst should be expected for them.

Where Muriel's dream involves a vain desire for fixity which becomes centered on the illumination of the Venini chandelier, Vic's
dream is an equally vain one of migratory flight, which becomes
centered on his vision of Australia and particularly on the stark
figures of the scarecrowlike explorers in the searing sun. Both their
visions contain the source of their dreams' destruction—but Muriel
sees no foreboding in the rat-infested chandelier, Vic no threat in
the stained shadows of the two explorers. Aisley's picture of God is
shadowed, like his own tubercular lung; Greta's cabbages are
stained with fungus; Russell sees a bride whose dress is stained.
Ideals, adapted to reality, become facts which help man to survive.
But if, like these characters, man seeks refuge from reality in a
dream of order, he will be destroyed by the flaws within his dreams.
The dreamers of *The Adaptable Man* are destroyed because they
are not adaptable men and women.

V *Adaptability*

Not everyone in the novel is destroyed, and there are reasons
why some survive. The apocalyptic moment at the end comes when
electricity is fed into Muriel's chandelier for the first time and it falls
in a circle of light to crush the dreams of Greta, Muriel, and Aisley
and to alter forever the lives of Vic and Russell. There are numerous
ways in which we can interpret this falling of the chandelier, from
seeing in it the yellow circle of fire of the shock therapy which
extinguishes the mind during the earlier fiction, to seeing in it the
grey circle of cloud in a nuclear explosion. But certainly it represents the disastrous, destructive collision of past and present, with
the triumph of man-made electricity (a false light, unlike the truth-
bearing sun, because a perversion of natural power) representing
the triumph of all that is destructive from the past.

Vic Baldry half-survives death because his vision embraced sunlight enough to gnaw the bones of Burke and Wills, and Russell lives
because he admits a little reality into his dull existence during his
bewildered trip to the airport. But Alwyn Maude has no dreams to
which reality needs admission: he is an incarnation of twentieth-
century man, utterly adapted to its amoral savagery. As Joan Stevens states, "he's built himself a sort of kitset identity, out of the
attitudes which his time and place assert for the young."[30] He is
adaptable in ways the others do not have—he wants to be a writer
but compromises and becomes a journalist when he sees that he will

never write a novel. But his adaptability has a more sinister aspect, for he is an incarnation of the destructive spirit of the twentieth century, actively destroying as well as passively contemplating reality. Thus, his vacation task is to knock down the walls of an old cottage that he is modernizing for a London executive; and Aisley sees him truly when he dreams of him as a skeleton-scarecrow, the monstrous child of the childhood photograph. He has grown "effortlessly into the space-age air, up through the everlasting pressures of history and habit, like a blade of grass innocently thrusting its way through concrete; dark crumbling fragments surrounded him."[31]

Adaptable in an unadapted family, Alwyn embodies the cosmic will and provides a mordant commentary on the direction the author envisages modern man to be taking: for "adaptability" is an evolutionary term, and Janet Frame is stating that his inhumanity is the only means of surviving a time as terrible as this. Jenny thinks of him as an astronaut far out in space staring with unblinking eyes at the twentieth century, and showing that he has adapted to it by murdering a man "whose only qualification for being murdered was that he belonged to the human race."[32] For Alwyn well knows that "If Raskolnikov had lived now . . . two pages rather than a novel would have been needed to describe his feelings after killing."[33] Alwyn will never be a Dostoevsky, for "the fattening purse within his skull" contains experience gained "simply by belonging to the twentieth century . . . as a birthright,"[34] and does not come from mature reflection. More than a knowledge of murder and hatred is needed in the writing of a novel: care for others is required, a compassion and love for mankind that Alwyn lacks. Novels need subtler authors than Alwyn Maude.

VI *The Adaptable Novel*

In the preceding chapter, the earliest evidence of Janet Frame's ability and desire to explore the limits of traditional fiction and its conventions was discussed. *Scented Gardens for the Blind*, it was suggested, was a half-novel whose other part was carefully concealed in "Snowman, Snowman." This was the result of a battle between formality and fluidity, and in *The Adaptable Man* this battle occurs again, although this time the different elements are contained in the same volume.

The writer's objective view of the medium she is using is well

shown at the beginning of the third part of the novel. Here, Jenny
Sparling teases Alwyn about the novel he wishes to write, giving
Janet Frame the opportunity to produce some amusing parodies:

Will your book be about us, Alwyn? You know, two students, two young
people trying to "fit in" with the world, and all that corn; rebelling, arguing;
every second word or phrase italicized; your mother uttering sentences
like, "*Don't* put your books there, Alwyn. I've told you. No-one in this
house *knows* anything. Can't you do *something* about Jenny. How can I
keep any kind of *order?* I can't think why I didn't give birth to a *normal*
son!" Is that the kind of novel, Alwyn? Or is it, "Looking at her with infinite
tenderness he sank on his knees before her and in response to her unspoken
appeal whispered, I can't manage. I thought I might be able to, but I can't
. . . Later he looked at her and murmured, a tremor in his voice, as he drew
her towards the bed, It's going to be all right, I know it's going to be all right
now."

Or shall it be—The bacon and egg is before him . . . his hungry eyes . . . he
will break it, plunge his fork in it, the punctured sun, the earth reeling . . .
noon . . . he is trying to escape the smear . . . afraid of too much daylight
. . . now the dark-red bacon . . . sandpaper surface . . . salt-filled newborn
skin . . . a moment ago . . . a moment ahead . . . he knows the significance
of *breakfast* . . . .

Or shall it be after the contemporary style, Alwyn? "Eccentric jackal, he he
palinode raw, human—once, once he was resolute lava."

Or shall it be, Alwyn, a novel to end all novels, one of the old style, "On
July twentyninth nineteen hundred and sixtythree a young man with fair
hair blue eyes humorously creased face . . . stood waiting at a number
fifteen bus stop to catch the two nought five bus to Port Strange to visit his
recently widowed aunt at number nine Chaucer Street . . . all the best
novels begin with such a plunge into numbers . . . .[35]

These skillful parodies are something more than the five-finger
exercises of an extremely gifted writer. They bespeak an attitude
which questions the ability of conventional forms of art to contain
life, and a desire to experiment with forms which expand the
boundaries of fiction. If one applies to fiction and its traditions Janet
Frame's dislike of the formal and the traditional as well as her distrust of man's verbal heritage as it has developed, certain contradic-
tions ought inevitably to occur. In *The Adaptable Man* the organic
and lyrical elements are set side by side with the traditional in a way

which sees the steady erosion of the latter. It is possible, in fact, to see the whole work as a quest for *fictional* adaptability.

The almost painful accuracy striven for in the fourth parody quoted above is also parodied in the body of the novel itself. *The Adaptable Man* is deliberately precise by comparison with the other fiction. It has a prologue, and its remainder is divided with almost mathematical accuracy into quarters. Its chronological location is almost as precise as its geographical setting, and the seasons pass carefully noted. The reader is always aware of the ages of the characters before him: Russell is fifty-three, Greta forty-seven, Aisley forty-five, Alwyn twenty-one, Jenny nineteen, and so on; Aisley was married at thirty-four when his nephew was ten, and subsequently exhausts his supplies of red and black ink in the precise jotting down of births, deaths, and marriages. But one would guess that a concern with measuring and weighing events is not Janet Frame's greatest passion in this work. Like a traditional novel, *The Adaptable Man* measures and weighs; but whenever it begins to do so, some opposite process of undermining or erosion begins.

This can be seen, for example, in the four sections of the book's prologue. In a traditional novel, the prologue might be expected to set out important themes and characters; this is certainly done in the prologue of *The Adaptable Man,* but in a way that is thoroughly unconventional and quite remarkable. Formal characterization prescribes traits and peculiarities; but this is how Aisley Maude is characterized in the prologue:

I, Reverend Aisley Maude, suddenly fashionable, but inwardly out of fashion, journeying the path of St. Cuthbert from the upstairs room of Clematis Cottage, Little Burgelstatham, where I cough and convalesce.[36]

And here, also mentioned in the prologue, is a "character" which might perhaps not be expected in a traditional novel:

I, the earth, fairly submissive, my seasons arranged beforehand; lifeless, but hopeful of the overflowing conceit and concern of man which spill life and feeling into my shell; man insists that I weep, groan, vomit, laugh; man reminds me that living is not much fun; but who wants fun?[37]

The traditional purposes of a prologue are undeniably fulfilled, but the manner of fulfillment is quite unexpected and unusual. The entire novel works in the same way, sketching the formal and the traditional but producing many imaginative insights and lyrical passages.

Its opening passages are remarkably like those of an English regional novel of the last century, with the tone perhaps of Mrs. Gaskell:

> Little Burgelstatham was in the part of East Suffolk which provokes little comment from the traveller when his train stops briefly, and will soon not stop at all, at the clay-coloured veranda-petticoated little station with its prize-winning beds of wallflowers and rock plants, and its station-master, shirt-sleeved, high-stooled in his office, surrounded by bicycles taken under his care and protection for the day while their owners travel north in the train to Tydd, the largest town within seven miles . . . .[38]

But this is a mere illusion; the mode of language soon changes after this passage and within a few pages the reader finds himself involved in a discussion of Anglo-Saxon and etymologies. In the same manner, the characterization of a figure in the novel can begin formally and then intensify with the language of poetry and insight, the "true" language of the novel. The same change can occur within the narration of the novel.

But formal characterization is not the only aspect of received fiction that is constantly tested here. In *The Adaptable Man* the concept of plot is attacked for its suggestion of consistent cause and effect and its implication of shape and order, its assumption of the existence of specific beginnings and endings. Plot here becomes not a means to an end (employed to promote a "meaning," for example) but an end in itself. Unable to adapt (as the process of characterization has adapted by compromising between the formal and the lyrical), plot joins the long list of traditions that are assaulted in the novel, along with Bert Whattling's altered bus timetables, Aisley Maude's Church, Russell Maude's practice, and so on. This novel constantly establishes cause and effect situations and just as constantly deflects them or deflates them.

Perhaps the most obvious of these gestures towards an apparent plot occurs with the murder of Botti Julio. It has no apparent motive, and the murderer's identity is withheld. Two questions are provoked: what has Botti done in the past to cause him to be murdered now, and who is his murderer? These questions are a conditioned response in the reader familiar with the kind of novel *The Adaptable Man* is pretending to be at this point. The game of cause and effect is played for some time: there is a discussion of Botti's background in a refugee camp and a small village, as if explanations could be found there. And the scene in Clematis Cottage when Russell reads to his family the newspaper report of the foreigner's death could come from any country house detective story. Something of Janet Frame's rather humorous attitude towards plot tensions can be glimpsed when, not long after the murder, Greta recalls that Alwyn has never cried and concludes that he must never have felt sorrow or needed "to contend with foreign bodies."[39]

Few readers will be gnawed by suspense when plot is treated in such a cavalier fashion. Aisley's dark suspicions about his nephew are clues enough to the identity of the killer. Instead of being held back, the fact that Alwyn is the murderer is revealed almost laconically in Part One (he "hadn't used an axe to kill the Italian. His hands had been strong enough"[40]). The apparent gratuitousness of the murder helps to erode the reader's confidence in the worth of artificial plot mechanisms in a novel which talks of the difficulty of finding and preserving shape and meaning in this chaotic century. A second similar use of plot occurs again at the beginning of Part Two, where there are several references to Greta's attraction to her own son. This notion appears not to have been in Greta's mind in the first part of the novel, but it is consummated all too literally at the climax of Part Two with the incestuous act in Greta's potting shed (a reference, perhaps, to all those "Potting Shed Mysteries" in detective fiction).

This incestuous act is of considerable significance in a novel with generic subject matter. Part Three contains a number of curious incidents for the life of the staid Clematis Cottage; for example, Greta and Russell have frequent intercourse after years of sleeping in separate rooms. This new-found virility on Russell's part makes the pregnancy of his wife crucial: will Greta bear the child of old-fashioned Russell, who for all his reclusiveness has some symbolic relation to authentic speech, or will she bear the child of Alwyn Maude, thoroughly adapted twentieth-century man? As I have remarked elsewhere:

What should concern us here is the means by which the pregnant Greta is bumped off. She is killed . . . when Muriel's antique Venini chandelier collapses on them at the Baldrys' dinner-table, seconds after electricity, come to the village at last, has briefly illuminated the chandelier. It is conceivable that the chandelier found its burden of symbol too much to support: its Fall follows the shabby Apocalypse of illumination; it symbolizes the collapse of tradition . . . .[41]

The question of who has fathered the child becomes less important than the need to destroy such formal, meaningful impulses within the novel, and this is accomplished by the symbolic means which renders all such elements of the work futile. Thus, the manner and the matter of *The Adaptable Man* become one, with the same task to perform, namely, finding new modes of thought and a new voice for our troubled century after showing us where the old ways have led. In the "overflowing" of *Scented Gardens for the Blind* there may be sensed a dissatisfaction with the form of the novel; in *The Adaptable Man* it is clearly felt that a novel about the destruction of old traditions of thought and behavior ought also to include the destruction of old traditions of fiction.

VII *Conclusions*

Janet Frame's fifth novel was received with considerable enthusiasm, particularly in North America, where its sophisticated stance found many appreciative readers. The few who did not fully appreciate it gave evidence, significantly enough, of not understanding that it contained evolutionary themes or that it was concerned with all forms of tradition. But to suppose that a work like *The Adaptable Man* is not a novel betrays a very limited understanding of what constitutes a novel.[42]

With the completion of this work, a substantial and important period of fiction ended for Janet Frame. During five years she had written six volumes plus an overflow of stories, poems, and articles; in the process, she had created for herself a style which was unmistakable and had tackled themes of undeniable seriousness and importance. The last two of these novels are quite remarkable, of a stature, it could be argued, to equal any work produced in the postwar period; and yet both are quite individualistic, owing little to outside influences. They transcend the personal and the regional, and belong to the literary heritage of the world, for they articulate experiences that are universal in the twentieth century. They complete an extraordinary period of literary inspiration, comparable perhaps to that which Rilke himself experienced as he wrote the "Sonnets to Orpheus."

There remains in this chapter the task of accounting for the uncollected stories of this period as well as for those that have not been related to the novels discussed so far. By far the greatest number of these are little sketches which have obviously been based upon observations of life made from directly above the typewriter, as it were, and which have found their way into the collections. "A Night of Frost and a Morning of Mist" is a meditation upon the ease with which the narrator kills a blowfly and his neighbors decide to kill a tomcat; like "The Press Gang" and "An Epidemic," which is about an epidemic of pure death, it shows the dominance of death in even the most innocuous surroundings. "One Must Give Up" sets out a desire for personal withdrawal and insularity against a meticulously drawn background of shops and suburban streets that are condemned in every detail.[43] "Flu and Eye Trouble" records a vacuous overheard conversation involving the narrator's landlord, who is a determined fixer of everything broken in his life—vacuum cleaners, taps, doorbells, windows—except, of course, his life itself. The last of these sketches, "The Linesman," again has a narrator peering out on the world through a window, this time at a linesman up a power pole; as the story concludes, the narrator realizes with horror that he has been hoping that the linesman might fall to his death.[44]

Some other stories are simply fantastic forms of the sketch: in "The Terrible Screaming," only a visitor to a town can hear the constant sound mentioned in the title; in the end he is consigned to a rest home. "Solutions" is about a man whose desire for freedom is so great that he progressively disembodies himself, ultimately finding that he is so free of the flesh that he does not exist at all. "The Man Who Lost Confidence" is a similar figure, who begins to see through all the certainties of existence and becomes aware of the absurdity and confusion of life seen in this naked way.[45]

As would be expected, some of these stories are autobiographical, like the story which gives the *Reservoir* collection its title. "Prizes" begins with the unforgettable aphorism, "Life is hell, but at least there are prizes": after recalling prizes from schooldays, the narrator concludes that in later life other people find that she is their prize. "Stink-Pot" is another story of bereavement in youth, and recalls the guilt felt when a sister dies shortly after an exchange of insults with the girl who narrates the tale. "Hecate, You Look Angerly" recalls a brief moment of glory in class readings during English lessons.[46]

Five of these stories deserve greater attention because they clearly are more ambitious works than those dealt with so far. "The Wind Brother" and "The Friday Night World" are children's stories,[47] but use images and techniques that have already appeared in the more serious fiction. "The Wind Brother" relies on a play upon the words "Air Mail" found on letters. Two young girls worry that all the letters posted in the local mailbox fail to reach their destination, and they wait up at night to catch the thief. After many nights they see a strange, cloudlike figure who seizes the letters from the mailbox, and they are themselves caught up in the folds of its misty cloak. They awake on a distant mountain which is covered in a snow of stolen letters to find that the figure who took them is the Wind Brother, a fabulous old man who has decided that Air Mail is so named that it belongs to him. After telling him what the words really mean, the girls are swept up in his cloak once again and returned to their home, and from then on no further mail goes astray. "The Friday Night World" is an even more fanciful tale. It begins with a description of evening shoppers at the end of the week who suddenly find themselves taken below the floor level of the shop they are in and deposited in the Friday Night World, which is ruled over by a king with eleven and a half eyes and an uncertain disposition. There they are entranced until their rescue by a young prince who is aided by the magical powers of a viola and a swarm of rather humanitarian bees.

The stories are both quite charming; but the equation of social communication with snow and the disdain for social institutions derive directly from the serious fiction. And the world of the children's stories is as divided as the "adult" world: a mundane existence regulated by parents, policemen, mailmen, and shopkeepers is opposed by the private world of childlike fantasy and innocence which redeems the lesser world.

"The Bath"[48] is a much grimmer story, about aging and death. The old woman who is at the center of the story is preparing herself to visit the grave of her husband, who has been dead for seventeen years. Gradually, as the difficulty of performing simple daily tasks becomes apparent, the old woman is seen to be enduring the living death of the aged, the bath she dreads because it threatens to entomb her every time she uses it being equated with the grave of her husband. "A Boy's Will"[49] is a somewhat more cheerful story of a young adolescent growing to a stage where he forms an identity of his own in the face of his family's attempts to impose a socially acceptable role upon him. All his individuality, a fusion of will and imagination, becomes concentrated on the task of making a box kite which will fly free of earthly restrictions. He makes and flies it, and when it is accidentally broken he has the strength of character to accept the blow calmly and to turn to the task of repairing it.

Two more of these longer stories belong to *The Reservoir*. "Burial in Sand" is about the slow fading of early ability in a young painter who travels overseas on a scholarship to Paris and later works in Spain. As the narrator of the story awaits the fulfillment of the young man's promise, he witnesses the painter's loss of his youthfulness, his marriage, the arrival of children, and no appearance of paintings. "The Triumph of Poetry" is simply an extension of this idea over the entire lifetime of a young man called Alan. After dazzling school years, he decides to become a poet, to the consternation of those who had foreseen a more useful career for him. But society buries him, and he becomes a university academic with a comfortable home, a matronly wife, children, and a sea of appliances and commodities in which he finally drowns quietly and without a struggle.

CHAPTER 7

Room for the Imagination

I A Diminished Scale

AFTER the enormously productive overseas years, Janet Frame's years in Dunedin from late 1963 to 1967 became a period in which she wrote a considerable amount of poetry and tidied up themes and ideas which had already found fictional form. The two main works of this period, *A State of Siege* and *The Rainbirds (Yellow Flowers in the Antipodean Room)* were written in rapid succession and may be taken as complementary works, although they do not have the deliberate unity which marked the first few novels. Both resemble stories written at length rather than full novels, for they are both essentially single parables explored in depth. Both show careful social observation by a writer who had returned to her home environment with increased objectivity, and both offer a certain amount of satirical humor.

A State of Siege contains three parts, "The Knocking," "Darkness," and "The Stone." It begins with a lurid description of an island called Karemoana, in the far north of New Zealand (actually based on Waiheke Island, near Auckland). There Malfred Signal, the fifty-three-year-old spinster and retired schoolteacher who is virtually the sole occupant of this novel, is preparing to spend her retirement. She has lived her entire life in the southern town of Matuatangi, which her father founded almost single-handed a number of years before. Her adult years have been divided between teaching art at the local girls' school and nursing her aging mother, who has recently died when the novel begins. Malfred is liberated by the old woman's death, severs her connections with her family home and early life, and sets out to become a creative artist, a painter, in the remaining years of her life.

Her journey northward is a harrowing experience, a steady translation from everything that is familiar to her to everything that is strange and bewildering. When, after a great effort, she arrives at Karemoana, she is disappointed by the barrenness of the island and the decrepitude of some of the buildings. She feels that the cottage she has bought is "hostile," and soon learns of its forbidding history: it is the former estate of a middle-aged woman who retired to the island and unexpectedly died there. The taxi driver who takes Malfred there hints at the presence of a mysterious, savage element on the island, and the day after, shopping in the township—known as "Kare" to its inhabitants—she becomes despondent at the islanders' lack of friendliness, for all show the same insularity and self-interest that she remembers from Matuatangi. "Few of the houses lining the streets were occupied . . . many of the people walking in the streets had grown to look like the summer baches: there was an appearance of rust in their skin and eyes, an unoccupied look on their faces."[1] When she returns home, a violent storm begins, and she enters her state of siege with the commencement of a mysterious and incessant knocking at the door, which continues even after the passage of the storm. She sees—or imagines she sees—a figure at the door, an Anyone to match her new view of Anywhere, the truthful vision of life she has gained as the first section nears its end:

She looked at the World, such a neat hollow schoolroom world, with coloured squares and writing on it; a touch of the finger could turn it; there was even a device behind it where the pencils could be sharpened! What a useful World! Then the schoolroom image faded and she saw the ugly, terrifying, beautiful Anywhere, no longer spinning at a touch, but motionless, not round but flat, yet with no danger to the inhabitants of falling over the edge, or of being trapped Down Under; and with no sharpening device.[2]

The section ends abruptly with the inexplicable turning off of Malfred's electric light from outside her cottage—and she is plunged into the dark night which provides the subtitle for Part Two.

Lying in the enforced darkness, she feels its gloom is the appropriate condition for modern man, "a part of [his] natural development to begin in light and move toward darkness."[3] In her terror, her past returns to her in memory and dream: she associates herself with a former colleague who has the appropriate name of Miss Float, and whose only venture outside the tiny cosmos of Matuatangi was a holiday trip to Scotland, from which she returned with her view of life unchanged and an unlikely Scottish accent. Malfred also recalls the only man who has ever loved her, Wilfred Anderson, the son of a respected local farming family, who became a soldier and died in the Second World War. During one of their last meetings, Malfred recalls, she and Wilfred went to the Matuatangi fernhouse where he made a sexual advance that she still associates with the cloying dampness of the ferns. Now she sees that this was her only chance for love and that in failing her lover she also failed herself and became doomed to live inauthentically. Now the storm begins once more outside her cottage, reminding her of the vast natural world from which she turned away years before in the fernhouse; when the storm dies, a pristine silence falls which is unlike anything she has experienced before. From this point on, in a series of imaginary telephone conversations with the local doctor and priest, and in brief dreams, Malfred's experience is almost complete fantasy, although as Part Two ends she realizes that she has always been caught in "a preliminary dream of which the one tragically constant feature was the way it stayed preliminary."[4]

Part Three, "The Stone," continues Malfred's prolonged self-analysis as the storm roars on outside and the mysterious figure returns to batter at the door. She compares her own life unfavorably with that of her sister Lucy, always a confused and disorderly girl who nevertheless has found happiness through marriage; and she compares herself equally unfavorably with her brother Graham, who, unlike Malfred, had the initiative to leave Matuatangi at an early age and to forge his own career and establish his own identity. She also comes to realize why her father used to spend so much of his time in direct contact with nature as he walked and camped in the dense native bush: he had an ability—a need—to confront the world authentically, which she has lacked. She now realizes that "the view of [her] life had so long been arranged with her mother in the foreground that her mother's death, though it set the View free, also left a hollow in the earth where the familiar tooth or tree stump had been removed, and where it was now too late for any other object to grow."[5] She withdraws into her imagination, which she has always thought of as a "room two inches behind the eyes."[6] There, at one point, she imagines that she has found the safely familiar fire shovel and brass tongs that she has spent years forcing her pupils to draw "correctly." The likelihood that she will achieve her new vision is now small, but towards the end of the novel she expresses her desire to explore the essence of her new surroundings, to see whether they contain life or "stone flames."[7] In the last pages, her window is shattered by a stone, around which is wrapped a piece of paper inscribed with a confused poem whose words are disordered. The novel concludes with the discovery of Malfred Signal's dead body three days later, the stone which has pierced her secondary reality still clutched in her hand.

II *Setting*

In this novel, as elsewhere in the fiction of Janet Frame, the south of New Zealand is seen as a place of stability and trustworthiness, without any particularly favorable connotations being necessarily implied in this kind of description—stability and trustworthiness being the hallmarks of inauthenticity. The north in this novel is a little like Conrad's Congo, a place of new experiences, half imaginary, where all is strange and frightening and beyond prediction. Malfred Signal's home town of Matuatangi is Malfred Signal herself: her father had been the town's principal founder, and the signs of his activity are visible everywhere, most obviously in a large, romantic statue of bronze which has been set on a nearby headland.

Drinking fountains, seats, gates, foundation stones, trees, all had been named after Francis Henry Signal. He was on the Mayoral roll in the Town Hall, in the records of past Library Committees (Atheneum and Mechanics Institute) and the Boys' High Honours Board. He had been a legend which Malfred found hard to reconcile with the slight, shy, brown-eyed man that she knew. He'd climbed mountains, too, named peaks in the Southern Alps, had been mentioned in the country's history; yet Malfred remembered most clearly his gentleness . . . . Malfred had been amused at the Apollo-like image cast of him in the bronze statue: his chin was firm, his head erect, his stance determined, almost regal. The sculptor had shaped him as the conventional Hero, and had got away with it, Malfred supposed, because her father, in life and in death, had been treated as time treats so many heroes: his exploits had been given physical expression.[8]

To a large extent, Malfred Signal is merely another of these exploits; furthermore, she is an expression of the dreams and desires of the remainder of her family. Her father died when she was twenty-three, and as the oldest unmarried daughter of the family she has been left with the responsibility for looking after her aged mother.

Her life has become an extension of the old woman's, and when her mother dies Malfred is left without an identity—she has only an orderly series of dimensions attributed to her by various relatives and townfolk.

Thus, she leaves Matuatangi (literally, "a place where one mourns an older relative") and travels to Karemoana (a name that refers to the lashing of a whip). Certainly Malfred Signal is lashed by reality in Karemoana, which is almost crammed with the more vivid images that have been associated with naked reality in Janet Frame's writing—a marauding sea, intense sunlight, an extinct volcano, and the besieging storm. She is overwhelmed by its vivid lushness:

A South Pacific paradise. An island where storms were stormier, rain was rainier, sun was sunnier; where figs, bananas, passion fruit, pawpaws, fijoas, custard apples, guavas, grew and ripened; where the cold pale narcissi opened their buds at the official beginning of winter, and violets bloomed all year; where the only enemies of man, apart from man, were wasps as big as flying tigers, a few mosquitoes breeding a giant island strain, and too many colonies of ants; and perhaps, though one does not explain why, the sullen grey mangroves standing in their beds of mud in the tidal inlets facing the mainland.[9]

There is another image connected with the mangrove swamps:

the winter pohutukawa, the coast tree, wind-fighting, gnarled, sprawling without decoration . . . in summer it would burst into flame and its flowers would die in a carpet of crimson ashes.[10]

Like Little Burgelstatham, Karemoana is a swampland, a primitive place where sea and land meet. And the swamp has its circle of fire in the blaze of pohutukawa blossom, like the gorse which surrounded the Waimaru rubbish dump, the nuclear explosion at the conclusion of the fourth novel, and the descending chandelier at the end of the fifth. It is a place in which Malfred Signal will be tested, to see if her imagination can pay the high price of authenticity.

III   *Vision and Imagination*

The story of Malfred Signal is in a sense a continuation of the story of Zoe Bryce and some of the characters in the shorter fiction. The figure of the spinster stands as typical of any human being who needs love but has not experienced it, as someone for whom no one has cared. The spinster schoolteacher is even more lost, in Janet Frame's world, for the schoolteacher imposes the false values of society upon the young. And to make Malfred Signal a teacher of art introduces the notion of vision and the issue of how society trains its young to see the world according to preconceived rules and proportions—how, to use terms that occur in Malfred Signal's own mind, we force ourselves to stop *looking* and start *seeing*:

> She remembered taking a class from the High School to Wellington for the Centennial Exhibition . . . when they returned to Matuatangi their paintings . . . had been so uninspired, so lacking in colour and originality, that it seemed as if the visit, far from giving the girls a spurt of mental growth, had had the effect of an application of DDT. Malfred knew that when she had said in despair, "What did you really *see* in Wellington, girls?" the disappointment had been directed chiefly at herself: what had *she* seen? The same dull uninspired images that yet had not seemed dull and uninspired, for they had been the result of the ingrained habit of dutiful looking, of seeing what was there, and what others agreed was there, which was a less arduous and hazardous way of coming to terms with the shapes and colours of everything, including wet and windy Wellington during Exhibition Week, than other ways of looking.[11]

As an art mistress, Malfred has been particularly strict, placing before her pupils inert objects and demanding that they be copied with careful attention to proportion, shading, and balance.

These values are a product of the more general obsession society has—the obsession with Safety:

> I remember that I've never known such a feeling of safety as I knew in Matuatangi when I woke each morning and knew that the school day, with its fire shovels, lay ahead; that my lessons were planned down to the last shadow. I knew which days I should prepare morning tea, supervise the playground, coach games after school. How can I ever explain to anyone my feeling of joy when I stood before my class and watched everyone busy with drawing or painting and knew that I had regretfully dispensed with the cliché comfort of the teaching profession—the discovery of genius—to replace it with shadows and with the calmer knowledge that no one in my classroom would ever "burst into that silent sea."[12]

No pupil will ever develop genius or even imagination in the classes Malfred conducts, in which all objects must be shaded "correctly." Her favorite pupil, a girl called Noni, used to shade "correctly": but "correct" shading is a concept at odds with the ever-moving sun of truth, from whose light there is no refuge. Malfred remembers—regretfully now, with her new knowledge—that she once punished a girl called Lettice Bradley, whose capacity to paint imaginative creative works was greater than her own, making her jealous.

Her mother's death has affected Malfred beyond the mere sense of physical release and without any sense of deep loss. "It was only the night her mother was dying that she realized what she had missed seeing by her dutiful habit of looking,"[13] and she comes to see that most people possess an "encircling tube of being."[14] Because she has always comforted her old mother by rubbing her body with lanolin, Malfred associates lanolin both with death and with man's feeble denial of death. From this association stems her desire to paint truthfully, and at Karemoana, disgusted with the wan, unconvincing colors which emerge from her tubes of paint, she mixes lanolin with them to make them more "real" and hence her pictures more authentic. She desires to absorb from her surroundings

a new intensity of vision, paint the manuka smoking with white flame, or the sky as manuka smoking with cloud; paint the shoals of light gulped down by the water; look at death, see it in the land, as I saw it in my mother's face, feel in seeing it, as I felt then; recognize it; wonder why; paint why; paint red, red, why? The glacier slides down the valley; my heart is too numb with its weight. There are some who, knowing my new purpose in painting, will remind me that I, Malfred Signal, may be promiscuous, even an adulterous woman, to lie so with the landscape of my country . . . I ask only that I be given the peace to live as I have decided to live, without my mother, father, sister, brother, lover knocking at my door; without being besieged by those who have been close to me . . . I want only to forget the years of rigid shading, obsessional outlining and representation of objects; I want in this, still my preliminary dream, to explore beyond the object, beyond its shadow, to the ring of fire, the corona at its circumference . . . . [15]

But Malfred fails to do all this—as the stone clutched in her dead hand finally suggests—and the circle of the fiery pohutukawa trees claims her as another victim.

The cause of Malfred's failure lies in the "room" she imagines to be two inches behind her eyes:

Malfred knew of the "room two inches behind the eyes"; it was filled almost to overflowing; yet for forty years she had kept it locked . . . . Malfred knew that she was on no human terms with the "room two inches behind the eyes," that what lay there, treasure or no treasure, did not belong to her, had not been captured by her and given a name.[16]

Thinking of the works of art she will create in Karemoana, she decides that she wants "first of all, to observe, to clean a dusty way of looking."[17] Years of passive living would then, she believes, become active and copulatory and she would "snarl at morning" and "tear the flesh of the killed beast."[18] Such vigorously authentic behavior is unlikely to be achieved, however, by one who has formerly shrunk from love in a fernhouse. When she first sees the lush vegetation of Karemoana, she thinks it is disturbingly fernlike and an improbable part of her future vision. The fern is evergreen and timeless, but she is condemned to autumn and decay, as much of the novel's color imagery suggests.

For the "room two inches behind the eyes" is a prison, and in the fantastic second half of *A State of Siege* Malfred's Karemoana cottage itself becomes the room of her imagination. Figuratively, she "becomes" the dead woman from whom she bought the cottage—the mildewed books and photographs she finds there are hers, and she realizes that she has entered her own mausoleum. From the first she has thought of herself as a "rectangular package" and felt that she contained the dead child of her dead lover[19]; she wears an autumn-tinted cardigan whose colors she finds on the hands of the dying woman who was her mother. And it is strongly implied that the squares of canvas upon which she paints and into which she has forced her pupils to fit their imaginations are also prisons, formal ways of thinking which invade her dreams of the past. In her dreams she moves from rectangle to rectangle viewing each evasion of reality that has made up her life, until she realizes finally that she has spent all her life dreaming, and that the mysterious element that has been battering to get into her room (both the room of her mind and the actual room she cowers in) is Light: the armies of eternal truth whose wounds she cannot bear and whose peace she cannot win.

IV   *Conclusions*

Some time after Malfred repelled Wilfred's advances, the fernhouse in which the incident occurred has been demolished and replaced by a formal, ornamental garden. This development suggests that Malfred Signal has turned from the chance to become a whole and hale human being and has consigned herself forever to the scented gardens planted for the blind. She herself realizes that this process occurs in most people around her: that the young have lost "the original vision, the primitive view"[20] and that it is part of man's natural development "to begin in light and move towards darkness."[21] People, she comes to realize, "had to be protected from living; living was a war that needed all the defences one could gather."[22]

It is illuminating to compare Malfred Signal with Istina Mavet, who constantly turns toward the painful, beautiful vision of authentic existence, and with Vera Glace, who creates the vestiges of an authentic language from such a vision. Malfred is of a lesser worth than her forerunners because of her failure to confront life, and the stone with its disordered language attached shatters her as it shatters her window. But this parable of the price the imagination demands of the artist is not wholly negative. It will be obvious that Malfred Signal reaches self-knowledge during the course of the novel in a way that adds much to the reader's understanding of the imaginative act, which is seen in particular as a means of realizing the need for communion and love all humans feel. Thinking, at one point in the novel, that New Zealand is isolated from war and social upheaval, Malfred realizes that experience will not force her countrymen to care about their fellows. But she has nevertheless a "dream of a vast imaginative force, its wealth drawn from its initial poverty, that quells prejudice, suspicion, that acts as a beam to draw distant countries close so that each sees, with instinctive vision, the needs of the other."[23] Her tragedy is that, having understood this, she cannot realize her part in such a dream, and the knowledge of this failure kills her.

V The Rainbirds

Where A State of Siege is the story of someone who fails to create an authentic imagination within herself, The Rainbirds is the story of someone who succeeds all too well in fulfilling this task. Godfrey Rainbird, the central figure of the novel, is an Englishman who at the age of twenty came to Dunedin as an immigrant, leaving behind him his only close relative, a much older unmarried sister named Lynley. Lynley has brought Godfrey up as if she had been his mother, because their actual mother died in an underground railway station during an air raid in the Second World War when the two children were living as evacuees in Scotland. During the ten years that follow Godfrey's departure from England, Lynley has kept a boardinghouse in London and then nursed an old man until his death. Godfrey, meanwhile, has been absorbed into the New Zealand way of life, and by the age of thirty has become a senior clerk in a travel office, married a Matuatangi girl named Beatrice Muldrew, fathered a daughter and a son, and settled into a comfortably anonymous existence in a Dunedin suburb. As the novel begins, the author is able to make some tart observations about the shortcomings of this kind of life. But a sense of brooding threat is also felt as the Rainbird family listens to the wind and rain outside their house and recalls their last Christmas holiday, spent away from home in a frail cottage amid a pine forest and in teeming rain. At the beginning of autumn, the Rainbirds prepare to withstand winter by purchasing a television set and installing an electric fire with artificial flames. But these potent precautions are ineffective: one evenning Godfrey is killed, struck down by a car as he walks home from a meeting.

A substantial portion of the remainder of the novel examines society's rituals and responses to death, chiefly with a satirist's eye. For Beatrice, whose vestigial imagination has long since been trimmed by schoolteachers and a pair of dull parents, bereavement is a puzzle. Before marriage she has dreamed of a romantic lover, but on meeting the utterly undistinguished Godfrey Rainbird at a dance decides that he will do. Now, having lost him, she finds it difficult to mourn him adequately. The impact of his death is numbed by a sedative process of ordering wreaths, sending telegrams, posting death notices, and receiving visitors; his clothes are given to charity and his place taken by Beatrice's parents, who travel from Matuatangi; and the Rainbird children find that they enjoy being without their father, since they are given toys and attention they never had with him. Death, it is made evident, promotes abundant life and activity, which culminates in this case in Lynley's sudden decision to come to New Zealand for her younger brother's funeral.

At this point, the smooth progression of affairs is interrupted by Godfrey's inconvenient return to life: he has merely been in a very deep coma. When he suddenly sits up in the morgue, the hospital staff are not terrified but annoyed—he has interrupted their morning tea break. His resurrection is an inconvenience to others. Lyn-

ley, who has had so much "experience in death,"[24] is a little startled
on her arrival in Dunedin to be greeted by Godfrey himself; Beatrice feels obliged to pay for the coffin and cemetery plot she has
ordered for her husband and has to retrieve the clothes she has
given to charity only a few days before; and the Muldrews return,
grumbling, to Matuatangi. When Godfrey goes back to work at the
Travel Bureau, he finds that he has been replaced.

For his "death" has altered everyone's attitude towards him; more
than this, it has altered his attitude towards himself. He realizes that
his life after death will be profoundly different from his life before,
since he is convinced that a strange, untranslatable message has
been given him which he must understand at all costs. Occasionally,
he is possessed by terrifying visions of great beauty which are new to
his experience, and he often becomes chilly and stiff like a corpse.
After a brief period, his wife begins to wonder whether his ordeal
has sucked the life from him, as a vampire sucks blood from a victim.
Others begin to sense that he has changed drastically, and he loses
his job on the not entirely unreasonable grounds that a man so
widely believed to have died can scarcely be expected to promote
holidays for tourists. Soon Godfrey begins to find himself unpleas-
antly recognized on the street, as if he were a famous criminal, and
the only employment he can find is as an elevator operator, an
occupation often reserved for the handicapped. The Rainbirds' children begin to feel awkward at school, resenting that their father has
lost his protective coloring of anonymity.

The turning point for Godfrey Rainbird comes when his recently
purchased electric blanket fails to save him from an icy, terrifying
dream which takes place during the first night of winter. All he can
recall of the dream is a forbidding and mystifying poem whose syn-
tax has begun to crumble till its words are disordered or reversed
completely. He has arrived at the edge of the alphabet, from which
position a letter of formal dismissal from the Travel Bureau seems
suddenly understandable and appropriate (it appears to be signed
"yours failfulthy"[25]). From this point on, Godfrey turns increasingly
away from society's values, refusing to find employment at all and
spending whole weeks in his garden or by his window staring at the
sea, whose secret significance he has begun to guess. Beatrice is left
to support the family, although Godfrey makes a little money by
assembling electric plugs at home. Lynley travels to Auckland
where she meets and marries the retired director of a chain of

cinemas, leaving the Rainbirds behind as social outcasts. Beatrice becomes an alcoholic and Godfrey is rumored to be a cripple and then a fraud. Their son is goaded into assaulting a schoolmate who jeers at Godfrey, then is taken from his parents by the Social Welfare Department and placed with foster parents; their daughter becomes an introvert whom the neighbors send north to be cared for by her Aunt Lynley and wealthy husband. As stones rain upon their roof and Godfrey spends his days alternately staring at the television set and at the sea, Beatrice drunkenly commits suicide by slitting her throat with a knife. Later, Godfrey too dies, and the novel ends with an epilogue much like that which concludes *Owls Do Cry*. In it, the action of the novel is placed in an almost mythical past, and the reader is told that Sonny Rainbird has grown to become the Town Clerk of Melbourne, Australia, while his sister, Teena, has become an internationally famous actress. The novel's last image is of the graves of Godfrey and Beatrice, and the sacrificial aspect of the imagination is strongly suggested.

VI   *The Cost of Imagination*

The first thing the reader will notice about *The Rainbirds* is its similarity to *A State of Siege*, particularly in the complementary nature of the experiences of the two central characters. There are obvious points at which the two novels come together, as in the replacement of living flame in the Rainbirds' hearth by the false flame of electricity (Malfred Signal thinks in these images late in her siege) and in the "death" of Godfrey on a stretch of marshy reclaimed land (described exactly as are the mangrove swamps where reality lies waiting for Malfred). In addition, the visions which illuminate the imaginations of both are expressed in the same vivid, pungent imagery. There is a less obvious similarity, too, in the fact that both characters are seen as being besieged in a room that is the literal counterpart of the "room" of the imagination: the room two inches behind Godfrey's eyes is also a holiday cottage, in this case among the pines and rainstorms of the Rainbirds' last holiday. Early in the novel, when both Godfrey and his daughter suffer a moment of deep and inexplicable misgiving during a period of heavy rain, they are reminded of the "thunder, lightning, torrential rains, gale force winds"[26] of their holiday, and the reader is probably reminded of the similar storms which gather round Malfred Signal. In both cases, the storms represent the enormous power of nature uncontrolled, and in both cases, the state of siege occurs figuratively first, in the mind of the central figure, and then actually, as a literal and physical predicament.

Something of Malfred Signal is called to mind, too, in the characters of Beatrice and Lynley Rainbird, the sisters-in-law. Beatrice is a Matuatangi girl whose imagination might well have been dulled in one of Malfred Signal's art classes; certainly, her father's paint and wallpaper shop could have contributed to the repetitive suburban smartness of Matuatangi homes that Malfred notes. Lynley's commitment to the nursing of a dying old man is familiar; as with Malfred, the death of her charge is a liberation and a moment of new knowledge. Lynley's journey to New Zealand serves to import from overseas an awareness of "the War," specifically the Second World War but mythically the war that has continued through the ages and, as the earlier novels suggested, reached a climax in this century, bringing a poverty and suffering which is beyond the knowledge of most New Zealanders:

And Lynley had had experience in death! Here she knew a feeling of triumph over Beatrice for no experience Beatrice had known in New Zealand would have taught her as much as Lynley knew about dying and being buried, and not only conventional death, but sudden ghastly explosions of bombs, mass killing and mass burial; and then there'd been this past slow quiet inevitable death of an old man who'd not loved life or people with much passion and whom few in their turn had known or cared for. Lynley felt superior in all her knowledge and prepared with the condescension of one sixteen years older to teach Beatrice what she had learned.[27]

Lynley ties together the novel's two main threads, which contrast the intensity of experience overseas and the degree to which New Zealanders have become insulated from such experience. The Englishmen and women she leaves behind her are "millions of people thrust together like lice on a penny,"[28] and London is remembered only as the tomb of her mother, buried under thousands of tons of rubble by the bombs of war. Feeling that she has failed to live well in England because she has lacked "room to breathe, move, grow, love,"[29] she hopes to find in New Zealand wide spaces—only to be reminded of the cry for living space over which the last war was fought. When she is in New Zealand, she finds that her wealth of experience in death is wasted, not simply because of her brother's thoughtless return from the grave but because the New Zealand way of death is so different from the way she knows. Godfrey begins to see this difference after he has been "reborn":

In the northern hemisphere he might have been better equipped to face death. Here in the south he had been overwhelmed by the greenness of the world, by the sun, the sea. The benign climate encouraged ease, relaxation, the urge to "give a hand" to help the grass to grow, and when it started to assert its growth and power, to put it in its place by cutting it down. Here, man and the natural scene were "cobbers" with nature still giving a reminder several times a year that being "just good friends" is as it states and is not an encouragement to take liberties with untamed personal snows and self-absorbed remote bush.[30]

He sees that the life of a small town is determinedly inauthentic, its shaven lawns and lacquered houses turned resolutely away from the chaotic tendencies of nature and particularly from the disorderly intrusion which is death.

But death itself is somehow different in the Southern Hemisphere, blandly and unimaginatively absorbed into life in a manner which ignores its true significance. Children play at the beach "gathering a different store of experience of different deaths. They were acquainted early with the bleached bones of animals, the overturned dinghy in the tidal river, the drowned classmates."[31] "Herbaceous borders are more precious than a display of bright ideas in the head," Godfrey begins to realize, and sees that scented gardens are a way of ignoring the existence of death.

Only "a trained, constantly used imagination had hope of 'facing' the terrors of being and not being,"[32] and when he understands this truth he determines to compensate for the inadequacies of his fellows by training his imagination, a process that involves learning to *see* correctly, as Malfred Signal's experience showed. Beatrice shares this task, although she never approaches the depths of her husband's visionary understanding, and quickly finds that her long-held suburban safety devices are detached from her. In fact, she changes roles with Lynley, as if each had infected the other: as Beatrice becomes more deeply aware of the frailty of her own existence and of the suffering and death which are common to life where Lynley comes from, Lynley becomes forgetful of all she has known and adopts the suburban ways and mentality which have kept Be-

atrice alive for so long. When she travels north to marry her wealthy
dream-merchant, the owner of cinemas, she leaves behind a sister-
in-law whose earlier certainties have all vanished.

One of the things that Godfrey first understands when he gains
his new vision is that his dead mother's experience can be seen as a
mythical form of his own, for just as he is cut down in the middle of
suburban routine and safety, so too was she, when a bomb directly
hit the tube station she and others were sheltering in during the last
war, burying them all:

That street and the Underground Station had been built by men. Men had
cared for the street, patched its skin, in winter lit their charcoal braziers by
its pavement, warming their hands before they mended the innocent street
that directed . . .   Walk On Me, the intestines of the city of Westminster
lay, planned and nursed by men; and further below them the Tube Station
and the railway lines . . . bleak surroundings like the inside of a sooty
skeleton yet how much a blessing during the raids! How safe they said it was
down there, with rugs and tea and people lying side by side head to the tiles
against, perhaps, a poster of Spain or a woman's legs and torso gripped by
Berlei; each person sharing body warmth with his neighbour. All over
London these dormitories of death had been arranged with the hope of
escaping death and almost all escaped but Balham Tube Station. After the
War Godfrey went one day to inspect the site of his mother's grave, the
rebuilt station. Even the thought that . . . hundreds of bodies still lay
buried did not rouse the horror that he felt now at *his* death and burial
alive.[33]

Godfrey sees that he has become a sort of "underground man": his
"death" felt as if it involved sinking into the bowels of the earth, and
his mind presents the horrible image of the earth "digesting" the
corpses interred within it. The act of imaginative inward journeying
that he cultivates is described as a descent into hell, from whose
impressive regions of majestic terror he returns to stare through the
tissues of the city and suburbs which surround him. Cold and
corpselike, he repels his fellows because he has become living evidence of their own mortality as well as proof of their inability to
accept that death has a place in life, to see that the first completes
the last.

But *The Rainbirds* would be misrepresented if this were all that
were said of it. Although its world is similar to that of the other
fiction, it presents that world with more wit and humor than

before—if one can accept the mordant quality in all the observations. The humor usually takes the form of pungently satirical comments on the ways of life in her own country. Here, for example, is a description of Easter celebrations in New Zealand:

Easter: the beach, the last supply of sun (but he dreamed; in this country the sun came in all seasons; but what use was it to him now?) Easter eggs, rabbits for the children; Good Friday changed to Dead Friday; death on the roads, in the mountains, the final drownings before summer came again . . . The Easter Show, the cattle and sheep and pigs. Farm implements, the Wall of Death, the Fijian Fire Walkers; Shoot and Win a Plaster Ornament; Alternate wails and cheers from the churches: He is dead. He is risen. Then Anzac Day most solemn: khaki and poppies.[34]

But the chief satirical idea is projected through Godfrey's "resurrection," with its suggestion that he is a sort of Christ-figure. Redemption and transformation might seem to be promised in this metaphor; but its point is to show that in Godfrey's world, there is *no* chance of transformation because of the lack of spirituality that characterizes so many of the figures in this novel. This barrenness and the forms it takes are suggested perfectly when Godfrey, after his "death," is offered a job for Easter as an elevator operator. Lo! He is risen again—with a weekly wage.

VII The Pocket Mirror

Although Janet Frame's original desire to become a poet had long been superseded by the need to write novels like *The Rainbirds*, she had frequently written poems which had the same relationship to the major fiction as did the stories and sketches. After many years away from Dunedin, however, she found that living in that city once more meant writing poetry about her life there, at a greater rate of composition than at any stage before. These and other poems were collected during the mid-1960's and published under the title of one of them as *The Pocket Mirror*.

Like the earlier stories and sketches, the Dunedin poems in *The Pocket Mirror* often seem spontaneous, to have been composed on the spur of the moment, as if flashes of sudden insight or understanding had provoked them. The resulting effect is not unlike that found in the Japanese *haiku*, although the form of the poetry is far from strict. "Dunedin Poem," which opens the volume, speaks of the passage of time since "down a long street lined with flowering

cherry trees I walked nineteen years ago/ to stare at the waves on
St. Clair beach,"[35] and contrasts the bland mutability of things with
the agonies that change brings to human beings. "Morning" is simply a picture of a wet Dunedin morning which appears to have a
mind of its own, unlike the scurrying people who shelter from it.
"Views" consists of four strongly visual images of Dunedin which
contrast the natural world of poplars, bush, fish, and seagulls with
the none-too-natural order of men. "At Evans Street" is written in
celebration of finding the house that was to be her home for several
years. Typically, it begins with a vivid description of the natural
things to be found in the garden but goes on to larger themes:

> It is not unusual to want somewhere to live but the impulse
> bears thinking about seriously and it is wise
> never to forget the permanent impermanence of the grave,
> its clay floor, the molten centre of the earth, its untiled
> roof, the rain and sunbeams arrowing through slit
> windows and doors too narrow to escape through,
> locked by the remote control of death-bed convulsions
> in a warm room in a cream-painted wooden house with
> a red roof, a white bargeboard, fallen roofbeam . . . .[36]

A similar contrast between day-to-day existence and larger issues
occurs in "Vacant Possession," where her "dead mother's best bedroom and fireside suite" seem determinedly immobile against the
telephone calls of someone who wishes to move into the house.[37]
"The Spell" makes the same contrast, but in a different manner:

> Into one medium-sized sliced-pineapple tin
> left overnight to gather Northeast Valley household
> smoke, and fog surrounding the green farm on the valley
> slope where each morning sheep bleat and dogs bark,
>   put one thread
> of crocus budded two days, one frost petal from a south-facing
> windowpane, one flame from a garden bonfire,
> one beam from a peak-hour television programme,
> enough light to flood, darkness to fill
> the four leaks in the kitchen roof that will never be mended.[38]

The ongoing, mundane processes of life surrounding the writer are
suddenly suspended in a flash of insight in which they appear

momentarily to be transformed. "A Golden Cat" achieves a lighter effect with the same purpose: the poet meets a beautiful animal which seems to symbolize the natural beauty of Northeast Valley and, again, to transform it.

Visions such as these make the poet feel very different from her fellows, and a number of the Dunedin poems show the same isolation of the poet from the citizen that can be seen in Godfrey Rainbird, whose vision of death in suburbia can be taken as merely a parabolic form of the vision of eternity which makes the poet an outcast from others. This vision becomes focused on an imagined being in "The Clock Tower," which seems to the poet to inhabit the building of the title and which supervises life from a mode of existence that is unimaginable. This angel is like the Angel of Rilke's *Duino Elegies,* and in fact shows openly what is evident in many of the poems in this volume, that Janet Frame's art is still animated and disciplined by the vision of Rilke. A twin poem is "Sunday Afternoon at Two O'Clock," which catalogues the monotonous, time-ensnared routines of suburbia:

> Having been to church the people are good, quiet,
> with sober drops at the end of their cold Dunedin noses,
> with polite old-fashioned sentences like Pass the Cruet,
> and, later, attentive glorying in each other's roses.
>
> Long past is Sunday's dinner and its begpardons.
> Cars start in the street. The ice-cream shop is open.
> The brass band gets ready to play in the Botanical Gardens.
> The beach, the pictures, the stock-car racing tracks beckon.

And then, as in "The Clock Tower," another order of existence, natural and eternal, announces itself:

> Seizing the time from the University clock, the wind
> suddenly cannot carry its burden of chiming sound.
> The waves ride in, tumultuous, breaking gustily out of tune,
> burying
>> two o'clock on Sunday afternoon.[39]

Sometimes this hidden order of existence can be thoroughly malevolent ("The hanging stairway in the library may well see/ some interesting executions"[40]), as it is in so many of the novels and stories.

At other times, its existence is merely accepted, and the reader is
assumed to infer its attributes by simple reversal of the mundane:

> this is an innocent birthday party where magicians
> dazzle with silk handkerchiefs and snow,
> think rabbits, live their habits,
> and never know, never know.[41]

Several of the poems in *The Pocket Mirror* strongly resemble in
tone the two novels of this period spent in Dunedin in the mid-
1960's: the focus is upon society and its blindness to the fullness of
existence, and frequently there occur flashes of that sense of autho-
rial alienation which was evident in *The Rainbirds*. Two poems tilt
at a favorite target, the accountant, whose ledgers divide life into a
profit that is always material and a loss that is never the loss inflicted
by suffering or bereavement. "Big Bill" is a "High School Boy,
Accountant,/ Cricket Star, hero of Plunket Shield Play" whose "neat
suburban street" with its "faded flowers in the garden" becomes the
scene of "madness, murder, suicide."[42] Similar themes occur in
"Dying":

> Dying, the accountant who skated
> on thin ice was rated
> an Obituary in the morning paper
> (the Otago Daily Times)
> that made no mention of crimes,
> called him neither embezzler nor raper
> but told of his various memberships sailing
> to charitable waters . . . .[43]

"Dunedin Story" is a parabolical poem very similar in method to the
earlier prose parables. "I brought a leper into my house," it begins,
and, in a perfect exposition of society's usual reactions to the disease
of artistic sensitivity, it outlines the horrified reactions of the poet's
neighbors which culminate in the sudden disappearance of the
leper, struck down by a disease caught from the neighbors themselves.

At times, the poems move to an opposite extreme from social
comment, and the anguish expressed in them becomes very personal, although not necessarily inwardly focused. Curiously, the
more intense the feeling of these poems, the wider the range of

reference in them seems to become, a development which corresponds with that of all the novels of Janet Frame's middle and later
period. "Napalm" and "Instructions For Bombing With Napalm"
are poems written in the context of the much-publicized Vietnam
War, whose remoteness from New Zealanders (observed by Godfrey Rainbird, who thought the entire world distant from the South
Pacific) is neatly expressed in "Comment":

> Smell of sweat in armpits dismays more
> than the distant smell of the dead in a jungle war.
> Possible and important are the blind date and alley but not
> the blind man and his plight.
>
> Heaven is curls in place
> guipure over fine embroidered lace, leather
> simulated, not mind membrane, human
> skin woven together on an unknown face.
>
> A clanger dropped at afternoon tea
> is more shocking than a plane-load of bombs on Hanoi.
> The cancelling of a rugby match through rain
> is more lamented than the cancelling of a thousand men. . . .[44]

"The Family Doom" is more openly pessimistic, recalling the earlier
themes of human evolution and man's inheritance of doom. Perhaps
the most intense and moving poem in the entire collection fuses the
general and the particular kinds of pessimism of the other poems:
this is "Yet Another Poem About a Dying Child," whose title implies the generality of the subject but which is nevertheless intensely compassionate towards the individual child it depicts. One is
inevitably reminded of Rilke's depiction of the slow spreading of
deadly disease through the young, growing body of Wera Ouckama
Knoop; the poetical ability is little inferior, but the most striking
difference lies in the increased emphasis in Janet Frame's poem
upon the destructive process of death. Certainly, like Rilke, she
brilliantly interfuses life and death within her imagery:

> He babbles, *they say,* of spring flowers,
>
> Who for six months has lain
> his flesh at a touch bruised violet,
> his face pale, his hate clearer
> than milky love that would smooth over
> the pebbles of diseased bone.

> Pain spangles him like the sun,
> He cries and cannot say why.
> His blood blossoms like a pear tree.
> He does not want to eat or keep
> its ugly windfall fruit.

But is life fused with death in the conclusion of the poem? The death of the young girl of Rilke's poem was a prelude to the honest celebration of the whole of life; but the death of the young boy in Janet Frame's poem leads to a horrifying image that is very far from celebration:

> He must sleep, rocking the web of pain
> till the kind furred spider will come
> with the night-lamp eyes and soft tread
> to wrap him warm and carry him home
> to a dark place, and eat him. [45]

Death is seen here as separate from life and threatening to it, although the reader's response will probably involve a battle between the intended attractiveness of death (the spider is "kind," and has a "soft tread" and "night-lamp eyes") and its repulsive voracity.

This emphasis upon death at the expense of life is something that may have become evident in this study so far, and it is a point that will be returned to in the last chapter. Most of the poems in *The Pocket Mirror* have this weighting, as has already been suggested, although there are several which are merely the five-finger exercises of a writer whose approach to language is almost that of a musician, as if the words had become objects in themselves without referents in the world of things. "My Mother Remembers Her Fellow Pupils at School" is one such poem:

> Dorcas Dryden
> Hetty Peak and Ruby Blake
> Kate Rodley
> Lucy Martella
> Dorcas Dryden
> Hetty Peak and Ruby Blake
> Kate Rodley
> Lucy Martella.
>
> Dorcas Dryden . . . . [46]

Several similar poems are equally pleasant and skilled, and the question raised by them and by the more serious verse is how to evaluate their author as a poet. The technical skill is unquestionably present in all her poetry, but the themes raised are those of her fiction rather than any that might be called inherently "poetical"—which may be another way of saying that she writes novels that are poetic. Certainly the poems are like the stories and sketches in being shards of the major works in most cases: they help to illuminate these both as parables and by showing the development of themes and figures in her writing (as the title poem of this collection shows admirably). At their least valuable, Janet Frame's poems are not trivial but, rather, too obscure; at their best, they are impressive and fully achieved pieces. "Some Thoughts on Bereavement," "Mevagissey Evening," "Beach," and "Declining the Offer of a Pair of Doves" are just a few of these in this collection, the last worthy of substantial quotation:

> Chiefly being, they may best be
> inside me where is room
> for their flying free,
> though how much room
> I do not know,
> I think more than a stone's throw;
> a stone will splash in the well,
> beneath the well is the fire,
> beneath the fire the impossible
> keeps warm and doves may also.
>
> They are said to be Peace. Nothing
> that feeds is Peace, peck
> and get, stab and bleed; would it not
> be wiser to have the reputation of a sea gull
> and improve slowly?
>
> Thank you. Though I do not accept your doves
> I think their twilight colour, their shape
> stay forever with me; a dove in its shape, anywhere
> is free. I who am free
> do not know how to borrow
> my clothes from the morning and night sky
> or the pearl cloud fed by thunder
> worn this year next year and forever . . . .[47]

VIII   Mona Minim and the Smell of the Sun

Even the more enthusiastic follower of Janet Frame's fiction
might be puzzled to see this title, which refers not to a novel but to a
storybook for children she wrote during her first trip to the United
States. A little under a hundred pages in length and charmingly
illustrated by Robin Jacques, it is of interest because, like the stories
and poems, it is basically a serious work.

Mona Minim is a house ant as likable as Uncle Black Beetle; but
she resembles most of Janet Frame's important characters by being
endowed with the subtle sensitivity and motivations of a young girl.
Although her ant community is antlike in many details (there are
references to scent-cones and the complicated procedures of mating), it is basically a human community, with sisters, cousins, and
aunts (parents of course are lacking). The opportunities for parabolic
emphasis are obvious. Mona Minim has reached a crucial point in
her life: she must make her first journey outside the nest and into
the bright sunlight above ground. But once outside, in an incident
reminiscent of the adventures of Lewis Carroll's Alice, she falls into
a crack in a staircase and is left for dead by her companions. When
she wakes, she finds herself adopted by a community of garden ants,
who soon replace the community she has left behind.

After some time, an ant-sized moment of apocalypse occurs: several ants are swept up in a glass by a human child and carried away.
As the only ant familiar with the houses of humans, Mona Minim is
sent by the others to rescue her friends. On her long journey she
finds the newly impregnated queen from her colony and suddenly
realizes the meaning of the courtship and mating ceremonies which
have been occurring for some time. When she finally crawls,
exhausted, into her former home she is appalled to find that she is
unrecognized and that many of her relatives are dead. She finds the
garden ants she is seeking sealed in an ant farm, happy to make their
new colony in a glass case, and also sees amongst them her best
friend, Barbara, now the colony's new princess. Observing their
contentment, she returns home, and finds that she has now
graduated to the status of aunt, experienced in the ways of life and
familiar with the smell of the sun.

This is another parable of the growth of the child to adulthood,
the theme which binds so much of her writing. But here the re-
quirement that children's stories not have sea serpents writhing out

of plugholes removes the customary emphasis upon death and bares some of the more optimistic attributes Janet Frame associates with reality. This does not mean death but change, and the measure of Mona Minim's growth to adulthood is her ability to accept and understand change. Thus, rituals which at first seem bewildering are revealed as meaningful parts of the life of the community— courtship, reproduction, and the establishment of fresh colonies. Life, seen in the previous fiction as being often overordered and sterile, is seen by Janet Frame's little ant as capable of meaning and purpose; the glimpse of the colony trapped behind glass but both aware of their predicament and happily reconciled to it is a key point in a process that is obviously meant to be taken as maturative. And the message is clear: such an optimistic vision is possible only because the ants make up a cooperative society in which every individual is subservient to the whole and each is protective towards the other. Briefly visible as it is, the sun of this children's story is far less searing than in the rest of the fiction.

CHAPTER 8

The Nightmare Garden

I Myth-Making

THE novels to be dealt with in this chapter, *Intensive Care* and *Daughter Buffalo*, belong to the most recent period of Janet Frame's writing, in which the influence of her frequent contact with North America becomes apparent. The focus of the two novels she wrote while based in Dunedin was local; these later works, reflecting the widening experience of their author, are less concerned with satire and parable and more concerned with morality and myth. Consummating the theme of New Zealand's isolation from the rest of the world and its suffering, *Intensive Care* conflates the two domains, bringing to the writer's own country the suffering and destruction that the war in Vietnam laid bare before the world. And *Daughter Buffalo* examines that society which became involved in yet another war after so many centuries of conflict.

The tendency towards mythicization is a fundamental part of Janet Frame's way of writing; yet it has clearly been enhanced by her North American experience. The persona of her writing is always the individual self besieged by a deadly, destructive world which has no other purpose than the annihilation of the individual. Long after the evolution of such a persona and such a vision of life, the writer found herself in a country where that predicament had suddenly become literal:

When you go to the United States, particularly to the cities or anywhere near the main highways, you find yourself almost licensed to be a paranoiac. You learn to be suspicious of every stranger—to fear certain streets during the daylight and the dark. To be a connoisseur of locks and keys, and bolts and chains and bars. Where one used to learn in geography that highways between cities were the life-lines—the life force of a great continent—one may speak now of them being a death force. The fear between person and person is almost palpable.[1]

168

Here is an experience in which the gaps between individuals become evident in bolts and chains, the materialism of society expressed in giant supermarkets and frenzied consumerism, its blind obsession with death revealed on the highways and in the alleys as well as in Southeast Asia. America, it might be said, resembles an enormous Janet Frame novel come to life, and to have witnessed this would have been deeply affecting for the writer. Many of her concerns, born in her own country, are symbolized in the American experience, and her running together of this experience with New Zealand's is an inevitable fulfillment of such themes. In the process, metaphor becomes myth, war becomes War, and a novel results which draws together all the themes of Janet Frame's first overseas period.

Intensive Care is divided into three parts, a practice common enough to the novels. Of these, the first two are realistic, apart from the usual leavening of dream and fantasy that the author sees as a part of everyday existence, while the third part can be seen as a long coda in which the themes of her fiction are cast in mythic form. Part One is subtitled "Kindness Itself, Happiness Itself, and Delphiniums," and is narrated, like the first novel, from a "dead room." The narrator this time is doomed not to an imaginative death but to a complete death—she is Naomi Whyborn, writing from a cancer ward where she is dying after numerous operations. Naomi Whyborn is the married daughter of Tom Livingstone, an elderly war veteran whose last months of life are the subject of this first section. Her opening lyrics are reminiscent of Daphne's in the first novel, although they depict the destructive forces that crush innocent childhood as the forces of war, and not the impersonal forces of nature. Her father is seen when he was a lad of eighteen wounded in the trenches during the Great War and cared for by a young English nurse called Ciss Everest, who becomes the obsession of his life. He returns to Waipori City in the south of New Zealand and to his wife, Eleanor, and lives a long, dull, orderly existence in which he fathers two girls, Naomi and Pearl, and works with the monotonous regularity of a machine, stoking the furnaces of a local cement factory.

When his wife dies and he retires from his job, Tom dashes back to England in an attempt to realize his dream of nearly half a century before. He breaks his leg in a fall and is sent to a "Recovery Unit," Culin Hall, a stately English home containing a grim assembly of the terminally ill, the artificially limbed, the maimed, and patients wearing "hairpieces," glass eyes, false teeth, and so on. There, to his horror, Tom Livingstone finds Ciss Everest at last, a bewigged old lady racked by the agony of terminal cancer. Because she refuses to remember him as the young soldier who loved her in the Great War, he stifles her with her own bedclothes and returns undetected to his home in Waipori City, New Zealand. There he immediately falls into the plump hands of Peggy Warren, a brassy matron known locally as "Furcoat Peg" as a result of her selfless hospitality to the American servicemen who had visited the country during the Second World War. Her motives in befriending Tom are equally generous—she wishes to secure a retirement nestegg for herself. Much of Part One describes Peg's determined invasion of Tom's life, of his ancient house, and finally of his rather seamy bed.

The reader also witnesses two fantasies by which Tom has managed to regulate his long and selfish life: in one of these, it is revealed that he has always imagined himself married to Ciss Everest and as the father of girls called Ciss and May; in the other, he faces the prospect of losing his job in the cement factory by fantasizing the destruction of the machine which threatens to replace him. In order to sustain the first dream, he also fantasizes the murder of Eleanor, imagining that he has pushed her into the slurry pool at the cement factory. There are other significant dreams: he tells his "daughter" May of a dream in which he is in a clearing in a pine forest during wartime, dancing with a group of mysterious figures who pause now and then to refresh themselves by drinking urine and eating rusty nails. At the end of his dream Tom tries to kill the beautiful girl he is dancing with by driving one of the nails through her heart. "May" tells Tom of a more esoteric dream that she has had: in it she is an underground dweller where "bone speech was the accustomed language,"[2] and she climbs to the surface only to find that it is exactly the same as the world she is used to. She is left at the end of the dream holding a stone in her hand.

Tom's actual family is explored in Part One, with some attention paid to his brother, Leonard, also a veteran of the Great War, a former tramp and now a derelict who lives in a cottage in the garden of the old Livingstone family home. Both men have only the Returned Servicemen's Association buildings for comfort and companionship, although of a meager sort. Leonard recalls his early love of books and the forces in society which have turned him away from their magic world forever and confronted him with scraps of reading from newspapers, comics, and hoardings. Tom's older daughter,

Pearl, is seen as a mountainous woman for whom growth has been chiefly physical; she is married to a dusty accountant named Henry Torrance and lives in suburban comfort in Auckland. Their son, Colin, is also an accountant living in a suburb with his family. Pearl is a part-time Child Welfare Officer, who must deal with innumerable victims of child beating and neglect with whom she cannot genuinely sympathize. This first section of *Intensive Care* draws to a close with the reminiscences of the stricken Naomi, Tom's younger daughter, who is married to an American and has three children. She idealizes her childhood in fantasy, imagining her sister and mother dead and that she has an unrecognizably lovable Tom all to herself as a father. But this fantasy becomes grotesque with an hallucinatory scene set on Guy Fawkes night, in which Tom entertains Naomi and the children of the neighborhood at the bonfire with a bizarre mime in which he wears a gas mask and carries a bayonet. A local boy, Donald Parker, hangs himself after indentifying with the dummy burning on top of the bonfire. Part One ends with the sudden death of Tom Livingstone—before marriage to Peggy, to her disgust and disappointment—and the passage of his effects to the local shopkeeper, named next of kin by a man he scarcely knew.

Part Two of *Intensive Care* is called "A Kind of Moss, A Sudden Cry," and transfers its attentions to old Leonard Livingstone in the last weeks of his life. He is different from Tom in certain ways, particularly in being inarticulately half-aware that the forces which produce war in society have also destroyed his chances of ever becoming a whole and hale human being. When he, like Tom, is suddenly stricken by illness, he finds himself being rushed to the next town for "cobalt bomb treatment" in the Maheno Memorial Hospital, a newly built unit in which the ill and dying receive intensive care amidst euphemistically pleasant surroundings. There, for reasons he cannot himself understand, he names Peggy Warren as his next of kin and receives a number of visits from this rather disappointed woman. Shortly after this, Leonard is suddenly sent home from hospital, knowing both that he is expected to die and that the impersonal lack of care shown him by the hospital authorities will continue until "people who speak, learn also to split and solve the alphabet."[3] He then dies, alone and unloved, like his brother.

The narrative of this part turns to Colin Torrance, grandson of Tom Livingstone and son of Pearl. Colin is a typically unimaginative denizen of the suburbs, an accountant who reduces words and values to numbers and appears to be well suited to life in a consumer society. But he too has his obsessive dream, and deserts his wife and children to travel to Australia with Lorna Kimberley, a nineteen-year-old girl from his office with whom he has fallen violently in love. For Lorna, their trip is merely an escapade, and a stern note from her parents sends her contritely back to her family. But Colin has come to rely completely upon her; he follows her to New Zealand and after spending many weeks pestering the girl and her parents, bursts into their neat suburban home one evening and murders them with a shotgun before taking his own life. The grief felt by his parents, Pearl and Henry, vies with their shame at becoming involved in a widely publicized scandal, their confusion over his motivation, and the pressing need to unpack the shopping. Part Two then concludes, with a brief return to Culin Hall and a glimpse there of Tom's former fellow patients now wonderfully adapted to their disabilities with new limbs and organs almost human in their inhuman artificiality, and with Naomi's last lyric, in which she confronts the silence that is her own death.

Part Three, "Pear Blossom to Feed a Nightmare," is set in New Zealand, and chiefly in Waipori City, somewhere in the twenty-first century after an apocalyptic Third World War has left the South Island of New Zealand one of the few places in the world to have escaped devastation. The first narrator of this last part is Colin Monk, one of an elite in Waipori City selected by the government to enforce its Human Delineation Act. This is a Swiftian piece of legislation conceived because the population of the world has exceeded its resources: New Zealand is once more to be the cradle of social legislation via a nightmare act dividing its population into Humans and Animals, the latter to provide the former with food as well as soap, lampshades, and other commodities that have become a little difficult to find since the war. Colin Monk, though he has "a feeling of cleanness" when working with numbers,[4] also has several moral misgivings about the scheme, but like most people manages to accept these after taking part in the mandatory sleep periods the Human Delineation Act insists upon.

Milly Galbraith, who may be thought of as the central figure of *Intensive Care*, takes over the narration at this point. The reader is presented with what she has quietly scribbled in an old notebook, which is later given to Colin Monk just before Classification

Day—Milly's twenty-sixth birthday, on which by coincidence she will be exterminated as an Animal. For Milly, like Erlene Glace, is an outcast because of her apparent abnormality: she is autistic, seeming to others to be sealed deeply within herself. She lives with her "normal" family (her father, a gardener, is in great demand in Waipori City) next to the house Tom Livingstone lived in, which is still vacant and whose old pear tree, massive and laden with fruit, is her favorite shelter. There she sits with a large tomcat called Sam, while she knits beautiful clothes to warm all the people she sees, and has imaginary conversations with "Sandy Monk," the twin she imagines for Colin Monk. Sandy is "a hero, the Reconstructed Man with the mechanical memory, the golden skin, the implanted glossily dead eyes, the Brand-X penis."[5] When she describes this imaginary being to Colin Monk, he feels reassured about the correctness of "H.D" (the Human Delineation Act and its agencies are soon swallowed into euphemistic acronyms).

Milly's diary, a sensitive account of her last weeks of life, survives to prove that she alone is sane and fully human. Unlike her parents, she knows that she is doomed and accepts the prospect calmly, watching the streets of Waipori City fill with the American soldiers who have been brought in to help control this important social experiment. She chooses friends from among the eccentric and the physically disabled who are condemned to die as Animals, and, unlike others, can understand what gifts make them human.

Although the morality of the population is anesthetized by a polished advertising campaign depicting families as "Happy and Free With H.D.,"[6] the smell of death is in the air, and with the approach of Classification Day widespread panic begins (the entire staff of the Botany Department at the local university barricades itself behind a stockade in a Waipori suburb, squirting weed killer and defoliant at all who come near). As winter draws to a close and the day of decision approaches with its meretricious spring, snows bend and break a branch of the old Livingstone pear tree, leading Milly's parents to saw it down in an act which signals the beginning of the end for the girl, removing from her an old friend and a familiar shelter.

Colin Monk narrates the final ten pages of the novel, describing the aftermath of Classification Day. There is an elegant cocktail party at which all present decently accept the rather unpleasant business of mass cremations on the plains beyond the city; all strive to present themselves as "normal," for with the slaughter of so much of the population normality becomes a fugitive concept. Even a lingering cold can condemn one to classification as an Animal. When Colin Monk reads the dead Milly's diary and realizes her gifts and understanding as well as his own moral repulsiveness, he is obliged to suppress his new self-knowledge for fear of appearing abnormal; like the others, he agrees that the diary is a forgery. But *Intensive Care* ends optimistically. It is revealed that Colin and a handful of others have surreptitiously avoided the mandatory sleep days that have numbed the conscience of many Humans; and in a final irony, it is shown that so many people have been condemned as "abnormal" that the population is nearly wiped out. The new elite is formed of the lame and the halt, people then cripple themselves in order to survive, and Colin Monk has to acknowledge the existence of his "twin," Sandy, in order to gain newly protective imaginative powers.

II *Dreams of Fair Women*

Like many of the earlier novels, *Intensive Care* is concerned with the difference between dream and imagination, with the destructive, sapping nature of the first and the vital, humanizing capacities of the second. In fact, its first and second sections are almost a handbook on the subject, recalling Bob Withers's escape into the yellow dream of newspaper and radio, as well as the fate of the dreamers of Little Burgelstatham. What makes *Intensive Care* such a distinctive—and ambitious—work is its desire to follow to a conclusion all the destructive processes of delusion and dream, in order to show how these processes relate to the barbarism of the Age of War. The novel shows that unfulfilled dreams lead not just to personal disappointment and tragedy but to violence and war, that the dreaming suburbs and cities produce a warring society, and that only the act of imagination can make people care enough to love and communicate and tame their desire to destroy.

This theme is worked out within the Livingstone family (a name which, like Withers, suggests a low capacity for life), where the effects of dreams upon generations of humans is explored. Tom Livingstone is the key figure: he is seen first as smooth-chinned youth caught up in the Great War not because he is committed to an ideal but because there had been company in killing and he liked company. After all, the world was full of people, wasn't it, ordinary people going their ordinary way and killing when they were asked to kill? And when he returned from the War he was a frightened man—afraid of poverty, of becoming a drunk like his father, known all over the pubs of Waipori City, of losing his job as furnace-man in the cement factory, of being overwhelmed by his wife's family with their oblong faces and large chins, her sisters like female cardinals and her brothers like bishops, all making blackmailing use of their exclusive personal God to form a protective body for Eleanor, trying to preserve Tom's inflexible love as if it had been a gold bar that no amount of heat or pressure could soften or twist . . . .

Returned from the War, Tom had become a member of the Union and the Lodge, a respected citizen. He who had fought and been wounded in the trenches attended lessons in the art of applying tourniquets . . . .

A returned soldier, entitled to wear the R.S.A. badge on his lapel . . . and a passion . . . for Ciss Everest alias the War . . . .[7]

In this crucial passage, Janet Frame traces the development of brutalizing instincts during the life of one man and shows how these instincts lead to a life that is conducted in fear and expressed in those numerous little acts of Safety which keep authentic experience at bay, and finally how it leads to an existence that is itself a form of slumber, producing only the cement of which the gray factories, mental hospitals, and prisons are made.

The dream which prolongs Tom's slumber is his dream of Ciss Everest, the English girl who nursed him in 1917; since it is incapable of fulfillment or of reconciliation with reality, it leads to violence and to the withdrawal of the love he ought to have given his wife and children. Nor is Ciss even a poignantly remembered lover: she is "Miss War of 1917," and in loving her, Tom is merely keeping alive his love of war. It is this that he brings home with him, symbolized by his gas mask and by the bayonet his brother finds after his death to have been regularly and lovingly polished for years. Ciss is an old flame he can never forget, but the metaphor is all too much alive, symbolized in the Flame of War he keeps alive for decades at the cement works' kiln. The brutality and violence of war lie in the gray factories and prisons formed of cement and in the slaughterhouse next door to the cement factory, outside which gather the sheep as Tom himself gathered with his company for the slaughter of the Great War. And for forty years, too, there is war between Tom and his wife, and with his two daughters, who abandon their father at the first opportunity.

The dream creates violence whenever it strikes against the reality it tries to deny. When Tom confronts the woman he has loved since the Great War, he rather unreasonably expects her not to have changed, although she is nearly seventy years of age. Instead, he sees what time and fevers have burned away from her:

an old tart with dyed hair, a life-sized doll mechanized to cry out in pain every few minutes, to groan in the night, to whisper her pleas for morphine. The Ciss Everest Cancer Doll. This way to see the Ciss Everest Cancer Doll. Real hair that can be washed, dried, combed, permed. Real face that can be made up to hide the age and the tears. This way, this way to the Ciss Everest Cancer Doll, Doll of the Years, Doll of Forty-Five years, This way to Miss World War I![8]

Worse than this, she counters his dream with one of her own and refuses to recognize him as an individual. The only alternative to the false dream is an attempt to alter reality till it conforms to the dream: and Tom stifles reality quite literally by pushing the old woman's face into her bedclothes. For years, this sort of violence has been his method of dealing with reality, as is suggested by the episode in which he fantasizes the destruction of the machine that has been designed to destroy his job.

Returning empty-handed to Waipori City, Tom needs a substitute for the dead Ciss. In Peggy Warren he finds a compromise between dream and reality. Her resemblance to Ciss Everest is repeatedly referred to; she is "Miss World War Two"[9]; "war" is imbedded in her name and, as a pun, in her occupation. But even this shabby dream-girl cannot be won—reality intervenes again with the sudden death of Tom.

The experience of Tom Livingstone dominates *Intensive Care*, since it is intended to be paradigmatic for his descendants. Self-interested people like Tom turn their love inward to form dreams which destroy their relationships with others because they attempt to subjugate others to their own demands. All the Tom Livingstones of the world have mind-mountains like Ciss Everest over whose cliffs their families and acquaintances are forced to tumble. A society of deluded dreamers cares only for itself and not for individuality, and produces the malevolent, impersonal "intensive care" found in the Maheno Memorial Hospital, with its terrifying "cobalt bomb treatment," and in Culin Hall (whose name contains "kiln" and "killing"), where the casualties of the war that has no end become fitted with the devices which symbolize the dehumanizing processes of the age. Intensive care is worthless, but individual care is vital, expressed as a love which radiates outward from each individual to join humans in a world of imaginative celebration.

Although far more clearly an outcast than Tom, Leonard Livingstone is caught up in his older brother's pattern of experience. He is possibly one of the most tragic figures created by Janet Frame, for he has once been a sensitive and imaginatively gifted child but has steadily moved through all those agencies society employs to rob such people of their gifts:

Leonard's formal education finished at primary school as soon as he found a job in a local garage. At school his most wonderful discovery had been books and reading. Then in his final year, because he was brighter than the other boys, he and the second boy in the class were given a reward by the headmaster—the task of weeding and planting the school garden, while the other pupils toiled at their lessons in the classroom. "There's nothing a boy likes better than to get out of the classroom, I know," the headmaster said. Remembering this exchange of pen, pencil, ink, and paper, for hoe, spade, and gardening fork, Leonard thought with bitterness of the long blue days outside in the garden planting, weeding, staking, and trying to understand why a supposed reward should have inflicted such punishment. That year he used to cry in bed at night, his tears dropping with the candlewax into the candlestick as he pored over a book that he'd had to steal from the classroom as he now spent so little time there. When he left school he gave up the habit of reading . . . .[10]

Ahead of this parabolic experience lies further stifling of the boy's individuality, as well as the inevitable reward of War. Both Leonard and Tom and all the young men they represent are sent to the Great War stripped of the imaginative innocence which alone could protect them from its horror, and they can find protection only in the false dream. Leonard's dream is far "purer" and more poignant than Tom's: with an imaginary wife and son he fantasizes a long period spent upon a balmy Mediterranean island whose language, although foreign, they all immediately and intensely understand. But this dream fades into the reality of his drunken, desolate later life in which he wanders about the countryside beyond Waipori City hunt-

ing food to eat, working casually in laboring jobs, and finally retiring
to a primitive existence in the hut in the garden of his brother's
home, surrounded by forbidding pine trees. He is at the rim of
society, neither a gifted outcast nor, on the other hand, a blind
ritualist like his brother. His only solace is in the Returned Servicemen's Association buildings about which he shuffles, endlessly
searching for "news" in the daily papers, a sad habit that is the only
remnant of his childhood obsession with the imaginative world of
literature. His imagination has atrophied, and all that remains is the
mindless physical action, the dried, repetitive habit.

The stories of Tom Livingstone's two daughters, Naomi and
Pearl, help to deepen this discussion of the individual and the family
in the society obsessed by violence and delusion. The mountainous
Pearl, herself an Everest of flesh, is a suburban ritualist like so many
of Janet Frame's disapproved characters. Her accountant husband is
almost completely devoid of a recognizable personality, and their
life together is organized to keep feeling, understanding, and emotion at bay. Now a grandmother herself, Pearl is associated with one
of society's many institutions which cares intensely but without true
feeling: this is the child protection organization in whose service
Pearl is daily exposed to the cruel wounds one generation inflicts
upon the next. She helps the scarred children efficiently, but never
understands that they are the victims of a war and that they have
suffered from a loss of their individuality which can only be repaired
through being given a selfless love that she herself does not possess.
But she has at least the acumen to perceive that her grandchildren,
whom she dominates and controls, need protection from their own
father, Colin; and finally, she realizes that his selfish neglect of them
and his violent murders are in some way the product of his society,
and specifically of her own relationship with her father.

Much of that relationship is filtered to the reader through the
lyrics of Naomi and by means of the prose reminiscences which
occur in Part One. In the lyrics, the innocence of childhood is
crushed by War and not simply by the destructive forces of life; in
the prose reminiscences, this process becomes mythical. During the
Second World War, as children, their play became infected by War.
In an imaginary submarine, "Pearl and Naomi, their pretty blue-
and white-print dresses with the gathered yokes and the puffed
sleeves, torn and stained with oil, died side by side with the sub-

marine crew"[11]; while, trapped within an equally imaginary bomber,

> Naomi and Pearl in their pleated skirts with the calico bodices and knitted jumpers, brown and green, died with the pilot and co-pilot when the plane crashed. Died. Died and died and died in the War. Because the War never ended, they forgot to find the trick of ending it, because they didn't know it was still going on and on and on, and if they saw it was there they kept looking away and pretending it wasn't there, like with the mental people.[12]

It is not only their inability to return from fantasy to reality which keeps the War alive; their father's obsession with War keeps its violence alive in his relationship with the two girls. This is the point of the Guy Fawkes scene, which casts his attitude in the form of a myth. His gas-masked war dance and the "death" of the local boy upon the fire (itself reminiscent of and related to the death of Francie Withers) are not Naomi's literal memories but a condensation of her childhood experiences with Tom, and the myth represents the behavior of all fathers who send all sons to be burned in the fires of War.

Naomi's sad fantasy in which she idealizes her relationship with her father is, again, the inevitable outcome of their destructive relationship. Once again it is a dream of love that has gone wrong, born in selfishness and expressed in the desire for the deaths of Naomi's mother and sister. But there is a little of her Uncle Leonard in Naomi, and through the idealizing untruths comes an important understanding about her father's experience. She wishes that he had brought back from the War not an identity disk on a string about his neck but "a clay tablet from Egypt pictured with storks and ibises and beautiful hieroglyphics—some of the first writing . . . a piece of civilization, to be rescued at all costs from the War . . . a piece of hope . . . for the future of man."[13] Instead, of course, the man brings back hopelessness and his inarticulate speech; their lack of communication forces both into their false dreams and causes Naomi's own cancerous decay. A man like Tom Livingstone produces the mountain of fleshly cares which is Pearl, or the steady decay of the flesh which engulfs Naomi.

Pearl's son, Colin Torrance, is also doomed to reenact the futile pattern of earlier generations; even his name promises torrents of

killing. Like his grandfather, he has a stable, repetitiously safe existence, but dashes overseas in an effort to realize an obsessive dream
of love. His act is far more disastrous than his grandfather's, for it
involves so many other people; it is also more realistically enacted,
its point being that it could happen to anyone, that all people carry
in their heads dreams which could destroy them. The woman he so
frantically loves is in reality a silly girl for whom the trip to Australia
is an exciting game which quickly bores her, although soon Colin
has surrendered his entire existence to her. She cannot return his
love, and marriage is out of the question; the wrongheadedness of
the whole affair is constantly hinted at in images of narcissistic
reflection in pools and streams, suggesting a self-love which will end
in the violent destruction of all things that do not match it. Colin's
final slaughter of the Kimberleys is an everyday event, the product
of the dreaming society in which it occurs.

Tragically, no character in the novel's first two parts breaks out of
his dream to understand that he has been asleep. Truth comes in the
guise of dream itself—in Tom's strange, parabolic dream of the
dance in the pine forest, and in May's dream of climbing from her
subterranean home to an everyday world which it exactly resembles. Just as two mirrors held together reflect a "correct" image of
the world, the dream within the dream shows truth to those who can
see it, namely, that "All dreams lead back to the nightmare garden"
of War.[14] But truths of this importance can be detected only by
those possessing a vital, creative imagination and a sensitivity to
language, capacities long lost to those who have been blinded by the
illusion of sight.

III   *Culin, Kiln, Colin, Killing*

Culin Hall, the stately English home where old Tom Livingstone
finds Ciss Everest, stands at the center of the novel's mythological
structure. It represents the brutality of the English aristocracy with
their ingrained habit of killing (each ward is named after an eminent
fox hunter). The implication is that the germs of the Great War are
to be found in institutions such as Culin Hall; and as a Recovery
Unit, it also stands for the kind of society produced by War and
producing War, specializing in an "intensive care" which leaves
Tom feeling "neglected and unwanted"[15] after he has been treated
as if he were a machine in need of oiling and repair. This metaphor
dominates all the Culin Hall sequences:

"Wheelchairs first, wheelchairs first."

It was tyrannical. Flashing silver, the seats and backs grained plastic, like frowning human foreheads, the wheels new hard rubber, the spokes whirling, the privileged wheelchairs moved towards the dining room.[16]

The humanity of individual bodies is confused—and sometimes fused—with mechanical things at Culin Hall: a woman is described, for example, as wearing "glasses with black rims like the rims of the wheels and the wheelchairs. Her eyes gave the impression of spinning, spinning, their spokes whirling."[17] The annihilation of the individual is illustrated in a remarkable hallucination in which people's bodies are taken apart in a search for their essential selves, a raid for their "me," as it is called.[18]

When the narrative of *Intensive Care* follows Tom back to Waipori City, the things Culin Hall stood for constantly reappear in words and images. This is one of the major triumphs of the novel, whose effectiveness relies upon its author's ability to dissolve the mythical in the everyday in a manner which reminds the reader of the presence of War in everything. The author's verbal dexterity is used in a medley of puns which, as has been seen, bare the truth in names like "Colin" and "Culin" and words like "kiln" by linking them to "killing," show "war" and "whore" lurking in "Warren," have the keeper of the Flame obsessed by his old flame, and so on. The same kind of echoing occurs in incidents. The inhumanity of "Killing" Hall is symbolized by the gas mask on the face of the old war veteran, which turns his appearance into that of a machine. In the realistic descriptions of Peg Warren lie features and actions that are those of the mythical Ciss Everest. The slaughterhouse next to the cement factory in Waipori City, with its mob of sheep queuing up to die, demands to be seen as a symbol of the Great War. The cement factory, with its Flame and its kiln, infuses the gray concrete walls of Waipori City with burning and killing. A harmless wait for a bus produces this disturbing vision:

All these women with their infants crowding from the bus, with never a thought for those in wheelchairs—ah, there was someone, a folding chair that the driver unpacked from the luggage boot and there was a young man—Peter?—being helped into it by his companion, a woman—his mother? his wife?—and now he was being wheeled away into the walking dancing skipping peopled world, as if the bus had delivered him, like a new product, all the way from the Recovery Unit.[19]

It is as if the bus had delivered all kinds of symbols like this straight from the noble Culin Hall, for its meanings steadily overlay the humble surfaces of Antipodean life.

The Maheno Memorial Hospital reminds the reader all too readily of Culin Hall, as it is expected to: it too is an institution which destroys people and then cares for their remains with the chill thoroughness of a computer. When Leonard Livingstone is sent there for the treatment with such a terrifying name, he finds himself wishing to die in peace amongst the hospital's trim lawns and artfully planted trees. But since he is a hopeless case, he is bundled back home to die, an act which makes him understand the true nature of the institution:

They were sending him home to die because they couldn't be bothered with him. They did that, he knew, with some patients, particularly the old and unwanted. In fifty or a hundred years' time maybe they'd get rid of them by killing them off. This was the way that sort of thing started. Not caring. People not caring for other people.[20]

And this mass slaughter is precisely what happens in the novel's final section.

IV   Intensive Care and After

After reaching back in time to the Great War for a myth that will help to explain the destructiveness of twentieth-century man, Janet Frame shows the forces of destruction in contemporary society leading inevitably, beneath their superficial order and goodwill, towards carelessness and failure of communication. Leonard sees this process at work as, near death, he contemplates the huge pear tree in his brother's garden:

Sycamore trees, pine trees, the big Livingstone pear tree might remain through centuries uncircled by human language. Unvoweled, unconsonanted, unexclaimed, a man must soon die. Even the alphabetical atom may be subdued by the hydrogen atom, unless those who work with language, unless people who speak, learn also to split and solve the alphabet.[21]

The fate of the pear tree represents the fate of mankind, and when it is cut down, near the end of the novel, its demise signals the death of hope, although the faint stirrings of originality and imagination in

Colin Monk's mind at the close of the novel keep alive a small possibility of human regeneration.

The futuristic section of the novel sees the extrapolation of the novel's earlier themes, and shows what lies ahead for the society which does not care. Although it contains flashes of humor (as with the vision of the hysterical Botany Department at bay in a Dunedin suburb), this section is fundamentally serious and literal. What gives it credibility is the familiarity of its picture of a brave new world. Milly Galbraith's scrawled diary is not new to those readers who know of Anne Frank; a "final solution" was reached in Nazi Germany during the Second World War, when human beings were defined as exterminable subhumans; neutral euphemisms such as "Humane Department," "Early Disposal Unit," and acronymical agencies like "DOSP" and "MOB" are a part of the contemporary sensibility and not merely a projection onto the future. The vision of a society turning to its gardens in order to avoid making moral decisions about the impending death of neighbors and friends, as the inhabitants of Waipori City do with the approach of Delineation Day, is not completely unfamiliar; while no reader could pretend that contemporary society has any special tenderness for those who do not conform to its patterns. And there is much that is familiar in the vision of American troops in a foreign country, helping an inept government to slaughter its own people. Milly, with her innocent wisdom, clarifies the significance of the section in which she appears:

if you think I paint a grim picture of what will happen, then I can only say that you who are reading this are lucky not to be living in the time I write of. Do not be deceived—you may be living in it and not know, because two times can live together and the one doesn't know that the other time is living because if you're in one time whatever would make you want to think there is another there going on through the light of day and the dark of night? Is your world my world?[22]

The twentieth century, it is stated, is an age of barbarism concealed by convenient fictions; what small steps, the author asks, need be taken before the euphemistic, anesthetized slaughter envisaged in the Human Delineation Act is reached? Is not the brave new world of the novel's final section merely a version of the present?

The significance of this section, and indeed of the entire novel, relies heavily on the credibility of the young autistic girl, Milly Galbraith, whose diary shames Colin Monk into self-knowledge. Milly is a touching figure, rather like a princess from a fairy tale, with her innocent desire to clothe the world and her amazing ability to knit and sew garments at a speed that is visible. Her clear fore-knowledge of what awaits her when she turns twenty-six and her record of her last days upon earth are unsettling to read, and far different from the parts narrated by Colin Monk. But she is also a familiar figure, despite all this, and it would be very difficult to argue that she represents any advance whatever upon the figure of Erlene Glace, or that her chats with the enviably equipped "Sandy Monk" offer more than a variation upon Erlene's conversations with Uncle Black Beetle. The language of her diary also presents difficul-ties, with its unconvincing misspellings and unusual command of grammar and self-expression for a girl who is supposed to fear words and whose speech is described as "mixed up too."[23] What she wants is her "own language, for if you have your own language nobody can take it away from you"[24]; but she writes her diary in the language of society, causing the novel to lack what it very much needs in order to consummate the themes it has set out. There is a need here for a virtuoso display of poetry, a performance from the edge of the al-phabet that will bring to life the novel's constant claims that a new, healing language is needed in the contemporary world. As it is, the prize for poetry in *Intensive Care* must go to Naomi Whyborn, a far less approved character than Milly, but one who is given the gift of tongues that Milly needs.

V   Daughter Buffalo

Despite these shortcomings, *Intensive Care* is a notable and dis-turbing work, containing writing that is often as impressive as any-thing written ten years before and also doing much to explain earlier themes. Nevertheless, the appearance of *Daughter Buffalo* so soon after is not surprising, as the earlier novel is not fully satisfying and needs a coda. The briefer novel requires a knowledge of *Intensive Care* for some of its difficulties to be overcome and for its hidden substantiality to be revealed, and in turn completes some of the ideas that that novel raised.

Daughter Buffalo is set almost entirely in America, the first of the author's novels to have this distinction. It consists, in effect, of a

dialogue between two personae, one American and the other New
Zealand by origin: these are presented as Talbot Edelman, a young
American Jewish doctor from a wealthy New York society family,
and Turnlung, a seventy-five-year-old writer from New Zealand
who is visiting New York. One of Turnlung's lyrics—speaking of age
and impending death and presenting a view of man as an animal—
opens the novel. It introduces the Latin phrase which becomes the
novel's refrain: "Squamata, sauria, serpentes".[25] There follows the
first part, entitled "D"—for "Death"—and narrated by Talbot
Edelman, who describes his privileged Long Island upbringing with
a mother who presides over a kitchen full of gadgets and a father
who spends his wealth upon paintings which look quite like the
works of acknowledged masters. Two events alter the course of
Edelman's early life: first, his father's revelation that he was brought
up in a Jewish ghetto in Brooklyn; and second, his family's treatment of his aged grandfather. The old man is ninety-three, "like a
character strayed out of *War and Peace* as Pierre strayed on the
battlefield."[26] Talbot's parents send him to a geriatric home where
he is proclaimed "happy and settled"[27] and given intensive and
impersonal care. The young Talbot is shocked by the callousness of
his family, and feels that the old man has been "dropped like a piece
of garbage" from the lives of the Edelmans,[28] as if flushed down the
garbage disposer of which his mother is so proud.

These events prompt Talbot Edelman to become a student of
death instead of a student of embryology. In his reshaped life, he
lives in a shabby apartment with a girl called Lenore, a student of
"sexually unfinished children"[29] and the daughter of a former minor
official in Nazi Germany. Talbot Edelman adopts a dog called Sally
for a pet, and proceeds to mutilate her in a series of operations,
removing an eye, numerous glands, and her sexual organs, and
breaking and resetting her limbs, while all the time attending to her
daily needs with the care and attention of a loving master. This
gruesome fusion of love and death is seen again when Edelman and
Lenore "share" the death of a boy of six and then copulate to consummate the experience. Then Edelman meets Turnlung, who
strikes him as resembling his own late grandfather. Turnlung too is a
self-declared student of death, who has come to a country which, he
thinks, is death's natural home. He settles, appropriately, in an
apartment between a funeral home and a terminal.

Part Two, subtitled "The Bees in the Flowering Currant," begins with Turnlung's long survey of the American landscape which surrounds him, where "death appears to be more important than life, where the secrecy of death is found even in the country's government,"[30] where death is domesticated, "a land as haunted by death and guilt as the Ancient Mariner, though here the mariner is young, he is the young Marine who has recently killed."[31] "I write from a land," declares Turnlung, "where the obsession is the death of all and the resurrection of all, including the people, if they can be found and distinguished among the dead and resurrected flavors, colors, fish, insects, animals, plants, seasons, images."[32] Where Edelman is making a scientific study of death, Turnlung prefers his own literary approach, for "Language, at least, may give up the secrets of life and death, leading us through the maze to the original Word as monster or angel."[33]

Turnlung then begins to recollect his own youth in the "cemetery wilderness" which is New Zealand.[34] One of his earliest memories is of finding a dead cat: "It lay under the flowering currant bush where honeybees swarmed about the clusters of tiny purple bell-like flowers, and for me the purple flowers and the golden bees became part of the smell and sight and sound of death."[35] Another memory recalls the death of his grandfather during his own childhood, a memory which leads to an exploration of the idea that death yields authenticity, a notion central to this part of the novel. He remembers the sudden importance of a man run over by a truck, and dwells on the mass suicide of a family which has elected not to let a backward son live on alone after the natural deaths of his parents. He remembers his Aunt Kate, whose wish to die an authentic death was thwarted by her family's desire that she die euphemistically. And he recalls two "literary deaths" described to him by a schoolmistress friend: the first is the death of the friend's older sister at sixteen, a loss which sent the surviving sister to Browning, Poe, and Whitman for Romantic verse about the death of maidens; the second is the later death of a younger sister, which presents itself as a shattering physical loss, something before which romantic escapism crumbles.

Part Three, "Down Instant Street, Jewels, and the Finishing Touch," returns to Talbot Edelman, with a glimpse of death upon the streets of New York in three briefly sketched scenes. Edelman then keeps an appointment with Turnlung at the Natural History Museum, and there follows the growth of a friendship between the two men which culminates in a lengthy embrace on a sofa in

Turnlung's apartment. Afterward, they go together to Central Park Zoo, where Turnlung becomes particularly fascinated by a mother buffalo and its six-month-old female offspring. Then Turnlung becomes faint and, recovering, begins to recall his former companion, a homosexual called Selwyn, now dead; Edelman, sensing that Turnlung's final decline has begun, offers him a home in his apartment. When he returns there it is to find that his dog, Sally, is dying, and he responds by becoming sexually aroused. When the dog dies he feels that his last substantial link with Lenore is severed and shortly afterwards she breaks her engagement to him and departs. Turnlung replaces her, making Edelman think increasingly of himself aged, as he himself reminds Turnlung of his own youth. But Edelman soon regrets his hospitality to the older man, and attempts to have him put in a geriatric hospital. His rejection is thorough: he gives up the shabby apartment and, to the joy of his parents, rents a new and expensive one overlooking Central Park South. But the announcement of the breaking of his engagement shocks them, and when his father shows him one of his newly bought paintings, entitled "Noon," Edelman finds that he sees through its safe forms and tints with a new vision which reveals its nightmare reality.

The fourth part of *Daughter Buffalo*, "Man, Dog, Buffalo, Do You Know Your Name?" opens with sixteen pages of Turnlung's poetry, in which he reviews aspects of his life and resolves that his future lies with the "daughter" born of the embrace with Edelman on the sofa—the young buffalo they saw at the zoo. Shortly afterwards, when Edelman contritely visits him, he finds Turnlung dead in his apartment. Edelman rejects him in death as he did in life, but is soon surprised when, inquiring at the embassy of Turnlung's country, he is told that Turnlung does not officially exist at all. Later, he finds it impossible to locate the whereabouts of Turnlung's old apartment, and when he goes to Central Park Zoo he is told that the baby buffalo has been transferred elsewhere. In a final dream, after the accidental death·of his parents, Edelman imagines himself surrounded by a swarm of people at which he himself is being auctioned, limb by limb and piece by piece. Only when disembodied does he feel that he exists authentically.

In a brief epilogue, a familiar revelation is made: the entire novel has been written by Turnlung, an eighty-five-year-old writer in a geriatric hospital in New Zealand, from which he has never travelled. He has written his novel outside, in the fierce sun, before a

scene exactly like the one in the last picture bought by Edelman's
father, entitled "Noon."

VI   *The American Way of Death*

Daughter Buffalo is undeniably an American novel in that an
awareness of the contemporary American experience permeates
nearly every scene and motivates the work. When Turnlung says of
America, "Here, death has been domesticated,"[36] or, "I write from
a land where the obsession is the death of all and the resurrection of
all,"[37] his voice is like the author's, his vision Janet Frame's own.
The novel is punctuated by scenes describing a land "which has fed
so many of the hungry and the poor" and yet will "at the same time
continue to secrete the milk of death."[38] Here is what Turnlung sees
as he tours New York:

When I set out toward the rivers, taking the crosstown bus part of the way, I
found that there was no place to *be*, and this, within my waking dream of
death, seemed ominous. The two rivers flow farther and farther from the
streams of man and if a man can get to stand near them he realizes that the
water does not even grant him a shadow, nor does it grant a shadow to the
city, while the sun itself cannot dredge from it a light-glimmer of gold. The
city rivers, filled with death, have long ago given up speaking of death;
indeed they are so far past speaking of it that as a kind of seasonal irony, in
springtime, they allow a green and yellow fire of grass and forsythia to break
out along the riverbanks of the Hudson Valley, above the opaque polluted
waters, flaunting the green and yellow life that bears the seeds of decay.[39]

And later Edelman, his awareness of such things maturing in his
relationship with Turnlung, sees a terrible truth in an everyday
American institution:

I remember what my race experienced, and sometimes as a child in our clean
home I would dream of what I had heard of the concentration camps, the
time and motion studies put into effect to enable an inmate to go from one
place fully clothed, and, divesting himself of everything without and much
within, arrive at the end-place with nothing, yet with an economic com-
pleteness for death; and I felt the strange parallel of the supermarkets
where instead of divesting ourselves of goods we collect them, we arrive
laden at the exits where, exchanging our goods and receiving the green or
blue stamp blessing, we come out into the street with the hope that in some
way we have replaced the processions of death with those of life.[40]

When he rents his new, expensive apartment, he looks at a city which is a living hell:

People in the streets ran in the rain-panic that overcomes those in the cities, cowering from the torrents of oil- and litter-filled water flung at them by lurching cabs and buses, while the vents in the street hissed their suddenly active hell-steam in hot wet spirals, all in a rain so remote from its original blessing that the people might have been forgiven for having the look of the damned in being forced to bear the meaninglessness and inconvenience of city weather. I looked out of my window at the darkened city with its lights already burning at midday and at the pall of unbreathable air breaking and sliding down the rain into millions of lung-closets beneath. Now and then lightning split the sky, scissoring the seams of the pall which closed them together after it had passed, invisibly stitched by the threads trailing from incinerator and factory chimneys and car and plane exhausts.[41]

The imagination is always conceived by Janet Frame as a process which detects the terrifying and the beautiful in the everyday; but here it is clear that the imagination needs to penetrate nothing in America, for the truth lies everywhere bared or at least visible beneath the barest membrane. In this novel, the skull is not beneath the skin but around it, in the helmets of the riot police and the "young Marine who has recently killed."

But America, on the other hand, is also the epitome of Safety, that talisman whose complicated rituals of worship Janet Frame has described so extensively in her fiction so far. This novel contains numerous descriptions of the American preoccupation with order and automation, with the retreat from a death which is nevertheless all too readily visible. These attempts to deny a death which is everywhere lead to some ludicrous situations epitomized in Turnlung's witty parody:

> At my back I hear
> the constant whirring of the air conditioner . . .[42]

—the chariot of modern times whose whizzing fan cleanses from the air the stench of death and decay. Edelman, with his death-student's eye for disaster, sees many of these ludicrous situations. As a medical student, he always marvelled at the efficiency with which hospitals dealt with automobile accidents. In "one automobile accident . . . the bodies and the wrecked car were removed at once and the lake of blood and oil erased so swiftly that unless I were to disbelieve what I had seen I was tempted to label it an instant Accident, a packaged deal like cornflakes, with the rescuers included in the bottom of the pack."[43]

But what Edelman refers to as "field deaths" are a different thing. One of these involves an elderly vagrant who collapses in a busy street before him and then expires lengthily. He watches the people in the street walk fastidiously around the old man's body as they try to ignore his existence, until their movements begin to look like a game. But Edelman soon realizes that he is no better than they:

Through about seven minutes of paralysis my body, my mind provided as though through a dispenser activated by the dying man, images of the warmth and comfort of my Long Island home. I saw, in particular, the bathroom. I felt the soothing touch of the hot water, the softness of the blue-furred toilet seat, the pleasurable texture of the big towels on the heated towel rack, and though I tried, with the dying man in front of me, to concentrate on his plight and his need for help, I found I could not concentrate; my mind groped about in search of all the known means of the instant disposal I was used to.[44]

This describes perfectly the Safety-obsessed mind threatened by danger. Moments later, he watches a man walking a dog, who stops by the corpse only to allow the animal to relieve itself into a plastic bag the man carries with him for such moments: the streets must not become littered, except with human bodies. A few nights later, Edelman is walking his deformed dog, Sally, through the streets and comes across another man, this time shot and robbed while walking his dog; he swings into a mindless routine of safe activities, summoning an ambulance through the entry phone of a nearby building and later calling the correct authorities in order that the man's dog might be cared for. But he realizes that he himself does not genuinely care for the fate of the wounded man.

VII *Man, Dog, Buffalo, Do You Know Your Name?*

Death dogs the footsteps of Edelman very literally; this concern with animal imagery needs careful scrutiny because it is relatively new to Janet Frame's fiction, having emerged only in *Intensive Care*. It can be seen, however, as a continuation of a pervasive theme, that of the evolution of man from his bright origins to a dark twentieth century in which all his powers are spent except his will to destroy. Edelman and Lenore are important agents of this particular theme, for they both bear a doomed heritage which makes their union a bizarre one. Lenore is a product of Nazi Germany, with its tradition of barbarism and legalized murder; Edelman is a Jew, with a tradition of suffering and persecution at the hands of the kind of person who has fathered Lenore. Their union is of persecutor and prey, and their love contains hate, while the product of their liaison is their "child," the mutilated dog Sally. Symbolically, they represent man and woman in contemporary America, practitioners of a sort of national necrophilia, of which many images occur in the novel. The most specific of these, perhaps, is the one Turnlung imports from New Zealand—a childhood memory of the fusion of love and death in which two dogs lock in coitus upon the street while a linesman lies in his death agony above them, entangled in the live wires at the top of a power pole. Edelman expresses his "love" for Sally by steadily mutilating her body, behavior that is the logical end point of the impersonal, inhuman way in which society cares for its members in the face of death. Sally's death is sexually arousing for Edelman, like the "shared" death of the small boy that was a prelude to intercourse with Lenore. Turnlung, even more aware of this national trait than Edelman, sees an image for the country—and for twentieth-century man himself—in a mulberry tree that is being consumed by silkworms which hatch and immediately copulate, reproduce and immediately die, in a senseless progression of events which have lost all meaning. Life and death come close together in another of Turnlung's images from childhood, this time of the dead cat under the flowering currant bush. By the time the novel proper concludes with Edelman's dream of being auctioned limb by limb, this image of cat and currant bush has developed into a metaphor for New York City itself, depicting a hive of fecund activity centered upon a rotting corpse.

The death of Sally and the departure of Lenore mark a turning point for Edelman, a chance to accept the possibilities represented by Turnlung. His actual family might be thought of as typically American in its middle-class wealth, bound by ritual and turning carefully away from an ugly past as they turn away from their ancient grandfather. Edelman's second "family," formed with Lenore and Sally, may be seen as a grim metaphor for the American and even human family, whose partners are doomed by years of tradition and blindness to make war in place of love, their product an innocent

victim that is perverted and then destroyed by the deliberate destructiveness of its parents. Sally—who is said to have died of a
human disease—stands for the neglected children of the earlier
fictional marriages, such as Colin Torrance's or that of his mother
before him; the visible scars of the maimed dog represent the bat-
tered minds of the young. And they also stand for false science,
something for which Edelman, as a doctor, is responsible. One
point made in this novel is that the scientific approach to life, found
in intensive care, is a powerful force in the dehumanization of society.

Turnlung represents for Edelman the possibility of forming a
third "family," of a metaphoric kind. Ever since the death of his
grandfather, Edelman has found himself sexually attracted to old
men, and his acceptance of the dying Turnlung would be, he
realizes, an act of acceptance of the authenticity of his death. Their
long embrace upon Turnlung's sofa is, for Turnlung, a copulative act
producing a daughter, the young buffalo they both saw at the zoo; it
is an act of sincere communion unlike the perverted sexuality of
Edelman's relationship with Lenore. Edelman is more reluctant
than Turnlung, however, not because of any homosexual overtones
in the relationship but because he feels that he is leaving Safety
behind to plunge into Experience. But once committed, he feels

love and gratitude, given and taken as a reward, and a sense of safety and
shelter which I had never known with Lenore with whom I had felt
trapped, unable to retreat. With Turnlung I felt protected by one whose
body was in my own image though aged and much used, so that when I felt
for him I also felt for myself; he gave me permission to mourn and rejoice
over my own life.[45]

Their communion comes close to being the ideal "mingling" of two
people, although it fails ultimately because of Edelman's all-too-
human misgivings. But Edelman begins to understand much of the
significance of Turnlung in his life, that "He was the jeweller (did he
not say the word 'Jewel' was set in the center of his life?) who makes
a long difficult journey to bring the genuine stone to one who has
been deceived in his life not only by an imitation jewel but by a
genuine imitation."[46] The jewel Turnlung brings is the gift of true
language, not the false language which separates words and things
and which, it is implied, leads ultimately to the separation of human

from human and finally to the separation of individual limb from limb. In one chilling scene, Edelman senses that he finds another man's body within his bed, lying as if shattered. It is a vision of himself, at the end of a process which divides instead of joining, shattering the race it should heal.

Thus the product of the union of Edelman and Turnlung is the buffalo, not a word but a thing, not the mutilated dog but the whole and hale animal, member of a race of animals which belonged to the North American continent long before man brought his gathering darkness there. What is desired, according to this novel, is a return to this condition, for the Daughter Buffalo that Turnlung imagines "shall not be tricked or threatened by words but she will race with the wind toward them, and trust them, and know the promises they give and those they withhold, and never confuse them with the promises she may make to herself."[47]

Although this possibility is established, the novel is not particularly optimistic, in its American context, about the ·chances of achieving such a state. Humans are seen as being imprinted with the wrong language from before birth, a thought which occurs to Edelman when a student presents him with a quantity of brains taken from aborted fetuses brought from Sweden wrapped in dry ice. Recalling the children Lenore treated for inadequate or incomplete development, Edelman looks at geriatrics who are presumably the end point of the process of individual development, and is convinced that *no* human beings develop fully or adequately. The old men remind him of children; Turnlung seems like a giant fetus:

the smooth soft skin . . . the thin strands of gray hair not quite concealing the blue-veined skull, vulnerable as a baby's, as if the fontanelle were not yet closed, and I thought of the newlyborn, how their organs, especially the vital organs—the heart, the lungs, the brain—are unfinished at birth, and yet having accepted life even they in their unfinished state must begin at once to struggle against death and secretly to complete their own birth— they like works of art, perfect through their built-in imperfections.[48]

A man of Turnlung's age and in his state of health is not, in Edelman's view, a promising representative of mankind, although with a knowledge that Turnlung is in fact imagining the whole work the reader realizes that he is an exceptional figure. Edelman is unsure of committing himself to him—hence his rejections and vacillations, his hasty switching on of all the lights in his apartment whenever he returns from Turnlung's unlit home—because, like all old men on the verge of death, Turnlung seems unequipped to face it.

Nevertheless, the epilogue gives qualified confirmation of the possibilities that the novel sets out—although considering that Turnlung has set them out and then confirmed them himself, one might feel that the work has become a rather closed system. The important point, however, lies in the setting of the epilogue, which is "within" the reality depicted in the safely framed picture belonging to Edelman's father. If no one else is capable of committing himself to authenticity, the epilogue implies, the creative artist always will, and *Daughter Buffalo* is created under the smarting rays of the vertical sun. And it is not only *named* after the buffalo: it *is* the buffalo itself—the living thing created from honesty and truth of vision, as all works of art honestly created must be.

CHAPTER 9

Epilogue

I T would have been impossible to write a study such as this without forming some clear general impressions of the nature and
value of Janet Frame's achievement as a writer, and a final chapter is
an appropriate place for a discussion of issues which are not intrinsi-
cally a part of the biographical approach to criticism. I hope that the
remarks I make in this chapter will not be taken as binding assess-
ments of the writer's worth, and that they will provoke discussion
and challenges and debate. To render the issues clearer I have
divided my comments into three main areas, the first treating Janet
Frame's relationship to the traditions of New Zealand fiction, as I
see them, the second discussing her stature as a writer of fiction in
the postwar world, the last attempting to provide material for a
balanced judgment of her work.

I *Janet Frame and New Zealand Fiction*

Earlier in this book I drew attention to the length of Janet
Frame's career, pointing out that a quarter of a century has elapsed
since it began. To acknowledge this is in effect to thrust her away
from us and to place her work against the earlier tradition of writing
in New Zealand; specifically, it helps us to test the common assumption that she is "the undisputed leader of a younger generation,"[1] as
one critic has put it. Certainly, in the early years of her career she
seemed to possess a new and distinctive voice, and this is still a valid
way to describe her work—she is quite original in much of what her
innocent eye sees and in her lyrical manner. But the more we
acknowledge that these qualities are inimitable, the less can she be
seen as a leader of a new generation of writers and the fewer are the
names of young writers we can call to mind who might be considered to "belong" to her in any way. One of the greatest—if
involuntary—achievements of Frank Sargeson has been perma-

nently to alter the style and many of the assumptions of younger writers; but in the case of Janet Frame, it is possible only to think of writers who (like Ian Cross, perhaps) *resemble* her in some of their interests and methods.

In fact, Janet Frame may eventually be seen as one of the last writers in a strongly established tradition of New Zealand writing, or at least as the last major figure of the tradition, able to take its themes and conventions and to use them in a consummate way. The further we move from her early work, the more clearly the later writing can be seen to resemble other works which have gone before. Like Jane Mander, Robin Hyde, Sargeson, John Mulgan, and others, she is a writer whose origins are in the first half of the twentieth century and not the second. The tradition shared by these writers is a provincial one, a single step beyond the colonial; and, as Frank Sargeson has said, "if you're provincial certain things happen."[2]

The view of Janet Frame's early years given in Chapter 1 tells much about the provincial experience as opposed to the metropolitan one.[3] From its colonial origins, the small provincial town retains a cohesiveness maintained by means of a common work ethic and a rigid morality, a reliance on material and utilitarian things, a tendency towards insularity, and a never-ending awe of a surrounding natural world that has originally been tamed only by the steady maintenance of these attributes. A provincial society is generally too young to have evolved wide distinctions between classes: its aristocracy and its poor still have a few things in common, and the dominance of the work ethic ensures that toil may end poverty. Thus, the outcast from such a society may only incidentally be poor: what particularly alienates him from his fellows is their disregard for the mind and for all those cultural refinements that are associated with the metropolitan experience. The outcast calls the provincial a puritan, accusing him of mindlessness and of possessing a narrow vision, of living a way of life that is devoid of purpose and meaning.

Inevitably, then, provincial literature divides its world picture in two. In its first aspect it represents the puritan; it devotes its second to the outcast, with whom the writer so deeply sympathizes that the outcast may himself be depicted as an artist, or be given the attributes of poetic imagination and imaginative insight. Robin Hyde's central figure, Eliza Hannay, evolves from a puritanical background to become an alienated figure with the sensibility of an artist. Asia, the daughter of the puritan of Jane Mander's *Story of a New Zealand River*, Alice Roland, grows out of her upbringing and must leave New Zealand for overseas in order to absorb the culture she needs; her mother, too, "educated" out of her narrowness, leaves a New Zealand that is just beginning to turn from the colonial to the provincial. The "waif" of Sargeson never puts pen to paper, and may indeed be unable to write at all; but he is distinguished by the childlike innocence which frees his eyes from the cataracts of convention and enables him to perceive truth and value. Bill, the narrator of the long story, "That Summer," is a parasite of the society he abhors—he steals suburban newspapers and money from nocturnal milk bottles and would be lost without free counter lunches—but he is aware of his reasons for disliking society, showing in particular a knowledge of its meanness and of the withering of the human spirit there. His positive side is seen in a typical moment of generosity when he deposits a coin under a tree in order to persuade a dreary child that the stuff grows amongst its leaves and that magic still lives in the world. The outcast from puritan, provincial society need not necessarily be an artist, as Bill shows; but he invariably possesses the innocent and imaginative qualities which inform the artist's vision.

Whatever interest is shown in the imaginative outcast, it cannot equal the enthusiasm with which the New Zealand writer examines and then attacks the puritan. Puritanism is at the heart of Jane Mander's writing, and Sargeson's earlier short stories when taken together form an anatomy of the subject. An underestimated contribution to the topic is John Mulgan's *Man Alone* (1939), a disturbing study of the dehumanizing effects of materialism. His central figure, an English migrant and veteran of the Great War, has come to New Zealand to make a new life only to find that the war has never really ended. Although almost completely without imagination or innocent vision, the nondescript Johnson can see the New Zealand landscape as a battlefield, and the ash and craters which pockmark farms as symbols of the struggle needed to maintain them. Mulgan's arid, lunar picture is of a New Zealand whose work ethic and materialism have been carried to an extreme where human relations become a commercial venture and human beings are automata motivated only by thoughts of profit.

A less doctrinal survey of the puritan came in the early 1950's when Bill Pearson published his essay "Fretful Sleepers." Although he does not use the term specifically in his long, informal essay, Pearson isolates many of the characteristics loosely associated with puritanism—the dreariness of small-town routine, the puritan's fear of change and especially of differences among people, the "aching need for art"⁴ and the general distrust of it. The metaphor he uses to describe this condition evokes a vision of a nation asleep:

Somewhere at the back of the outlook of the New Zealander is a dream, a dream of security in equality. Everybody acts the same, receives the same amount of the world's goods, everyone moves in the same direction. Everyone has simple tastes, explainable desires which can be satisfied with proportionately simple effort. No one has any grievance and accidents don't happen. It is a version of a human dream, which I believe one half of the world is on the right road to bringing off as nearly as can be under the conditions of existence. The special quality of the New Zealander's version is that the evil is to disagree or be different. The chaos of existence is to be legislated into shape; the varieties of human quality and personality are to be levelled into conformity with the legislation. It is the development of individual talent that destroys the conformity: some men are left resenting their lack of another man's talent, so he must not use it, it is an unfair advantage. If life is (as the New Zealander assumes) a race, it is to be run by handicap. If nature can't be controlled then man must be: social boycott must keep the talented man in his place . . . I see it as the human dream of security perverted by the fears of the middle class hiving off from the threats of communism, the coloured races and the bland terror of infinite space; trying to give their customs a universal validity flouted by life, time, and the multiplicity of planets.⁵

Pearson too sees that the artist differs from his fellows, being the only person awake and therefore entrusted with the difficult task of waking others from a slumber only briefly and rarely disturbed by moral doubt. Later, in his novel, *Coal Flat* (1963), Pearson drew a remarkable picture of a provincial community in accordance with the observations made in "Fretful Sleepers," again showing the narrow-mindedness and latent violence of a small town.⁶

Pearson sees a slumbering country; Janet Frame states that her fellows are blind. Only the metaphor is different: both have diagnosed the same problem and made similar responses to it. And generally, the world depicted by Janet Frame, conceived so early in her career, is strongly in the tradition of New Zealand provincial fiction which Pearson describes. She has not built this world by imitation; it is simply that the invariability of the New Zealand experience has dictated similar responses amongst different writers. The blind men and women of her novels have ancestors who live in earlier fiction; and the figure of the outcast with a vivid mind is not altogether new in New Zealand's literature. But one of the outcast's attributes *is* new. The composite outcast of the Withers trilogy feels as alienated from society as does, for example, one of Sargeson's outcasts, and shares many of his reasons for feeling so. But nowhere in New Zealand literature is there a comparable concern with death and its place in life. It is this concern which begins to release her fiction from its local context and which gives her the stature of a considerable writer.

II *Janet Frame and Postwar Fiction*

And so, curiously enough, Janet Frame gains stature as an author the further her work is removed from its regional provenance. Looking back, one could guess that without the tragic bereavements of her early years she might have become a minor novelist with a flair for satire but without a reputation overseas. As soon as death enters her vision, her art breaks the limitations of the provincial mode and begins to speak to all readers; her concern is not merely with what it means to be a New Zealander but with what it means to be a human being living in the twentieth century. The breakthrough in the fourth novel is just the kind of liberation which elevated other provincial writers (George Eliot and Joyce have been cited as similar cases[7]) and enabled them to speak *for* men and women and not simply *of* men and women. It is from this point that her fiction gains overseas recognition; the American critic, Stanley Edgar Hyman, for example, has described *Scented Gardens for the Blind* as one of the best novels written since the war and "a brilliant and overwhelming tour de force."[8] Steeped from girlhood in the tradition of world fiction, she has inevitably entered that world in her own right.

Her place in it can be deceptive. Some critical space has been devoted to the relationship between the world of her fiction and the world of twentieth-century existentialist philosophy. Jeanne Delbaere-Garant, for example, has said of *Scented Gardens for the Blind* that "there is only one series of events which are seen differently by each of the three 'selves' and there gradually emerges from the apparently fragmentary book the three-dimensional structure of Heidegger's *Dasein*."[9] She goes on to describe Erlene Glace as representing Heidegger's "being-ahead-of-itself," Edward Glace as "already-being-in-the-world," and Vera Glace as "being-with." There is no proof whatever that this novel, or any other, has been shaped by a reading of Heidegger, and the resemblance discerned must surely be coincidental. But it remains an interesting resemblance, for it demonstrates that Janet Frame's artistic response has been to a general experience, not simply to a local one: the forms she has produced resemble those of Heidegger (including a common belief in the authenticating power of death) because both have responded to a common experience.

This common experience has produced a distinctive body of mid-twentieth-century fiction which knows no national boundaries and which might loosely be defined as sharing existentialist values and coloring. In its earliest stages of development one must obviously place the fiction of Sartre and Camus—*La Nausée* is an extremely influential novel—while its later developments become so broad as to include theorizing novelists like Robbe-Grillet, the English writer John Fowles, the Australian Patrick White,[10] the Argentinian Borges, and, in particular, several contemporary American writers. While all of these writers have individual characteristics and concerns, they share many common attributes, and I think it will eventually come to be acknowledged that Janet Frame's novels belong to this world tradition. Like the other writers I have mentioned, she is concerned with the effects of bourgeois existence, and particularly with bourgeois life in an industrialized society. Kierkegaard showed a similar concern one hundred and fifty years ago; Rilke, as we and Janet Frame have seen, responded to bourgeois life after the Great War, and Sartre's Roquentin is repelled and sickened by it before the Second World War.

The problems of life in a materialistic, industrialized society dominated by its middle class have recently been described by Erich Fromm, who has mentioned the levelling effect of capitalism upon human variety and its creation of simulated demands for material things and a common desire for progression instead of progress. Then he asks,

What is the outcome? Modern man is alienated from himself, from his fellow men, and from nature. He has been transformed into a commodity, experiences his life forces as an investment which must bring him the maximum profit obtainable under existing market conditions. Human relations are essentially those of alienated automatons, each basing his security on staying close to the herd, and not being different in thought, feeling or action. While everybody tries to be as close as possible to the rest, everybody remains utterly alone, pervaded by the deep sense of insecurity, anxiety and guilt which always results when human separateness cannot be overcome.[11]

Much of what Fromm and similar writers have said has been anticipated in Janet Frame's novels, as Anna Rutherford has pointed out[12]: again, both are responding to a common experience. And anticipating Janet Frame is the distinguished American novelist Walker Percy, himself deeply influenced by Heidegger and Sartre. In the 1950's he constantly diagnosed his own society's malaise as resulting from materialism and its dehumanizing effects upon the individual. In addition, Percy has done much to explain the effect of this kind of existence upon our language; he has suggested, for instance, that a gulf has grown between words and world because language is orderly while the world is not. Percy's linguistic theories read like explanations of Janet Frame's attitude to language, for he strongly implies that individual wholeness and fulfillment come not amongst the orderly slogans at the center of the alphabet but in the alienation which lies at its edge.[13] The subjective approach to language in which literature itself becomes the subject of literature, seen in the "New Novel" in France, the stories of Borges, and some of the fiction of John Barth, Saul Bellow, and Thomas Pynchon, lies farther along the same path.[14] It is an approach taken by Janet Frame herself in *The Adaptable Man,* where one of the author's concerns is with the capacity of literature to represent life adequately.

There is no doubt that her writing has earned the right to be discussed in the company of the writers I have mentioned. Even her most purely provincial novels, the first and second, can be compared with others in that international subgenre which chooses mental disturbance as its subject matter—novels such as Ken Kesey's *One Flew Over the Cuckoo's Nest,* Sylvia Plath's *The Bell Jar,* and Jennifer Dawson's *The Ha-Ha.* Like these, and like the other writers referred to in this chapter, Janet Frame's fiction impresses by the range of its referents and by its ambition. Like all these, too, it has its flaws and its shortcomings, and no critical study should close without some assessment of these. To undertake such a project as is represented in this book is inevitably a mark of respect and commitment in itself, and these are not diminished by an attempt to form a rounded and balanced judgment of her achievement.

III *Inward and Outward Suns*

There are two critical reactions I have not yet mentioned in this chapter, and they represent the two extremes of critical opinion which have been accorded Janet Frame so far. One is V. Dupont's general assessment of her as one of the greatest writers of the century[15]; the other is Lawrence Jones's more moderate assessment, carefully based upon the first novel alone:

Can we share her dark vision of the narrow limitations placed upon human possibility? Put another way, although we may grant the book a "willing suspension of disbelief" in experiencing it as a self-consistent world, can we accept that world as an adequate image of the world as we know it? Any answer to such a question must be personal, for it depends on the relationship between the "idiosyncratic mode of regard" of the author and that of the reader. To me, the vision of the novel seems intense but incomplete. Some things Janet Frame seems to see very clearly: the intrinsic value of the intense, aesthetic, intuitive vision of childhood; the restrictive, unimaginative, misdirected nature of the values of our culture; the ultimate tragedy of the tyranny of Time. But there is so much that she does not seem to see, so much that is left out of the world of *Owls Do Cry* or hastily dismissed from it: the self-justifying experiences of intellectual understanding, of intellectual and emotional communication between equals, of non-possessive parental love, of significant work, of adult sexuality. Compared to, say, the world of Tolstoy or George Eliot or even Joyce, the world of this novel is a narrow one, one that does not fully justify the claims of universality made by the Epilogue.[16]

Here is an interesting moderation of any overgenerous claims that might be made on behalf of Janet Frame's fiction, and a fine exposition of values that cannot be said to have worked their way into that fiction yet. Jones does not deny her generic place (the novel, he says, "ranks with Malcolm Lowry's *Under the Volcano* as one of the very few novels of the last twenty-five years written any place in the English-speaking world that can be put next to the work of Faulkner and Joyce without being dwarfed"[17]). But he suspects limitations to the range of her writing and in doing so focuses upon what is perhaps the central problem of her art, its inward orientation and the many personal factors which seem to prevent its turning fully outward. Her imaginative world is possessed by a force of gravity that draws all things to a center at which she herself stands; as a result, the statement which turns the specific and personal into the universal is made only with difficulty. This is not to say that such statements are worthless, nor does it deny the heroism of the effort involved. But it does mean, as we shall see, that at times her art is laid open to charges of obsessiveness or even narcissism.

The charge that Janet Frame as a writer is sequestered from the world which should shape and temper her art is substantiated, surprisingly, by the author herself. When asked during an interview in recent years how she saw life, she replied:

> I'm not sure that I see life at all. What I do see is life within. I suppose you would call it the imagination. I'm rather unconscious of things around me, in a way. I've a kind of arrangement with a part of myself which is given the menial task of absorbing things. It takes over the menial task and I don't know what these things are until I see them in an imaginative light—which is a bright light, without shade—a kind of inward sun.[18]

To a certain extent, there is described here a process that any worthwhile artist would recognize and acknowledge—the ignition of the imagination which creates the world eventually to be depicted on the page or canvas or in wood or stone. But should the "task of absorbing things" be delegated to so obviously a menial part of the mind? Should a writer so deliberately obscure the world which, however much she may dislike the fact, probably exists around us all? For centuries, artists like the painter Bosch or the writer Céline have been doing this and producing remarkable works. But we do not see in them a significant, compassionate view of mankind; instead, as with all inward-looking artists, we see the artist himself, his obsessions and fears and fantasies. The handful of writers who might deserve the accolade Dupont bestows upon Janet Frame have regulated and humanized their vision by constant recourse to their fellows, to life, and to history. Although, at her best, she shows evidence of having undertaken this process, it does not occur constantly as she writes.

The single trait which most often reveals the introspectiveness of her writing is her obsession with language. Words are of course mined brilliantly for their poetry and as a source of humor and wit; but the more often this occurs, the more world and word become divorced. The Orphic commitment to celebrate things in poetry,

often so dazzlingly fulfilled, is not served when the things celebrated obviously hold less fascination than the language that is used
to celebrate them. Occasionally, the reader will find the narrative
held up as an echo or verbal association grasps the imagination of the
writer, and demands—usually with success—to be explored. This
technique can be dazzlingly successful, as it is, for example, in the
last novel where a reference to the guilt of the Ancient Mariner of
Coleridge suddenly leads the writer to the modern mariner, the
young American Marine who has become a killer in Vietnam. But
the process which produces this sort of felicity appears to be involuntary, a product of a long association with language and literature in which, as R. T. Robertson has said, "The books she read, the
phrases she heard were only half-comprehended and so took on an
independent existence in her mind."[19] Her prolonged immersion in
worlds made of words has elevated the status of language in her art.
The rewards of this have been noted; but the penalties—digression
and "difficulty" in texture and references—must be noted too.

We could in fact widen these charges that a world lit by an inward
sun is difficult for others to see clearly. A number of people have
recently drawn my attention to the story called "The Day of the
Sheep," which was published before she had begun work on her
first novel.[20] In every case, the point of the reference has been to
contrast the realism of this story with the general tendency of the
subsequent fiction towards a sort of unreality. In this story, the
illusion that we are witnessing a slice of life is successful and consistent: the characters are closely observed, they appear to emanate
from the actual world, and their motivations stem from their apparent characters. While it would be wrong to expect that Janet Frame
should have continued in this manner simply because it was successful, the reader of the subsequent fiction ought to ask himself or
herself whether the characterization there is as convincing. For it
could be maintained that many characters in the novels are insufficiently differentiated. The Withers family, because they are so
close to Janet Frame's own, neatly balance realistic individuality and
the figurative need for unity. But is Zoe Bryce genuinely different
from Malfred Signal? Is Pat Keenan a development of Bob Withers
or a repetition of the same character? Does he differ significantly
from the "blind" figures of the later fiction—from Tom Livingstone,
say? And it is worth noting that her most successful characteriza-
tions, which occur in the densely populated novel *The Adaptable*

Man, are the product of a period she spent far from the society in which she was bred and which figures in so much of her writing. Objectivity, it seems, may have geographical dimensions in this case.

It need scarcely be said that there is a corollary to these conclusions. If Bob Withers, a character created in 1955, resembles even in his name a character created fifteen years later, Tom Livingstone, and if such resemblances can be seen between other characters situated at different points in her work, it might seem that there is a certain inertia, a sort of stasis, in her art. Her vision, I have suggested, was formed very early, becoming tinted and intensified with each successive novel and, in the early 1960's, widening its themes as it aimed for greater significance. But because of this admitted lack of copulation with the outside world the artistic vision of Janet Frame has become rather doctrinaire, inductively producing characters and situations which are impelled by a theoretical view of life rather than by a pragmatical one.

I cannot help feeling that this vision is also a little uncompromising, too rigidly the vision of the outsider. Her picture of the cheerfully blind society wandering beneath sunlight it refuses to see is very accurate in many ways and is worth having; her understanding that such a society breeds its own violence and danger as it craves safety for itself is quite brilliant. But these are generalizations, and when they are insisted upon they exclude life from her fiction. We can see a deep irony in this situation: while she places at the core of the society she depicts a stone representing utter rigidity, conformity, and inability to adapt to the changes of life, her own vision can be stonily intransigent, betraying a fear of change and particularly an inability to adapt the innocence of childhood to the rigors of adult life. It is this inflexibility which cuts her fiction off from the positive qualities Lawrence Jones identifies as missing from it.

For her art was born from a predicament, and although it transcends that predicament, there are occasions when personal limitations show through. The reader must make a personal judgment as to the validity of some of her claims in the light of this personal element. Her dislike of institutions, her insistence that we all belong to the waters of the lagoon, her view of society as exclusive and overmaterialistic—these beliefs, rooted in the experience of her own impoverished and often tragic childhood, must not be accepted without careful evaluation. We must also ask whether she has remained true to the beliefs of Rilke which helped form her art, whether she has continued to celebrate the unity of life and death and the wholeness of existence or has allowed death to become an alien force in her imaginary world, an intruder and destroyer and not a giver of strength when confronted.

It is possible that the charges I have indicated here could be swiftly and easily rebutted—and I hope that the foregoing chapters have provided ample material for such a rebuttal. The remarks I have made are offered in the interests of fairness and balanced appraisal, and are not binding claims requiring articulate defense. There remains, therefore, only a need to redirect attention to the undeniable and abiding strengths of this writer—to the beauty of her language, the tragedy and pathos of her most moving scenes, the sharpness and accuracy of her social satire, the brilliance of the formal conception of the middle novels, and, above all, the moral concern of these novels which raises them to the company of the best. It is right that we should conclude with Janet Frame's voice and not mine; it is the voice of an important writer:

> It is easy, in a well-fed land full of sun, sea, sky, for the mortal people to forget their mortality. Yet we don't need a hurricane, a revolution or national disaster to make us more aware and alive. We need only to be human beings; not animals which are without pity or guilt or the need to judge and compare or the magical power of naming things which is the basis of art; not vegetables which grow in silence, sweating dewdrops instead of tears.
>
> We need only to remember that we are human, to forget our preoccupation with distances between continent and continent, the measurement of physical miles, and remember the unbearable closeness of one human being to his neighbour. Unless we have the courage to use our inherited human riches to name, name, name things visible, things invisible in our land, to play the thought-game from time to time, to raise a few more rich fat dreams and poems and get a fair price for them, we'll be spiritually hungry and poor; we may not even survive.[21]

Notes and References

Chapter One

1. I have based this outline of the origins of Oamaru on K. McDonald's *History of North Otago* (Oamaru: Oamaru Mail Co., 1940), Chapters 1 & 2. For a general outline of New Zealand's development in the nineteenth and early twentieth centuries, see W. H. Oliver, *The Story of New Zealand*, (London: Faber & Faber, 1963). I am grateful to Mrs. P. Hill of Christchurch for telling me the etymology of the Frame's family name.

2. See *History of North Otago*, Chapter 3.

3. Janet Frame, "Beginnings," *Landfall*, 19, 1 (March 1965), 40. The names of Alexander and Mary Frame and the date of their marriage were supplied to me by the Oamaru branch of the New Zealand Department of Justice.

4. George Samuel Frame's name and date of birth were supplied by the Oamaru branch of the Department of Justice.

5. The date of the marriage of Janet Frame's parents was supplied by the Oamaru branch of the Department of Justice.

6. All details relating to the Frame children were supplied by the Dunedin and Oamaru branches of the Department of Justice.

7. Janet Frame's family name was mentioned to me in a letter from Miss Janet Gibson dated 11 June 1975.

8. "Beginnings," 42.

9. *Ibid.*, 42.

10. "Janet Frame: It's Time For France" (interview), *New Zealand Listener*, 27 October 1973, 20.

11. "The Foxes," *The Pocket Mirror* (Christchurch, 1968), 120–21.

12. *History of North Otago*, Chapter 10.

13. "University Entrance," *New Zealand Listener*, 22 March 1946, 18.

14. See "Beginnings," 44.

15. *History of North Otago*, Chapter 11.

16. Many of Janet Frame's former fellow-pupils have mentioned her love of nature to me in their correspondence.

17. "Beginnings," 43.

18. Mrs. Frame's successes in publishing her writing were mentioned to me by a former Headmistress of the Waitaki Girls' High School, Mrs. J. Banks-Kirkness, in a letter dated 19 August 1975.

19. "Beginnings," 43.

20. *The Lagoon* (Christchurch, 1951), 63.

21. *Ibid.*, 79

22. *The Reservoir* (New York, 1963), 33.

23. *Ibid.*, 67.

24. *Owls Do Cry* (New York, 1960).

25. Mentioned to me in a letter from Miss Janet Gibson, 15 August 1975.

26. The drowning was reported in *The Oamaru Mail*, 5 March 1937, from which these details are taken.

27. Janet Frame's impressive academic record was reproduced for me by the present Headmistress of Waitaki Girls' High School, Miss J. J. Jarrold.

28. Letter from Miss Janet Gibson, 11 July 1975.

29. "Janet Frame: It's Time For France," 20.

30. Letter from Miss Janet Gibson, 15 July 1975.

31. Letter from Miss Janet Gibson, 11 July 1975.

32. "Beginnings," 44.

33. *Ibid.*, 44.

34. Printed in *The Oamaru Mail*, 26 April 1940.

35. Letter from Mrs. Banks-Kirkness, 19 August 1975.

36. Letter from Miss Jarrold, 22 July 1975.

37. For details concerning the Frames' shift of house I am grateful to Mr. K. Small of Oamaru.

38. Mentioned in a letter from Miss D. Logie of Oamaru, 22 June 1975.

39. Janet Frame's impressive performance as a University Scholarship candidate has been described to me in a letter from Miss Janet Gibson, 15 August 1975.

40. Mentioned in a letter from Mrs. Judith Powell, 19 September 1975.

41. "Beginnings," 45.

42. *Faces in the Water* (New York, 1961), 10–11.

43. This was Mrs. Judith Powell; the anecdote is mentioned in her letter of 19 September 1975.

44. At this time, university units (i.e., a year's work in a single subject) were credited to Teachers' College students in pairs or not at all. Thus, for the purposes of her teaching career, Janet Frame had wasted her 1944 academic year.

45. "Beginnings," 45.

46. Referred to by R. T. Robertson in his article, "Bird, Hawk, Bogie: Janet Frame, 1952–62," *Studies in the Novel*, 4 (Summer 1972), 196.

47. "Beginnings," 45.

48. *Ibid.*, 45.

49. Details of this tragedy were given in *The Oamaru Mail*, 19 February

1947. Supplementary details were given me by Miss Janet Gibson in a letter dated 27 July 1975.

50. "Beginnings," 46.

51. The date of Janet Frame's entry to hospital was given me in a letter by Mrs. A. J. Hubbard of Timaru, dated 23 July 1975. R. T. Robertson, who appears to have received his information from the New Zealand writer, Maurice Shadbolt, identifies the hospital as Seacliff, near Dunedin, and also mentions that Janet Frame was a patient at Avondale hospital, near Auckland. See "Bird, Hawk, Bogie: Janet Frame, 1952–62," 196.

Chapter Two

1. "Memory and a Pocketful of Words," *Times Literary Supplement*, 3240, 4 June 1964, 487. According to a letter from Frank Sargeson dated 18 October 1975, Janet Frame's reading during these years was voracious, taking in New Zealand literature as well as world literature.

2. "Memory and a Pocketful of Words," 487.

3. *Ibid.*, 487.

4. Quoted by J. B. Leishman in his introduction to his translations of R. M. Rilke, *Sonnets to Orpheus* (London: The Hogarth Press, 1949), 17.

5. *Ibid.*, 17.

6. *Ibid.*, 19

7. *Ibid.*, 172.

8. *Ibid.*, 19.

9. See also Jeanne Delbaere-Garant, "Daphne's Metamorphoses in Janet Frame's Early Novels," *Ariel*, 2 (April 1975), 73.

10. Mentioned in a letter from Frank Sargeson, 11 July 1975.

11. See for example Patricia Guest's review in *Landfall*, 6, 2 (June 1952), 153.

12. *The Lagoon*, 8.

13. *Ibid.*, 10.

14. *Ibid.*, 17.

15. *Ibid.*, 17.

16. *Ibid.*, 18.

17. *Ibid.*, 25.

18. *Ibid.*, 27.

19. "Beginnings," 47.

20. *The Lagoon*, 47.

21. *Ibid.*, 50.

22. *Ibid.*, 51.

23. *Ibid.*, 52.

24. *Ibid.*, 113.

25. *Ibid.*, 38.

26. *Ibid.*, 101.

27. *The Reservoir*, 11.

28. *Ibid.*, 12.

29. *Ibid.*, 9.

30. *Ibid.*, 15.

31. *Ibid.*, 42.

32. *Ibid.*, 42.

33. H. W. Rhodes, "Preludes and Parables: A Reading of Janet Frame's Novels," *Landfall*, 26 (1972), 135.

34. Sargeson's letter of 18 October 1975 specifically confirms Janet Frame's knowledge of *The Godwits Fly*.

35. Cherry Hankin, "New Zealand Women Novelists: Their Attitude Towards Life in a Developing Society," *World Literature Written in English*, 14, 1 (April 1975), 158.

36. Michael Beveridge, "Conversation With Frank Sargeson," *Landfall*, 24, 2 (June 1970), 158.

37. These dates were provided for me in a letter from Frank Sargeson dated 9 August 1975.

38. Unsigned review, *Free Lance*, 7 June 1975.

39. Unsigned and undated review, *Otago Daily Times*.

40. Unsigned review, *New Yorker*, 13 August 1960.

41. "Beginnings," 46.

42. *Ibid.*, 46.

43. *Ibid.*, 46–47.

44. *Ibid.*, 47.

45. Geoffrey Moorhouse, "Out of New Zealand," *The Guardian*, 16 November 1962.

46. R. T. Robertson quotes Maurice Shadbolt in claiming this. See "Bird, Hawk, Bogie: Janet Frame 1952–62," 196.

47. These details were mentioned to me in a letter from Frank Sargeson dated 18 October 1975.

48. These details were supplied to me by the Oamaru branch of the New Zealand Department of Justice.

49. "This Desirable Property," *New Zealand Listener*, 1292, 3 July 1964, 12.

50. Mentioned to me in a letter from Miss Janet Gibson dated 27 July 1975.

51. "At Evans Street," *The Pocket Mirror*, 22–23.

52. Review of Terence Journet's *Take My Tip*, 309.

53. "This Desirable Property," 12.

54. These incidents were described in Frank Sargeson's letter to me of 9 August 1975.

55. Mentioned to me in a letter from Miss Janet Gibson dated 27 July 1975.

56. See "Artists' Retreats" (interview), *New Zealand Listener*, 1605, 27 July 1970, 13.

57. *Ibid.*, 13.
58. "Janet Frame: It's Time For France," 21.

Chapter Three

1. *Owls Do Cry*, 13.
2. *Ibid.*, 26.
3. *Ibid.*, 14.
4. *Ibid.*, 46.
5. *Ibid.*, 12.
6. *Ibid.*, 132.
7. *Ibid.*, 129.
8. *Ibid.*, 124.
9. *Ibid.*, 210.
10. *Ibid.*, 63.
11. *Ibid.*, 61.
12. *Ibid.*, 11.
13. *Ibid.*, 11.
14. *Ibid.*, 13.
15. *Ibid.*, 23.
16. *Ibid.*, 60.
17. *Ibid.*, 53.
18. *Ibid.*, 53.
19. *Ibid.*, 80–81.
20. *Ibid.*, 196.
21. *Ibid.*, 117.
22. *Ibid.*, 67–68.
23. *Ibid.*, 37.
24. *Ibid.*, 130.
25. *Ibid.*, 39–40.
26. *Ibid.*, 38.
27. *Ibid.*, 42.
28. *Ibid.*, 94.
29. *Ibid.*, 16.
30. *Ibid.*, 13.
31. *Ibid.*, 51.
32. *Ibid.*, 87.
33. *Ibid.*, 33.
34. *Ibid.*, 38.
35. *Ibid.*, 58.
36. *Ibid.*, 96.
37. See "Daphne's Metamorphoses in Janet Frame's Early Novels," 23–29.
38. *Owls Do Cry*, 19.
39. *Ibid.*, 20–21.

40. *Ibid.*, 21.
41. *Ibid.*, 46.
42. *Ibid.*, 46–47.
43. *Ibid.*, 47.
44. *Ibid.*, 24.
45. *Ibid.*, 45.
46. *Ibid.*, 94.
47. *Ibid.*, 161–62.
48. *Ibid.*, 27.
49. *Ibid.*, 70.
50. *Ibid.*, 83.
51. *Ibid.*, 14.
52. *Ibid.*, 71.
53. *Ibid.*, 91.
54. *Ibid.*, 154.
55. *Ibid.*, 161.
56. *Ibid.*, 180.
57. *Ibid.*, 180.
58. *Ibid.*, 190.
59. *Ibid.*, 191–92.
60. *Ibid.*, 196.
61. *Ibid.*, 196.
62. *Ibid.*, 205.
63. "Bird, Hawk, Bogie: Janet Frame, 1952–62," 195.

Chapter Four

1. Joan Stevens, *The New Zealand Novel 1860–1965* (Wellington: A. H. & A. W. Reed, 1966), 127.
2. "Preludes and Parables: A Reading of Janet Frame's Novels," 135.
3. *Ibid.*, 136.
4. "Bird, Hawk, Bogie: Janet Frame, 1952–62," 196.
5. *Faces in the Water*, 46.
6. *Ibid.*, 65.
7. *Ibid.*, 129.
8. *Ibid.*, 69.
9. *Ibid.*, 75.
10. *Ibid.*, 87.
11. *Ibid.*, 107.
12. *Ibid.*, 225.
13. *Ibid.*, 9.
14. *Owls Do Cry*, 156.
15. *Faces in the Water*, 150.
16. *Ibid.*, 104.
17. These interpretations were suggested to me by Janet Frame herself

in a letter dated 13 November 1974. "Istina," as she pointed out, is Serbo-Croatian for "truth."

18. *Faces in the Water,* 139–40.

19. *Ibid.,* 152.

20. *Ibid.,* 152.

21. *Ibid.,* 241.

22. *Ibid.,* 241.

23. *Ibid.,* 239.

24. *Ibid.,* 239.

25. *The Edge of the Alphabet* (New York, 1962), 35.

26. *Ibid.,* 49.

27. *Ibid.,* 44.

28. R. T. Robertson briefly discusses this reference to the "Lost Tribe of Manapouri" in "Bird, Hawk, Bogie: Janet Frame, 1952–62," 195.

29. *The Edge of the Alphabet,* 3.

30. *Ibid.,* 142.

31. *Ibid.,* 51–52.

32. *Ibid.,* 30.

33. *Ibid.,* 70.

34. *Ibid.,* 131.

35. *Ibid.,* 280.

36. *Ibid.,* 249.

37. *Ibid.,* 249.

38. *Ibid.,* 249.

39. *Ibid.,* 249.

40. *Ibid.,* 244.

41. *Ibid.,* 4.

42. *Ibid.,* 238.

43. *Ibid.,* 104.

44. *Ibid.,* 238–39.

45. "Daphne's Metamorphoses in Janet Frame's Early Novels," 35.

Chapter Five

1. *Scented Gardens for the Blind* (New York, 1964), 12.

2. *Ibid.,* 10.

3. *Ibid.,* 12.

4. *Ibid.,* 19.

5. *Ibid.,* 252.

6. This epigraph does not occur in the North American edition of her works.

7. "Preludes and Parables: A Reading of Janet Frame's Novels," 136.

8. *Ibid.,* 125–30.

9. *Scented Gardens for the Blind,* 25.

10. "Preludes and Parables: A Reading of Janet Frame's Novels," 139.

11. *Scented Gardens for the Blind*, 41.

12. *Ibid.*, 31.

13. *The Reservoir*, 27–32.

14. *Scented Gardens for the Blind*, 61.

15. *Ibid.*, 144.

16. *Ibid.*, 61–62.

17. *Ibid.*, 61.

18. "Preludes and Parables: A Reading of Janet Frame's Novels," 138.

19. *Scented Gardens for the Blind*, 147–48.

20. *Ibid.*, 49.

21. *Ibid.*, 151.

22. *Ibid.*, 118.

23. *Ibid.*, 227.

24. *Ibid.*, 153.

25. *Ibid.*, 252.

26. *Ibid.*, 251.

27. *Ibid.*, 83.

28. *The New Zealand Novel 1860–1965*, 128.

29. *The Reservoir*, 131–40.

30. "Snowman, Snowman," *Snowman, Snowman* (New York, 1963), 32–33.

31. *Ibid.*, 39.

32. *Ibid.*, 43.

33. *Ibid.*, 3.

34. *Scented Gardens for the Blind*, 25.

35. "Snowman, Snowman," 4.

36. *Ibid.*, 4.

37. *Ibid.*, 4.

38. *Ibid.*, 34.

39. *Ibid.*, 12.

40. *Ibid.*, 26.

41. *Ibid.*, 6–7.

42. *Ibid.*, 14.

43. *Ibid.*, 57.

44. L. O. Jones, "No Cowslip's Bell in Waimaru: the Personal Vision of 'Owls Do Cry'," 295.

45. "Preludes and Parables: A Reading of Janet Frame's Novels," 139–40.

46. Stanley Edgar Hyman, "Reason in Madness," *Standards: A Chronicle of Books for Our Time* (New York, 1966), 239–43.

Chapter Six

1. *The Adaptable Man* (New York, 1965), 6.

2. *Ibid.*, 64.

3. *Ibid.*, 65.
4. *Ibid.*, 72.
5. *Ibid.*, 72.
6. *Ibid.*, 79.
7. *Ibid.*, 97.
8. *Ibid.*, 99.
9. *Ibid.*, 2.
10. *Ibid.*, 162.
11. *Ibid.*, 12.
12. *Ibid.*, 12.
13. *Ibid.*, 11–12.
14. *Ibid.*, 92.
15. *Ibid.*, 92.
16. *Ibid.*, 54.
17. *Ibid.*, 55.
18. *Ibid.*, 62.
19. *Ibid.*, 63.
20. *Ibid.*, 32.
21. *Ibid.*, 63.
22. *Ibid.*, 34.
23. *Ibid.*, 33.
24. *Ibid.*, 24.
25. *Ibid.*, 5.
26. *Ibid.*, 77–78.
27. *Ibid.*, 243.
28. *Ibid.*, 204.
29. *Ibid.*, 88.
30. Joan Stevens, "The Art of Janet Frame," *New Zealand Listener*, 1593, 4 May 1970, 52.
31. *The Adaptable Man*, 86.
32. *Ibid.*, 149.
33. *Ibid.*, 150.
34. *Ibid.*, 62.
35. *Ibid.*, 138–40.
36. *Ibid.*, 5.
37. *Ibid.*, 6–7.
38. *Ibid.*, 11.
39. *Ibid.*, 50.
40. *Ibid.*, 66.
41. Patrick Evans, "Janet Frame and the Adaptable Novel," *Landfall*, 25 (1971), 455.
42. Perhaps the least sympathetic review came in *Time* magazine, which described the novel as "emptiness puffed up."
43. These four stories are from the *Snowman, Snowman* collection.

44. These two stories are from the collection, *The Reservoir*.

45. These three stories are from *Snowman, Snowman*.

46. These three are from *The Reservoir*.

47. These appeared in the *New Zealand School Journal*, which is specifically devised for school use.

48. "The Bath," *Landfall*, 19 (1965), 225.

49. "A Boy's Will," *Landfall*, 20 (1965), 314.

Chapter Seven

1. *A State of Siege* (New York, 1966), 56.

2. *Ibid.*, 74.

3. *Ibid.*, 87.

4. *Ibid.*, 167.

5. *Ibid.*, 173.

6. *Ibid.*, 9.

7. *Ibid.*, 239.

8. *Ibid.*, 8,

9. *Ibid.*, 3.

10. *Ibid.*, 62.

11. *Ibid.*, 19–20.

12. *Ibid.*, 117–18.

13. *Ibid.*, 20.

14. *Ibid.*, 93–4.

15. *Ibid.*, 238–39.

16. *Ibid.*, 8–9.

17. *Ibid.*, 9.

18. *Ibid.*, 40.

19. *Ibid.*, 28.

20. *Ibid.*, 87.

21. *Ibid.*, 87.

22. *Ibid.*, 87.

23. *Ibid.*, 70.

24. *Yellow Flowers in the Antipodean Room* (New York, 1969), 47.

25. *Ibid.*, 160.

26. *Ibid.*, 13.

27. *Ibid.*, 47.

28. *Ibid.*, 47.

29. *Ibid.*, 50.

30. *Ibid.*, 65–66.

31. *Ibid.*, 66.

32. *Ibid.*, 66.

33. *Ibid.*, 59–60.

34. *Ibid.*, 113.

35. *The Pocket Mirror*, 1.

36. *Ibid.*, 23.
37. *Ibid.*, 24.
38. *Ibid.*, 68.
39. *Ibid.*, 3–4.
40. *Ibid.*, 6.
41. *Ibid.*, 9.
42. *Ibid.*, 5.
43. *Ibid.*, 67.
44. *Ibid.*, 30.
45. *Ibid.*, 22.
46. *Ibid.*, 81.
47. *Ibid.*, 100.

Chapter Eight

1. "Artists' Retreats," 13.
2. *Intensive Care* (New York, 1970), 51.
3. *Ibid.*, 166.
4. *Ibid.*, 217.
5. *Ibid.*, 247.
6. *Ibid.*, 270.
7. *Ibid.*, 3–4.
8. *Ibid.*, 19.
9. *Ibid.*, 35.
10. *Ibid.*, 71–72.
11. *Ibid.*, 104.
12. *Ibid.*, 105.
13. *Ibid.*, 112.
14. *Ibid.*, 5.
15. *Ibid.*, 32.
16. *Ibid.*, 9.
17. *Ibid.*, 17.
18. *Ibid.*, 54.
19. *Ibid.*, 58.
20. *Ibid.*, 160–61.
21. *Ibid.*, 166.
22. *Ibid.*, 240.
23. *Ibid.*, 235.
24. *Ibid.*, 238.
25. *Daughter Buffalo* (New York, 1972), "Prologue," xii.
26. *Ibid.*, 9.
27. *Ibid.*, 11.
28. *Ibid.*, 13.
29. *Ibid.*, 16.
30. *Ibid.*, 28.

31. *Ibid.*, 32.
32. *Ibid.*, 32.
33. *Ibid.*, 29.
34. *Ibid.*, 35.
35. *Ibid.*, 35–36.
36. *Ibid.*, 29.
37. *Ibid.*, 32.
38. *Ibid.*, 102.
39. *Ibid.*, 102.
40. *Ibid.*, 127.
41. *Ibid.*, 154.
42. *Ibid.*, 33.
43. *Ibid.*, 79.
44. *Ibid.*, 80.
45. *Ibid.*, 144.
46. *Ibid.*, 143.
47. *Ibid.*, 147.
48. *Ibid.*, 86–87.

Chapter Nine

1. Peter Alcock, Introduction, *World Literature Written in English*, 14, 1 (April 1975), 11.

2. Michael Beveridge, "Conversation With Frank Sargeson," *Landfall*, 24, 1 (March 1970), 23.

3. The best analysis of the provincial origins of New Zealand society is given in Robert Chapman, "Fiction and the Social Pattern," *Landfall*, 7, 1 (1953), 26–58. The term, "metropolitan," suggesting the reverse of provincialism, is used by R. T. Robertson, "Bird, Hawk, Bogie: Janet Frame, 1952–62," 187.

4. Bill Pearson, "Fretful Sleepers," *Landfall Country* (Christchurch: Caxton Press, 1962), 345.

5. "Fretful Sleepers," 354.

6. *Coal Flat* (Auckland: Paul's Book Arcade, 1963) is a classic study of New Zealand's provincialism, the story of a young schoolmaster on the west coast of the South Island, who is handicapped by an active moral conscience. Pearson's portrait of Mrs. Palmer, the publican's wife, epitomizes the narrow-minded puritan; it may usefully be compared with similar figures which appear in Janet Frame's fiction. Mrs. Seldom, an ancient, static woman who rejects the entire town—including her daughter—as a result of an old feud, is as blind to reality as are any of Janet Frame's disapproved characters, and equally hostile to change. Several of Maurice Shadbolt's stories in *The New Zealanders* (London: Eyre & Spottiswoode, 1959) are studies of puritanism and its reverse, as are Ian Cross's novels, *The God Boy* (London: Andre Deutsch, 1958) and *The Backward Sex* (London: Eyre & Spottiswoode, 1960). For an interesting study of the origins of

materialism in pioneer New Zealand see James McNeish's novel, *McKenzie* (London: Hodder & Stoughton, 1970), whose hero is a mysterious, poetical outcast from a blindly money-grubbing society.

Pearson's vision of a nation of dreamers has provoked two recent literary responses—C. K. Stead's novel, *Smith's Dream* (Auckland: Longman Paul, 1973), a study of moral commitment and violence in New Zealand, and Janet Frame's *Intensive Care*, which has similarly shown the nightmare of violence as coming from the sleep of morality. For an interesting examination of the origins of violence in middle-class New Zealand society, see Michael Henderson's recent novel, *The Log of a Superfluous Son* (Dunedin: John McIndoe, 1975), which, like those mentioned above, questions New Zealand's supposed insulation from a violent world and its moral problems.

7. By R. T. Robertson; see "Bird, Hawk, Bogie: Janet Frame, 1952–62," 187.

8. "Reason in Madness," 239.

9. "Daphne's Metamorphoses in Janet Frame's Early Novels," 30.

10. I have noted some of the similarities between the early fiction of Janet Frame and that of Patrick White in "Alienation and the Imagery of Death: the Novels of Janet Frame," *Meanjin Quarterly*, 32, 3 (September 1973), 294–302. See too Anna Rutherford, "Janet Frame's Divided and Distinguished Worlds," *World Literature Written in English*, 14, 1 (April 1975), 51.

11. Erich Fromm, *The Art of Loving* (New York: Harper, 1956), 63. My attention was drawn to Fromm by Anna Rutherford; see "Janet Frame's Divided and Distinguished Worlds," 57–58.

12. "Janet Frame's Divided and Distinguished Worlds," 57–58.

13. Walker Percy, "The Message in the Bottle," *Thought* XXXIV (Fall 1959), 405–33.

14. See in particular John Barth, *The Sot-Weed Factor* (New York: Doubleday, 1960), Saul Bellow, *Henderson the Rain King* (New York. Viking, 1959), and Thomas Pynchon, *V* (London: Jonathan Cape, 1963). Although Percy's linguistic theories do not overtly enter his novels, the novels make an interesting comparison with Janet Frame's. See, for example, *The Moviegoer* (London: Eyre & Spottiswoode, 1963), a novel based on European existentialist philosophy, but with an atmosphere much like that of Janet Frame's fiction.

15. V. Dupont, "Janet Frame and the Psychological Novel," *Commonwealth Literature Conference*, Aarhus, Denmark, 1971.

16. "No Cowslip's Bell in Waimaru—the personal vision of *Owls Do Cry*," 295.

17. *Ibid.*, 296.

18. "Artists' Retreats," 13.

19. "Bird, Hawk, Bogie: Janet Frame, 1952–62," 195.

20. In *The Lagoon* collection.

21. "This Desirable Property," 12.

Selected Bibliography

PRIMARY SOURCES
(arranged chronologically)

1. Novels

Owls Do Cry. Christchurch: Pegasus Press, 1957; New York: George Braziller, 1960; London: W. H. Allen, 1961; Melbourne: Sun Books, 1966.

Faces in the Water. Christchurch: Pegasus Press, 1961; New York: George Braziller, 1962; London: W. H. Allen, 1962; New York: Avon Books, 1971.

The Edge of the Alphabet. Christchurch: Pegasus Press, 1962; New York: George Braziller, 1962; London: W. H. Allen, 1962.

Scented Gardens for the Blind. Christchurch: Pegasus Press, 1963; London: W. H. Allen, 1963; New York: George Braziller, 1964.

The Adaptable Man. Christchurch: Pegasus Press, 1965; London: W. H. Allen, 1965; New York: George Braziller, 1965.

A State of Siege. New York: George Braziller, 1966; Christchurch: Pegasus Press, 1967; London: W. H. Allen. 1967.

The Rainbirds. London: W. H. Allen, 1968; Christchurch: Pegasus Press, 1969.

Yellow Flowers in the Antipodean Room (American edition of *The Rainbirds*). New York: George Braziller, 1969.

Intensive Care. New York: George Braziller, 1970; Wellington: A. H. & A. W. Reed, 1971; London: W. H. Allen, 1971.

Daughter Buffalo. New York: George Braziller, 1972; Toronto: Doubleday, 1972; Wellington: A. H. & A. W. Reed, 1973; London: W. H. Allen, 1973.

2. Translations

Visages Noyes (French translation of *Faces in the Water* by S. Lecomte). Paris: Editiones du seuil, 1963.

Rostros en el agua (Spanish translation of *Faces in the Water* by Alfredo Percovich). Buenos Aires: Plaza & Janes, 1965.

Al margen del alfabeto (Spanish translation of *The Edge of the Alphabet* by J. Ferrer Aleu). Barcelona: Ediciones G. P., 1966.

221

3. Children's Literature

Mona Minim and the Smell of the Sun. Illustrated by Robin Jacques. New
    York: George Braziller, 1969.

4. Collections of Short Stories

The Lagoon. Christchurch: Caxton Press, 1951; 2nd ed., *The Lagoon and
    Other Stories.* Caxton Press, 1961.

The Reservoir. New York: George Braziller, 1963; Christchurch: Pegasus
    Press, 1966; London: W. H. Allen, 1966.

Snowman, Snowman. New York: George Braziller, 1963.

The Reservoir and Other Stories (selection of stories from *The Reservoir* and
    Snowman, Snowman). Christchurch: Pegasus Press, 1966; London:
    W. H. Allen, 1966.

5. Uncollected Stories

"University Entrance." *New Zealand Listener,* 22 March 1946, 18.

"The Gravy Boat." *New Zealand Listener,* 18 December 1953, 10.

"Lolly-Legs." *New Zealand Listener,* 15 October 1954, 8.

"I Got Shoes." *New Zealand Listener,* 2 November 1956, 26.

"The Wind Brother." *School Journal,* 3 (Autumn 1957), 57.

"Face Downwards in the Grass." *Mate,* I (September 1957), 7.

"The Friday Night World." *School Journal,* 3 (Autumn 1958), 58.

"The Bath." *Landfall,* 19 (1965), 225.

"A Boy's Will." *Landfall,* 20 (1965), 314.

"Winter Garden." *Cornhill Magazine,* 1063 (Spring 1970), 11.

"Flo." In Helen Hogan (ed.) *Nowhere Far From the Sea* (Christchurch:
    Whitcombe & Tombs, 1971).

"The Dreams." In Helen Hogan, *Nowhere Far From the Sea.*

6. Collection of Poems

The Pocket Mirror. New York: George Braziller, 1967; Christchurch:
    Pegasus Press, 1968; London: W. H. Allen, 1968.

7. Poems in Anthologies

"The Clown," "Rain on the Roof," and "Wet Morning." In V. G. O'Sullivan,
    (ed.) *An Anthology of Twentieth Century New Zealand Poetry.* Lon-
    don: Oxford, 1970.

"As I Walked Along the Street," "Beach," "Cat Spring," "The Chrysalids,"
    "Complaint," "Lament for the Lakes," "Leith Street," "Sunday After-
    noon at Two O'Clock," "Three Black Mice," and "The Tree." In Helen
    Hogan, (ed.) *Nowhere Far From the Sea.*

8. Uncollected Poems

"The Waitresses." *New Zealand Listener,* 9 July 1954, 11.

"The Liftman." *New Zealand Listener,* 13 August 1954, 22.
"On Paying the Third Instalment." *New Zealand Listener,* 10 September 1954, 25.
"Trio Concert." *New Zealand Listener,* 29 September 1954, 11.
"Timothy," *New Zealand Listener,* 26 November 1954, 11.
"The Transformation." *New Zealand Listener,* 28 January 1955, 15.
"The Ferry." *New Zealand Listener,* 13 July 1956, 24.
"The Dead." *Landfall,* 11 (1957), 148.
"The Senator Had Plans." *Landfall,* 18 (1964), 210.
"Scott's Horse." *Landfall,* 18 (1964), 210.
"The Road to Takapuna." *Mate,* 12 (June 1964), 33.
"The Death of Twoot-Noodle." *Craccum,* 40, 3 (April 1966), 5.
"White Turnips." *New Zealand Monthly Review,* 67 (May 1966), 24.
"In Mexico City." *New Zealand Listener,* 3 December 1968, 20.
"Jet Flight." *New Zealand Listener,* 8 August 1969, 12.

9. Non-fiction Prose
"A Letter to Frank Sargeson." *Landfall,* 7 (1953), 5.
"Artists' Retreats" (interview). *New Zealand Listener,* 27 July 1970, 13.
"Beginnings." *Landfall,* 19 (1965), 40.
"The Burns Fellowship." *Landfall,* 22 (1968), 237.
"Memory and a Pocketful of Words." *Times Literary Supplement,* 4 June 1964, 487.
Review of Terence Journet's *Take My Tip. Landfall,* 8 (1954), 309.
"This Desirable Property." *New Zealand Listener,* 3 July 1964, 12.
"Janet Frame: It's Time For France" (interview). *New Zealand Listener,* 27 October 1973, 20.

SECONDARY SOURCES
(arranged alphabetically)

ALCOCK, PETER. "Frame's Binomial Fall, or Fire and Four in Waimaru." *Landfall,* 29 (1975), 175. A late addition to criticism of *Owls Do Cry,* Alcock's article attacks dualistic analysis of this work, proposing instead a four-part division reflected in the four Withers children. Aggressive and rather dogmatic, it offers a refreshing approach that is increasingly hard to accept, however, when applied to Janet Frame's later fiction.

DELBAERE-GARANT, JEANNE. "Daphne's Metamorphoses in Janet Frame's Early Novels." *Ariel,* (2 April 1975), 23. A valuable discussion of the first four novels as an expression of the novelist's Rilkean vision, this article leaves certain aspects of the topic open for further discussion. A discussion of Heidegger's similar world vision is less valuable.

————. "Death as the Gateway to Being in Janet Frame's Novels." In Hena Maes-jelinek, (ed.) *Commonwealth Literature and the Modern World*

(Brussels: Librairie Marcel Didier, 1975) 147–55. Based on a paper delivered at the Liège conference of the Association for Commonwealth Literature and Language Studies in 1974, this article covers similar ground to the one noted above.

DUPONT, V. "Janet Frame and the Psychological Novel." *Commonwealth Literature Conference*, Aarhus, Denmark, 1971. Based on a paper given at the Liège conference on Commonwealth literature in 1971, this article offers a rudimentary overview of Janet Frame's work, with some errors *(The Rainbirds* and *Yellow Flowers in the Antipodean Room* are referred to as different novels, for example). Generous claims are made for Frame's standing as a writer, although the basis for such claims is economically expressed.

EVANS, P. D. "Alienation and the Imagery of Death: the Novels of Janet Frame." *Meanjin Quarterly*, 32, 3 (September 1973), 294. An overview of the first seven novels, with an attempt to form a generic background by placing Frame's fiction against the early novels of the Australian writer, Patrick White. Similarities in the treatment of Antipodean society are noted, but the writers differ in their attitudes to language and mysticism.

————. *An Inward Sun: The Novels of Janet Frame*. Wellington, N. Z.: N. Z. U. P., 1971. A monograph primarily devised to introduce school children and college students to the novels, this work covers the first seven in a fairly simplified manner, making no attempt to provide background material. Each chapter contains a series of questions for discussion and written work.

————. "Janet Frame and the Adaptable Novel." *Landfall*, 25 (1971), 448. An attempt to interpret *The Adaptable Man* as a novel written under the influence of the objective approach to literature shown by Robbe-Grillet, Borgès, Nabokov, and the Americans, James Purdy and Donald Barthelme.

HANKIN, CHERRY. "Language as Theme in *Owls Do Cry.*" *Landfall*, 28 (1974), 91. A highly detailed and lengthy analysis of the novel in terms of its approach to language. Lacks discussion of similar themes in the later fiction and occasionally comes close to stating the obvious, but offers nevertheless a clearly-argued and workmanlike approach to the work.

HARRIS, WILSON. "Scented Gardens for the Blind." This is a chapter in an as yet unpublished work of criticism to be entitled *Enigma of Values*.

HYMAN, STANLEY EDGAR. "Reason in Madness." *Standards: A Chronicle of Books For Our Time*. New York: Avon Books, 1966, 239. Originally a review of *Scented Gardens For The Blind*, this article describes Frame's novel as one of the best written since the war and gives a succinct and valuable analysis of its aims and attributes. A useful example of reaction to Frame's work outside her own country.

JONES, L. O. "No Cowslip's Bell in Waimaru: The personal vision of *Owls Do Cry.*" *Landfall,* 24 (1970), 280. The first attempt to analyze the novel as a major work of fiction, this excellent article is necessary reading for anyone wishing to approach Janet Frame's fiction. Jones sees her world as dualistic and the novel as rejecting middle-class values. There is a tendency to refer to the imaginative domain of the novel as "insanity," but his summary of the worth of the novel is extremely valuable.

MALTERRE, MONIQUE. "Myths and Esoterics: A Tentative Interpretation of Janet Frame's *A State of Siege.*" This is an unpublished paper read at the conference of Commonwealth literature held at Liège University in April 1974.

MOORHOUSE, GEOFFREY. "Out of New Zealand." *The Guardian,* 16 November 1962. An interesting article written after an interview with Janet Frame, this contains some pleasant anecdotes as well as useful background information on the writer's life.

RHODES, H. WINSTON. "Preludes and Parables: A Reading of Janet Frame's Novels." *Landfall,* 26 (1972), 135. An invaluable discussion of the early novels as part of a larger continuum of writing, this article relates the longer fiction to some of the shorter works in the collections in order to interpret the former correctly. Although more could have been done in greater space to show how all the fiction is interrelated, this remains an important article, and no reader should approach Janet Frame's early fiction without reading it.

ROBERTSON, ROBERT T. "Bird, Hawk, Bogie: Janet Frame, 1952–62." *Studies in the Novel,* 4 (Summer 1972), 186. A useful discussion of the unity of the earliest short stories and *Owls Do Cry,* this was at the time the first critical study to acknowledge that Frame's first three novels form a trilogy. Robertson also discusses her work in terms of provincialism, regionalism, and metropolitanism.

RUTHERFORD, ANNA. "Janet Frame's Divided and Distinguished Worlds." *World Literature Written in English,* 14, 1 (April 1975), 51. Originally a paper delivered at the Liège conference, this article takes the customary dualistic approach to Janet Frame's fiction, which it usefully places in the context of other contemporary writing and social philosophy.

STEVENS, JOAN. "The Art of Janet Frame." *New Zealand Listener,* 4 June 1970, 13. Originally a talk broadcast over radio, this discussion of the first half dozen novels is a clear and valuable introduction to Frame's fictional world, especially useful because of its inclusion of discussion of some of the poetry.

Index

(Janet Frame's works are listed under her name)